FARMING AND DEVELOPMENT

TECHNOLOGICAL PERSPECTIVES

ENV BOOKS SERIES

FARMING AND DEVELOPMENT

TECHNOLOGICAL PERSPECTIVES

Editors

Dr. Pawan Kumar 'Bharti'

Society for Environment, Health
Awareness of Nutrition and Toxicology (SEHAT)
B-225/5D, Top Floor, Subhash Gali, Road No. 7, Block B
Ashok Nagar, Shahdara
Delhi-110093
(India)

&

Dr. Jaswant Ray

Society for Environment, Health
Awareness of Nutrition and Toxicology (SEHAT)
F/119, Pandav Nagar
Meerut-250003 (U.P.)
(India)

DPH

DISCOVERY PUBLISHING HOUSE PVT. LTD.
INDIA

Published by:
Namit Wasan
DISCOVERY PUBLISHING HOUSE PVT. LTD.
4383/4B, Ansari Road, Darya Ganj
New Delhi-110 002 (India)
Phone : +91-11-23279245; 23253475; 43596065
E-mail : discoverybooksindia@gmail.com
discoverypublishinghouse@gmail.com
namitwasan9@gmail.com
web : www.discoverypublishinggroup.com

***First Edition:* 2019**

ISBN: 978-93-88854-08-5

Farming and Development: ***Technological Perspectives***

Printed at:
Infinity Imaging Systems
Delhi

FOREWORD

M.S. Swaminathan
Founder Chairman
Ex-Member of Parliament (Rajya Sabha)

I am very glad to know that a several books are being edited under the aegis of ENVBOOKS series Delhi, India on various sub-themes of Agriculture and environment like:

- Heavy Metals and Pesticides in Environment
- Heavy conservation and renewable sources Climate Change and Agriculture Production
- Geospatial Technology and Ecosystem Assessment
- Food Technology and Agriculture Advancement
- Vermicompost and Vermitechnology
- Pest Control and Management
- Plant Response to Environmental Stress
- Bioremediation and Biotechnology
- Noise and Air Pollution
- Risk and Disaster Management
- Agro-ecology and Environmental Biotechnology
- Water and Wastewater Management
- Soil Pollution and Lithosphere
- Earth Ecosystem and Pollution
- Microbial Ecology
- Waste Recycling and Product Development

I am very happy to learn that a number of editors and authors from different institutions and university of different nations are involved in editing these books. The books are the compendium of screened-in manuscripts received from different countries like UK, Canada, Egypt, Nigeria, Ghana, Ethiopia, China, South Africa, Japan, Guyana, PNG, Nepal, South America and various parts of India. I am feeling delighted in writing forward to these books and congratulate to Dr. Pawan Kumar 'Bharti', Editor-in-Chief and founder of ENVBOOKs series and of course his team for their tenacity and hard work in compiling these valuable compendiums.

I hope these books will be beneficial for academician, researchers, industrialist policy makes and students as study material and will work as reference for further research work.

M.S. Swaminathan

PREFACE

Farming has been innovated at multiple different points and places in human history. The transition from hunter-gatherer to settled, agricultural societies is called the Neolithic Revolution and first began around 12,000 years ago, near the beginning of the geological epoch of the Holocene around 12,000 years ago. It was the world's first historically verifiable revolution in agriculture. Subsequent step-changes in human farming practices were provoked by the British Agricultural Revolution in the 18th century, and the Green Revolution of the second half of the 20th century. Farming spread from the Middle East to Europe and by 4,000 BC people that lived in the central part of Europe were using oxen to pull plows and wagons.

A farm may be owned and operated by a single individual, family, community, corporation or a company, may produce one or many types of produce, and can be a holding of any size from a fraction of a hectare to several thousand hectares. A farm may operate under a monoculture system or with a variety of cereal or arable crops, which may be separate from or combined with raising livestock. Specialist farms are often denoted as such, thus a dairy farm, fish farm, poultry farm or mink farm.

Some farms may not use the word at all, hence vineyard (grapes), orchard (nuts and other fruit), market garden or "truck farm" (vegetables and flowers). Some farms may be denoted by their topographical location, such as a hill farm, while large estates growing cash crops such as cotton or coffee may be called plantations. Many other terms are used to describe farms to denote their methods of production, as in collective, corporate, intensive, organic or vertical. Other farms may primarily exist for research or education, such as an ant farm, and since farming is synonymous with mass production, the word "farm" may be used to describe wind power generation or puppy farm.

The present book updates the subject content of agriculture farming, issues related to farms, advanced techniques in farming, organic farming, farm credit, farm machinery, integrated farming, sustainable development, farm enterprises and farm technology commercialization.

Thanks are due to publisher and contributors from various institutions and universities.

The book will be helpful for the researchers, academia working in the field of agriculture farming, issues related to farms, advanced techniques in farming, organic farming, farm credit, farm machinery, integrated farming, sustainable development, farm enterprises and farm technology commercialization.

Editors
(envbooks@gmail.com)

PREFACE

CONTENTS

Farming and Development : *Technological Perspectives*
***Edited by:* Dr. Pawan Kumar 'Bharti' & Dr. Jaswant Ray**
ISBN: 978-93-88854-08-5
***Edition:* 2019**
***Published by:* Discovery Publishing House Pvt. Ltd., New Delhi (India)**
Pages 1-8

1 Introduction

Agriculture is the cultivation of land and breeding of animals and plants to provide food, fiber, medicinal plants and other products to sustain and enhance life. Agriculture was the key development in the rise of sedentary human civilization, whereby farming of domesticated species created food surpluses that enabled people to live in cities. The study of agriculture is known as agricultural science. The history of agriculture dates back thousands of years; people gathered wild grains at least 105,000 years ago and began to plant them around 11,500 years ago before they became domesticated. Pigs, sheep, and cattle were domesticated over 10,000 years ago. Crops originate from at least 11 regions of the world. Industrial agriculture based on large-scale monoculture has in the past century come to dominate agricultural output, though about 2 billion people worldwide still depend on subsistence agriculture.

Modern agronomy, plant breeding, agrochemicals such as pesticides and fertilizers, and technological developments have sharply increased yields from cultivation, but at the same time have caused widespread ecological and environmental damage. Selective breeding and modern practices in animal husbandry have similarly increased the output of meat, but have raised concerns about animal welfare and environmental damage through contributions to global warming, depletion of aquifers, deforestation, antibiotic resistance, and growth hormones in industrially produced meat. Genetically modified organisms are widely used, although they are banned in several countries.

The major agricultural products can be broadly grouped into foods, fibers, fuels, and raw materials (such as rubber). Classes of foods include cereals (grains), vegetables, fruits, oils, meat, milk, fungi and eggs. Over one-third of the world's workers are employed in agriculture, second only to the service sector, although the number of agricultural workers in developed countries has decreased significantly over the past several centuries.

The development of agriculture enabled the human population to grow many times larger than could be sustained by hunting and gathering.

Agriculture began independently in different parts of the globe, and included a diverse range of taxa. At least 11 separate regions of the Old and New World were involved as independent centers of origin. Wild grains were collected and eaten from at least 105,000 years ago. From around 11,500 years ago, the eight Neolithic founder crops, emmer and einkorn wheat, hulled barley, peas, lentils, bitter vetch, chick peas and flax were cultivated in the Levant. Rice was domesticated in China between 11,500 and 6,200 BC with earliest known cultivation from 5,700 BC, followed by mung, soy and azuki beans. Sheep were domesticated in Mesopotamia between 13,000 and 11,000 years ago. Cattle were domesticated from the wild aurochs in the areas of modern Turkey and Pakistan some 10,500 years ago. Domestic pigs had multiple centres of origin in Eurasia, including Europe, East Asia and Southwest Asia, where wild boar were first domesticated about 10,500 years ago. In the Andes of South America, the potato was domesticated between 10,000 and 7,000 years ago, along with beans, coca, llamas, alpacas, and guinea pigs. Sugarcane and some root vegetables were domesticated in New Guinea around 9,000 years ago. Sorghum was domesticated in the Sahel region of Africa by 7,000 years ago. Cotton was domesticated in Peru by 5,600 years ago, and was independently domesticated in Eurasia. In Mesoamerica, wild teosinte was domesticated to maize by 6,000 years ago. Scholars have developed a number of hypotheses to explain the historical origins of agriculture. Studies of the transition from hunter-gatherer to agricultural societies indicate an initial period of intensification and increasing sedentism; examples are the Natufian culture in the Levant, and the Early Chinese Neolithic in China. Then, wild stands that had previously been harvested started to be planted, and gradually came to be domesticated.

In the past century, agriculture has been characterized by increased productivity, the substitution of synthetic fertilizers and pesticides for labor, water pollution, and farm subsidies. In recent years there has been a backlash against the environmental effects of conventional agriculture, resulting in the organic, regenerative, and sustainable agriculture movements. One of the major forces behind this movement has been the European Union, which first certified organic food in 1991 and began reform of its Common Agricultural Policy (CAP) in 2005 to phase out commodity-linked farm subsidies, also known as decoupling. The growth of organic farming has renewed research in alternative technologies such as integrated pest management and selective breeding. Recent mainstream technological developments include genetically modified food. Demand for non-food biofuel crops, development of former farm lands, rising transportation costs, climate change, growing consumer demand in China and India, and population growth, are threatening food security in many parts of the world. The International Fund for Agricultural Development posits that an increase in smallholder agriculture may be part of the solution to concerns about food prices and overall food security, given the favorable experience of Vietnam. Soil degradation and diseases such as stem rust are major concerns globally; approximately 40% of the world's agricultural land is seriously degraded. By 2015, the agricultural output of China was the largest in the world, followed by the European Union, India and the United States. Economists measure the total factor productivity of agriculture and by this measure agriculture in the United States is roughly 1.7 times more productive than it was in 1948.

Farm

A farm is an area of land that is devoted primarily to agricultural processes with the primary objective of producing food and other crops; it is the basic facility in food production. The name is used for specialised units such as arable farms, vegetable farms, fruit farms, dairy, pig and poultry farms, and land used for the production of natural fibres, biofuel and other commodities. It includes ranches, feedlots, orchards, plantations and estates, smallholdings and hobby farms, and includes the farmhouse and agricultural buildings as well as the land. In modern times the term has been extended so as to include such industrial operations as wind farms and fish farms, both of which can operate on land or sea.

Farming originated independently in different parts of the world, as hunter gatherer societies transitioned to food production rather than, food capture. It may have started about 12,000 years ago with the domestication of livestock in the Fertile Crescent in western Asia, soon to be followed by the cultivation of crops. Modern units tend to specialise in the crops or livestock best suited to the region, with their finished products being sold for the retail market or for further processing, with farm products being traded around the world.

Modern farms in developed countries are highly mechanized. In the United States, livestock may be raised on rangeland and finished in feedlots and the mechanization of crop production has brought about a great decrease in the number of agricultural workers needed. In Europe, traditional family farms are giving way to larger production units. In Australia, some farms are very large because the land is unable to support a high stocking density of livestock because of climatic conditions. In less developed countries, small farms are the norm, and the majority of rural residents are subsistence farmers, feeding their families and selling any surplus products in the local market.

Farming has been innovated at multiple different points and places in human history. The transition from hunter-gatherer to settled, agricultural societies is called the Neolithic Revolution and first began around 12,000 years ago, near the beginning of the geological epoch of the Holocene around 12,000 years ago. It was the world's first historically verifiable revolution in agriculture. Subsequent step-changes in human farming practices were provoked by the British Agricultural Revolution in the 18th century, and the Green Revolution of the second half of the 20th century. Farming spread from the Middle East to Europe and by 4,000 BC people that lived in the central part of Europe were using oxen to pull plows and wagons.

Types of Farm

A farm may be owned and operated by a single individual, family, community, corporation or a company, may produce one or many types of produce, and can be a holding of any size from a fraction of a hectare to several thousand hectares.

A farm may operate under a monoculture system or with a variety of cereal or arable crops, which may be separate from or combined with raising livestock. Specialist farms are often denoted as such, thus a dairy farm, fish farm, poultry farm or mink farm.

Some farms may not use the word at all, hence vineyard (grapes), orchard (nuts and other fruit), market garden or "truck farm" (vegetables and flowers). Some farms may be denoted by their topographical location, such as a hill farm, while large estates growing cash crops such as cotton or coffee may be called plantations.

Many other terms are used to describe farms to denote their methods of production, as in collective, corporate, intensive, organic or vertical.

Other farms may primarily exist for research or education, such as an ant farm, and since farming is synonymous with mass production, the word "farm" may be used to describe wind power generation or puppy farm.

Farm Equipment

Farm equipment has evolved over the centuries from simple hand tools such as the hoe, through ox- or horse-drawn equipment such as the plough and harrow, to the modern highly-technical machinery such as the tractor, baler and combine harvester replacing what was a highly labour-intensive occupation before the Industrial revolution. Today much of the farm equipment used on both small and large farms is automated (e.g. using satellite guided farming).

As new types of high-tech farm equipment have become inaccessible to farmers that historically fixed their own equipment, Wired reports there is a growing backlash, due mostly to companies using intellectual property law to prevent farmers from having the legal right to fix their equipment (or gain access to the information to allow them to do it). This has encouraged groups such as Open Source Ecology and Farm Hack to begin to make open source hardware for agricultural machinery. In addition on a smaller scale Farmbot and the RepRap open source 3D printer community has begun to make open-source farm tools available of increasing levels of sophistication.

Forest Farming

Forest farming is the cultivation of high-value specialty crops under a forest canopy that is intentionally modified or maintained to provide shade levels and habitat that favor growth and enhance production levels. Forest farming encompasses a range of cultivated systems from introducing plants into the understory of a timber stand to modifying forest stands to enhance the marketability and sustainable production of existing plants.

Forest farming is a type of agroforestry practice characterized by the "four I's": intentional, integrated, intensive and interactive. Agroforestry is a land management system that combines trees with crops or livestock, or both, on the same piece of land. It focuses on increasing benefits to the landowner as well as maintaining forest integrity and environmental health. The practice involves cultivating non-timber forest products or niche crops, some of which, such as ginseng or shiitake mushrooms, can have high market value.

Non-timber forest products (NTFPs) are plants, parts of plants, fungi, and other biological materials harvested from within and on the edges of natural, manipulated, or disturbed forests. Examples of crops are ginseng, shiitake mushrooms, decorative ferns, and pine straw. Products typically fit into the following categories: edible, medicinal and dietary supplements, floral or decorative, or specialty wood-based products.

Forest farming, though not always by that name, is practiced around the world. For centuries, humans have relied on fruits, nuts, seeds, parts of foliage and pods from trees and shrubs in the forests to feed themselves and their livestock. Over time, certain species have been selected for cultivation near homes or livestock to provide food or medicine. For example, in the southern United States, mulberry trees are used as a feedstock for pigs and often cultivated near pig quarters.

In 1929, J. Russell Smith, Emeritus Professor of Economic Geography at Columbia University, published "Tree Crops – A Permanent Agriculture" which stated that crop-yielding trees could provide useful substitutes for cereals in animal feeding programs, as well as conserve environmental health. Toyohiko Kagawa read and was heavily influenced by Smith's publication and began experimental cultivation under trees in Japan during the 1930s. Through forest farming, or three-dimensional forestry, Kagawa addressed problems of soil erosion by persuading many of Japan's upland farmers to plant fodder trees to conserve soil, supply food and feed animals. He combined extensive plantings of walnut trees, harvested the nuts and fed them to the pigs, then sold the pigs as a source of income. When the walnut trees matured, they were sold for timber and more trees were planted so that there was a continuous cycle of economic cropping that provided both short-term and long-term income to the small landowner. The success of these trials prompted similar research in other countries. World War II disrupted communication and slowed advances in forest farming. In the mid-1950s research resumed in places such as southern Africa. Kagawa was also an inspiration to Robert Hart pioneered forest gardening in temperate climates in the sixties in Shropshire, England.

In earlier years, livestock were often considered part of the forest farming system. Now they are typically excluded and agroforestry systems that integrate trees, forages and livestock are referred to as silvopastures. Because forest farming combines ecological stability of natural forests and productive agriculture systems, it is considered to have great potential for regenerating soils, restoring ground water supplies, controlling floods and droughts and cultivating marginal lands. In addition to these benefits for re-establishing productive forests on marginal lands, forest farming is way to add financial value while conserving land that is currently forested, as discussed in the methods section.

In more recent years, there has been growing interest in locally grown and organic foods throughout the United States. There has been an increase in farmer's markets and community-supported agriculture small enterprises. These have also become outlets for NTFPs. In order to stay competitive, many farmers look to add unique crops to their product line. With the quantity and quality of resources developing online that offer tutorials and educational information on how to create and maintain forest farms, forest gardens, how to cultivate specific crops such as shiitake mushrooms and how to successfully market these items, forest farming is expanding as a viable land management practice. Good places to look for research-based resources are the USDA National Agroforestry Center's publication section, the Center for Agroforestry at the University of Missouri, the Cornell Cooperative Extension, the Non-Timber Forest Products website by The Virginia Tech Department of Wood Science and Forest Products, the USDA Forest Service Southern Research Station and the Top of the Ozarks RC&D in Missouri and the collaborative Forest Farming community of practice on eXtension.org, the online presence of the Cooperative Extension System of the US Land Grant Universities.

Principles

Forest farming principles constitute an ecological approach to forest management. Forest resources are judiciously used while biodiversity and wildlife habitat are conserved. Forest farms have the potential to restore ecological balance to fragmented second growth forests through intentional manipulation to create the desired forest ecosystem.

In some instances, the intentional introduction of species for botanicals, medicinals, food or decorative products is accomplished using existing forests. The tree cover, soil type, water supply, land form and other site characteristics determine what species will thrive. Developing an understanding of species/

site relationships as well as understanding the site limitations is necessary to utilize these resources for production needs, while conserving adequate resources for the long-term health of the forest.

Apart from the environmental benefits, forest farming can increase the economic value of forest property and provide short- and long-term benefits to the landowner. Forest farming provides economic return from intact forest ecosystems, but timber sales can remain part of the long-term management strategy.

Methods

Forest farming methods may include: Intensive, yet careful thinning of overstocked, suppressed tree stands; multiple integrated entries to accomplish thinning so that systemic shock is minimized; and interactive management to maintain a cross-section of healthy trees and shrubs of all ages and species. Physical disturbance to the surrounding area should be minimized.

Level of Management Required

1. Forest gardening is the most intensive of forest farming methods. In addition to thinning the overstory, this method involves clearing the understory of undesirable vegetation and other practices that are closely related to agronomy (tillage, fertilization, weeding, and control of disease and insects and wildlife management). Due to input levels, this method often produces lower valued products compared to other methods. Forest gardens take advantage of the vertical levels of light availability and space under the forest canopy so that more than one crop can be grown at once if desired.

2. Wild-simulated seeks to maintain a natural growing environment, yet enriches local NTFP populations to create an abundant renewable supply of the products. Minimal disturbance and natural growing conditions ensure products will be similar in appearance and quality of those harvested from the wild. Rather than till, practitioners often rake leaves to expose soil, sow seed directly onto the ground, and then cover with leaves again. Since this method produces NTFPs that closely resemble wild plants; they often command a higher price than NTFPs produced using the forest gardening method.

3. Forest tending involves adjusting tree crown density to manipulate light levels that favor natural reproduction of desirable NTFPs. This low intensity management approach does not involve supplemental planting to increase populations of desired NTFPs.

4. Wildcrafting is the harvesting of naturally growing NTFPs. It is not considered a forest farming practice since there is no human involvement in the plant's establishment and maintenance. However, wildcrafters often take steps to protect NTFPs with future harvests in mind. It becomes agroforestry once forest thinnings, or other inputs, are applied to sustain or maintain

plant populations that might otherwise succumb to successional changes in the forest. The most important difference between forest farming and wild crafting is that forest farming intentionally produces NTFPS, whereas wild crafting seeks and gathers from naturally growing NTFPs.

REFERENCES

https://en.wikipedia.org/wiki/Agriculture
https://en.wikipedia.org/wiki/Farm
https://www.pghfarmandforest.com/
https://en.wikipedia.org/wiki/Forest_farming
https://www.iso.org/ics/65.020/x/

Farming and Development : *Technological Perspectives*
Edited by: Dr. Pawan Kumar 'Bharti' & Dr. Jaswant Ray
ISBN: 978-93-88854-08-5
Edition: 2019
Published by: Discovery Publishing House Pvt. Ltd., New Delhi (India)
Pages 9-34

2 Eco-Issues in Grape Farming Systems

[1]Jebapreetha D and [2]Esakkimuthu M

Introduction

Grapes cultivation in India has been commercially taken up under a wide range of soil and climatic conditions. Grapes is an important commercial fruit crop which is mainly used for table purpose. It's productivity is also very high. It is grown in tropical condition (Maharashtra, Karnataka, Tamil Nadu and Andhra Pradesh), using double pruning system. Further, a special type of pruning regulated the cycle of vine growth and fruiting. These technologies have made it possible to ensure two harvestings in a year and upto two to five harvestings in two years during summer in tropical regions and during autumn in sub-tropical regions. The current area and production under grapes in India is estimated at 64,400 ha with an annual production of 1.68 million tonnes (2007-08). While 80% of grapes produced are used for table purpose, nearly 20 percent is dried for raisin production and 2% is used for manufacture of juice and wine. The grapes export from India started in 1991 with the initiation of economic liberalization. India's export to the Middle East accounts for 90% of the total exports while 8% is exported to European countries and the rest to the South East Asian countries. Exports from the country have grown from a level of 15,932 tonnes in 1993-94 to the present level of 96,723 tonnes in 2007-08. Though there has been a steady growth from the year 1993-94 to 1995-96 and from 1997-98 to 2001-02 there were sharp declines during the year 1998-99 and 2001-02. This was the result of rejection due to the pesticide- residues found in the lots sent from Maharashtra and some other regions (Parate, 2006). According to Borkar (2007) reported that with the advancement of technologies, the cultivation practices of grapes had improved increasing the yield and quality of grapes. However, to control the tremendous losses occurred due to pests and diseases in grapes, thousands of hundreds of kilograms of pesticides were dumped into the environment causing pollution. Grapes require frequent spraying of pesticides. The application of various pesticides by the

1 Tamil Nadu Agricultural University, Madurai, Tamil Nadu, India
2 Kerala Agricultural University, RARS, Pilicode, Kerala, India

vine growers is mainly based on the experience of their friends and on the information given by the profit-motive pesticide-dealers rather than following the recommended package of practices.

Environment and Its Issues in Practicality

Environmental issues is operationalized as the harmful effects caused to the environment and the agricultural system due to the mismanagement of agricultural practices in grapes cultivation. According to Maliwal (2005) Environment is all external forces, influences and conditions which affect the life, nature, behaviour and the growth, development and maturation of living organism; Jelinek and Corneliussen (1977) inferred that the use of arsenic containing compounds as pesticides and insecticides may result in translocation of this metal to ground water, fruits and vegetables; Steven and Dipasquale (1979) inferred that pesticides often translocate from soil to food crops. Human beings consuming fruits, vegetables and food grains having high amount of pesticides accumulated through translocation become victims of toxic effect of pesticides; Knight and Norton (1989) reported that pesticide use could result in water pollution, residues in food and dangers to human health and non-target species; Ramesh (1994) stated the problems encountered by farmers due to dust emission from the cement industry as reduction in crop yield, hardening of the top soil, reduction in cattle strength, ground water depletion, quality reduction of ground water in agriculture and respiratory disorders, eye and skin irritation, stone formation in the urinary tracts with regard to human beings.

According to Paroda (1995) opined that indiscriminate use of pesticide had adversely affected the ecological balance resulting in pest resurgence, pesticide resistance, pollution of environment and the food chain with pesticide-residue at toxic level; Haverkort (1997) found that the use of tractors was increasing the risk of environmental damage by soil erosion, soil compaction, deforestation and pest hazards; Alexandratos (1998) stated that the environmental problems of developing countries were large due to exploitation of land, extensive cropping and deforestation; Murthi (1998) observed that the agricultural lands were becoming unfit for cultivation as could be seen from the stunted growth of crops and the diseases affecting the saplings; Babu *et al.* (1999) reported that the honey samples from five southern states were contaminated with DDT, HCH, lindane, aldrin and heptachlor. He also found that sixty six per cent of the butter samples were contaminated with DDT above MRL. The average HCH level in ghee samples collected was 2.49 ppm, which varied from 0.3 – 6.65 ppm.

According to Singh *et al.* (2000) indicated that as a result of unprincipled use of natural resources, the component of environment got impaired raising threats to survival of human beings. Unscientific use of agricultural inputs (either natural or manmade) and inefficient farming systems were resulting in aggregation of too many environmental disorders such as acid deposition in air, green house effect, depletion of ozone layer in stratosphere, soil erosion, contamination of ground water and loss of diversity of flora and fauna; Naidu (2000) reviewed that though productivity had gone up significantly in the agricultural sector, indiscrimate use of chemical pesticides had turned fertile lands barren; Paneerselvam and Manuel (2004) reported that continuous and frequent cultivation of soil resulted in breaking down of crumbs of aggregates and destruction of organic matter leading to depletion of soil fertility.

According to Prasad *et al.* (2004) made it clear that the long-term effects of pesticide-residues in human body includes carcinogenicity, reduced life span and fertility, increased cholesterol, high infant mortality, varied metabolic and genetic disorders; Gupta *et al.* (2005) stated that air pollution had been associated with a variety of adverse health effects such as impairments in lung function, increased incidence of chronic bronchitis, asthma, premature mortality, cardiovascular diseases etc. The costs of air pollution in terms of damage to human health, vegetation, buildings, and of reduced visibility are serious problems in the cities of developing countries; Fulekar (2005) warned that the climate change was one of the major global environmental challenges. About 80 per cent of the greenhouse gas emissions were from human activities particularly burning of fossil fuels and remaining 20 per cent was associated with agriculture and changes in land use.

According to Tripathi and Singh (2005) explained that the intensive, indiscriminate, non-judicious use of chemicals to increase the production had not only polluted the soil, water and environment but also affected human beings. In addition, adverse effect on non-target organisms and destruction of beneficial organisms like honey bee, pollinators, parasites and predators was also confirmed; Lailk and Pandeya (2005) inferred that the excessive use of pesticides in agriculture resulted in widespread decline of birds, beneficial insect population which can disrupt the balance between predator and prey. The pesticides produce both short and long term effects on human health, of which long-term effects includes elevated cancer and disruption of body's reproductive, immune, endocrine and nervous systems; Mohideen (2005) found that when insecticides were sprayed, 20 per cent of the bee population had decreased due to the toxicity of insecticides and when pesticides were used 305 types of insects had developed immunity against insecticides.

According to Murugesan *et al.* (2005) revealed that qualitative changes occur in ground water due to pollution, indiscriminate disposal of industrial, human and agricultural wastes, which pose great threat to the quality of ground water in many regions. Water quality deterioration had made the potable water resources a scarce one and endangered for living systems; Pariyar (2006) concluded that the uncontrolled and non-scientific use of pesticides was a great threat to our environment because pesticides (Insecticides, nematicides, weedicides etc.,) leave long term residual effects in the soil and ground water. The use of pesticides at higher dose causes environmental imbalance, continuous loss of quality of land, adverse effect on flora and fauna, pollution of drinking water, increased economic burden on the common farmer. The residues of these pesticides directly come in the food chain of human beings through crop uptake and adversely affects the human and animal health; Pariyar (2006) observed that due to mismanagement of water resources, around six million hectare of area is under water logged condition in India. With four per cent water resources plus 16 per cent of the world's population, the situation will soon worsen. Farmers are exploiting ground water by means of modern technologies at an alarming rate without considering it as a precious natural resource.

Pesticide Residue in Soil, Water and Crop Produce

Residues in soil: According to Chechani and Gupta (2006) found that the spray of 1000 and 2000 g ai/ha of ethion resulted in the initial deposits of 3.76 – 3.85 and 5.82 – 5.98 ppm on soyabean leaves, 2.87 – 2.99 and 4.661 – 4.74 ppm on pods of soyabean and 0.51-0.56 and 0.81 – 0.87 ppm in soil; Chechani and Gupta (2007) found that the spray of 100 and 200 g ai/ha cypermethrin resulted in the initial deposits of 2.33 – 2.54 and 3.94 – 4.04 ppm on leaves and 2.00 – 2.12 and 3.38 – 3.41 ppm on pods. The soil was found to be contaminated as a result of drift during the spraying of crop to the extent of 0.19 – 0.21 and 0.30 – 0.39 ppm; Singh *et al.* (2007) inferred that successive use of nitrogenous fertilizers to the soil make plant less resistant to diseases. Though the total crop yield increases there is a decrease in the protein content; Kanjana and Kannathasan (2007) analysed soil samples at periodical interval and tomato fruit drawn at post harvest stage found that carbofuran had higher initial residues in soil as compared to endosulphan. The residues of endosulfan in tomato fruit were higher than that of carbofuran; Safiatou *et al.* (2007) revealed that pesticides were detected in 77 per cent of the collected soil samples .Eight pesticides were detected in water samples used for human and animal consumption.

Residues in water: According to Edward (1982) found that pesticides are present in water than in air. The main source of pesticides in water are effluents from pesticide manufacturing plants, run-off from agricultural fields, leaching of pesticides from farm soil and from washings and cleaning of pesticide using equipments; Mohapatra *et al.* (1994) detected the presence of monocrotophos in many samples of ganga river water while malathion and monocrotophos were frequently detected in ground water samples. Quinalphos, methyl parathion and ethion were detected in a few samples of river water; Guzzella *et al.* (1996) investigated the pesticide content of agricultural soil and groundwater was by monitoring three sampling sites located in the Northern Italy and cultivated with maize crop. The GC (Gas chromatography) analyses of soil samples allowed the description of vertical distribution of pesticide-residues in the soil profile. High concentrations of pesticide were determined in the superficial horizons while in the deeper layers the contamination reached values less than 0.2 ìg/kg; Babu *et al.* (1999) reported the contamination of river, tank and canal water of four districts of Andhra Pradesh *viz.*, Krishna, Mahaboobnagar, Godavari and Nellore with HCH residues. Lindane residues were highest in canal water of Godavari district; Prasad *et al.* (2001) reported that the various species of fresh water mussels, snails, prawns, insects and fishes collected from Jamuna river contained DDT and its metabolites. The fish, Mystus sp. contained maximum total DDT of 10.59 ppm. Fish were unable to breed in water polluted with endrin, thiodan or malathion. Insecticides also reduced the fecundity of fish. Rajagopalan (2006) reported that pesticides have settled on the soil and washed into the streams below. Further he stated that pesticide residues were found in 34 common brands of bottled water. The residue included deadly pesticides like lindane, DDT and malathion; Singaravel *et al.* (2007) assessed the quality of irrigation water samples from the coastal areas of Cuddalore and Nagapattinam district. The results of the study indicated that pH ranged from 7.2 to 9.2 and EC (Electrical conductivity) from 0.4 to 8.3 dsm^{-1}. Thus the waters were medium to highly saline and low to medium in sodicity hazard. The use of such waters for irrigation would develop salinity of soils and affect the crop yield.

Residues in crops and crop produces: According to Bindra and Kalra (1971) estimated insecticidal residues in vegetables collected from different markets of Delhi, Hyderabad and Punjab. The analysis indicated that 75 per cent of the samples were contaminated and 50 per cent contained residues higher than the tolerance limits; Lakshminarayan and Krishnamenon (1975) reported the presence of DDT, BHC and endosulfan pesticide-residues in vegetables like potato, tomato, brinjal, cauliflower and cabbage; Siddiqui *et al.* (1981) found the vegetable oils like mustard oil, ghee, coconut oil and groundnut oil have also been reported to contain residue of organochlorine pesticides like DDT, DDE, HCH (Hexachlorocyclohexane) and heptachlor; Sukul and Handa (1986) reported that high deposit of 9.02 and 14.02 ppm of cypermethrin on leaves of chickpea and green gram respectively after spraying the crop with 140 g ai / ha of cypermethrin; Chaudary (1990) reported that after spraying 0.005 and 0.01 per cent cypermethrin on soybean an initial deposit of 1.62 to 1.67 and 2.31 ppm on leaves and 1.36 – 1.40 and 1.94 – 2.00 ppm on pods was observed.

According to Bhatnayar *et al.* (1997) reported that out of the 55 samples of tomato analysed for pesticide-residues, 41 samples were contaminated and three samples showed insecticides above MRL (Maximum Residue Level); Chandrasekaran *et al.* (1997) analysed brinjal for contamination of residues of thirteen insecticides and reported that out of thirty samples, three with fenvalerate and one with endosulfan were exceeding the MRL. Among the thirty okra samples, three samples had fenvalerate, endosulfan and cypermethrin exceeding the MRL and four out of ten cauliflower samples exceeded the MRL with cypermethrin, fenvalerate and monocrotophos; Kumar and Yadav (1998) found that spraying cauliflower crop blindly throughout the growing period on calendar based interval would be wasteful of the pesticides, which would unnecessarily increase the cost of production, contaminate the human diet and environment; Jain and Gupta (1999) reported the initial deposit of 1.4792 and 2.6965 ppm on cabbage head after application of cypermethrin @ 50 and 100 g ai/ ha respectively.

According to Babu *et al.* (1999) reported that the most common pesticide contaminants found in vegetable oils and oil seeds were DDT and HCH. Out of 12 brands of edible oil collected during 1992, six were contaminated with HCH and DDT. Most of the vegetable samples collected from Delhi, Haryana, Punjab, Karnataka, Andhra Pradesh and Maharashtra had been found to be contaminated with DDT and HCH and a few were contaminated with aldrin, heptachlor and endosulfan; Singh *et al.* (1999) reported that among fifty samples of green chilli monitored for different pesticides applied to the crop, 30 samples showed contamination of phosphamidon, HCH, carbofuran, monocrotophos, endosulfan and fenvalerate. Eight samples showed insecticide residues above MRL; Shah *et al.* (2000) concluded that out of 214 samples of brinjal cauliflower, chilli, bhendi, cabbage, Indian bean and other minor vegetables 145 (68 per cent) were found contaminated with organochlorine, organophosphorous, synthetic pyrethroids and dithiocarbamate group of pesticides. However 14 (6.5 per cent) samples exceeded the tolerance limits wherein monocrotophos was the major one.

According to Gupta (2001) stated that although DDT and HCH had been banned for use in agriculture but their residues in mothers' milk had not yet been declined significantly in Himachal Pradesh. When mother's milk was analysed for contamination of pesticide-residues such as organochlorine, organophosphorous and synthetic pyrethroids, 49 samples were found to be contaminated with HCH isomers out of 51 samples and all contained DDT isomers and nine samples contained dicofol; Kumar *et al.* (2005) reported that, of the 30 vegetable samples collected and analysed for endosulphan residue, 29 samples were found to be contaminated. Among the 29 contaminated samples, 3 samples were of brinjal and 2 samples of cauliflower showed insecticides above MRL (<2 ppm); Chahal *et al.* (2006) revealed that all samples of mushroom were found to be contaminated with one or more insecticides and 57 per cent of these samples contained residues of chlorpyrifos above MRL of 0.05 mg kg^{-1}.; Pokharkhar *et al.* (2007) reported that monocrotophos recorded maximum of 95.56 per cent mean mortality and proved to be highly toxic to the grubs, followed by malathion with 83.33 per cent mean mortality.

It was obvious that the higher concentrations of pesticides showed maximum of 73.06 per cent average mortality, followed by the recommended and below recommended concentrations.

According to Seshabala and Chandrasekhar (2007) found that bottle gourd had the ability to uptake the heavy metals through their roots and transport them to the edible portion of the plant. The heavy metals may accumulate in the edible part of the crops that are consumed by the people or fed to the animals. Their increased concentration in human food chain over a long period can provoke detectable damage to health (Carcinogenic and mutagenic effects).

Pesticides and health: In a joint statement, the United Nations-Food and Agricultural Organization and the World Health Organization had warned that around 30 per cent of pesticides marketed in developing countries with an estimated market value of $900 million annually did not meet internationally accepted quality standards and they were posing a serious threat to human health and the environment; Braid and Carthy (1972) reported that volatile organochlorine pesticides causes epithelial damage of respiratory tract of spray workers. Consumed accidentally or deliberately may cause various type of damage to our body systems. Persistent organochlorine group of pesticides have a tendency to accumulate in adipose or fatty tissues of the body, because the mammalian system is deprived of the enzyme required to hydrolyse most of them; Strect (1981) said that the pesticides besides posing grave health hazards to people exposed to their handling, chemical pesticides also cause immunologic suppression of the hosts living in the environment and can cause various forms of toxicity even in low doses; Antle and Pingali (1994) concluded that pesticide use had a negative effect on farmer's health. Farmer's health had a positive effect on productivity, and that they were likely to be social gains from a reduction in insecticide use.

According to Gupta *et al.* (1995) found that the socio economic status and health of the mango workers were below that of workers in comparable industries who were not engaged in pesticide use and other agricultural work. A high occurrence of respiratory problems among the workers surveyed was highlighted; Bakhetia and Udean (1998) stated that pesticide poisoning in India had caused dwarfism, handi Gods Syndrome, loss of memory, effect on reproduction, skin and allergic reactions, behavioural changes, miscarriages and epileptic outbreaks. They also quoted the ICMR (Indian Council of Medical Research) study on bovine milk from 12 states showing presence of DDT complex and HCH isomers above the tolerance limits; Fernandez -Cornejo (1998) stated that the pesticides posed risk to human health and the environment if people are exposed to the pesticides; Verma and Singh (2000) reported that exposure to organophosphates (OP) produced depression, a major risk factor in suicides. Research from Spain had shown that suicide rates were higher in areas of greater OP use.

According to Bay (2000) indicated that prolonged exposure to pesticides could produce chronic ailments such as cardiopulmonary, neurological and skin disorders, adverse reproductive effects such as foetal deformities, miscarriages, lowering the sperm count of applicators etc. In Philippines, of the 4031 acute pesticide poisonings reported between 1980-87, 608 were fatal; Ali (2001) cautioned that the spraying of pesticides in the fields was particularly dangerous for the women because it not only affected their health but also jeopardizing the health of the generations to come. Reproductive performances of the males exposed to pesticides also get reduced; Lofquist (2002) reported that children exposed to toxic, urban pesticides like bug sprays, pet flea and tick products, hair treatments for lice and especially "cosmetic" pesticides to control weeds and insects in lawns and gardens are susceptible to health hazards.

According to Jyotsna *et al.* (2003) found that 85 healthy male pesticide spray men in grapes garden exposed to different class of pesticides for three to ten years experienced significant decrease in serum cholinesterase, serum total proteins, albumin and hematological parameters viz. Hb, Hct and RBC and significant increase in lipid peroxidation. He concluded that the long term exposure of various pesticides on spray men of grapes garden affect liver, heme biosynthesis and decrease serum cholinesterase; Prasad *et al.* (2004) made it clear that the long term effects of pesticide-residues in human body includes carcinogenicity, reduced life span and fertility, increased cholesterol, high infant mortality, varied metabolic and genetic disorders.

According to Brown (2004) in a new study opined that an apple a day may not keep the doctor away. Research by a Liverpool University lecturer has found that children who eat an apple or pear a day may be exceeding the pesticide safety level and calculated that each day some children would get a toxic level because of the residues on fruit; Mahindra and Kaur (2004) said that as a result of indiscriminate use of pesticides, air, water, soil and food commodities had become loaded with pesticide-residues. The situation was so alarming that even mother's milk was not free from pesticides. Consumption of pesticide contaminated food had put the survival of mankind of danger by causing various fatal diseases; Arora and Trivedi (2006) reported that the poisonous effect of pesticides like DDT, BHC, malathion, quinalphos have been reported in the blood samples of human beings and the farm workers were reported to suffer from headache, numbness, lethargy, allergies, dermatitis, epigastric pain or blurred vision; Miles (2006) indicated that regular pesticide exposure may play a role in some cases of deadly motor neuron disease and found some patients with the progressive paralysing disease. Preliminary results from a survey of 900 Australians, including 300 people with motor neuron disease, suggested regular exposure to pesticides may increase a person's risk of neuron disease.

According to Subramaniam *et al.* (2006) analysed the blood of the patients with minimum health complaints and skin diseases for the residue of the banned organochlorine pesticides DDE and BHC using Gas Chromatography. High concentrations of both BHC & DDE were observed in the serum samples of the people who had direct exposure to the pesticides, namely agriculturalists and public health workers with few exceptions. The pesticide-residue concentration in serum ranges from 0.006 to 0.130 ppm for BHC and 0.002 to 0.033 ppm for DDE. The significance of this study revealed that human serum contained these banned pesticides; Grace *et al.* (2006) studied the relationship between the extent of pesticide-use and signs and symptoms of illnesses due to exposure among farmers of Thanjavur District (South India) and reported that the 433 (68.6%) farmers (of whom 4 were women) sprayed pesticides by themselves were directly exposed to pesticides. More than 75% of farmers used either "moderately" or "highly hazardous" pesticides. Eighty eight per cent did not use any form of protection, while handling pesticides. About 50% of spray men mixed different brands of pesticides, many of which were substitutable to each other. More than half of the respondents obtained information on pesticides from retail shop owners. Farmers reported the following acute signs and symptoms: "excessive sweating" (36.5%), "burning/ stinging/ itching of eyes" (35.7%), "dry/sore throat" (25.5%), "excessive salivation" (14.1%). These signs and symptoms had a higher prevalence among the spray men; Cohen (2007) opined that exposure to pesticides can occur directly from occupational, agricultural and household use and indirectly through the diet. He also suggested that pesticides may be related to various diseases, including cancers, as well as having neurological, mental and reproductive effects. Children may be more susceptible to the effects of pesticides due to increased exposure via food and breast milk, underdeveloped detoxification pathways, and longer life expectancy in which to develop diseases with long latency periods; Singh and Kadam (2007) reported that when fluoride content in ground water is between 1.5 to 4.0 mg/l, it causes mottling and staining of teeth, 4.0 to 8.0 mg / l causes dental carrier and minor skeletal deformation and above 8.0 mg/L causes acute osteofluorosis, stiffness in joints, skeletal deformation, thyroid changes, and kidney damage.

Pesticide residue in grapes: According to Brown (2004) opined that apples and grapes had high levels of toxic residues from pesticides. He advised the parents to stop feeding their children with fruits and vegetables and encouraged consumers to consider buying organically grown varieties of foods; Cabras and Conte (2001) expressed that, out of 1532 grapes samples analyzed for pesticide residual contamination, around 8 per cent were contaminated; Subramani (2003) stated that the pesticide-residue committee of the UK (United Kingdom) had found 0.07 milligram per kg of methomyl against the permitted level of 0.05 mg/kg and 0.04 mg / kg of alephate against the acceptance level of 0.02 mg / kg in atleast two samples of grapes.

According to Manoj (2006) stated that grapes sold in the market contained high levels of residues of dimethoate, lindane, chloropiriphos and malathion. These residues were much above the stipulated limits; Kumari (2006) stated that fruit samples of ber, grapes and guava analysed for pesticide-residues were found with HCH, DDT and endosulfan in almost all the samples. Residues of HCH and DDT were maximum in ber followed by grapes and guava whereas of endosulfan were maximum in guava followed by grapes and ber; Venkateswarlu *et al.* (2007) using a sensitive and selective liquid chromatography method found that the fresh grapes samples collected from an agricultural area in Hyderabad, South India, contained monocrotophos, above the permissible limits.

According to Anil *et al.* (2008) reported that the insecticides cypermethrin (0.025 per cent) fenvalerate (0.125%), malathion (0.05%), methomyl (0.05%), were highly toxic to all the bio stages of *S. coccivora*. Imidacloprid (0.045%) and acetamiprid (0.05%) were toxic to all the stages of *S. coccivora* Thiamethoxam (0.01%) were toxic to egg and grubs of *S. coccivora*. Among the fungicide carbendazim (0.1%) were more toxic to egg and grubs of *S. coccivora*; Cesnik *et al.* (2008) reported that 28 samples (59.6%) of grapes contained residues lower or equal than maximum residue levels (MRLS) and 18 samples (28.3%) exceeded National MRLs, for cyprodinil and fludioxonil. Multiple residues were found in 41 samples (87.2%) and highest number of pesticide detected per sample was seven. Tolpet (97.9%), cyproclinil (51.1%) dithiocarbamates (44.7%), chlorothalonil (23.4%), chloropyriphos (19.1%), pyrimethanil (14.9%) were the most frequently found pesticides in grapes.

Socio-conomic and Communication Characteristics of Eco-farmers

Age

Age was operationalised as the number of completed years of the respondents at the time of enquiry and the chronological age was taken as the measure. According to Mansingh (1992) found that 38.00 per cent of the grapes growers belonged to old age category followed by 32.00 per cent in the middle age and nearly one-third (30.00%) of the grapes growers were found to be in young age; Illayaraja (2001) observed that more than fifty per cent of the grapes growers (55.84%) were old aged followed by middle aged category (35.83%) and young aged (18.33%) category; Sukitha (2003) indicated that more than half of the grapes growers (54.17%) belonged to old aged category, followed by 33.33 per cent and 12.50 per cent in middle and young aged categories respectively; Ramani (2004) stated that majority of the grapes growers (81.67 %) distributed were between the old and middle aged categories. Only 18.33 per cent of them were in young age category.

Educational Status

Educational status referred to number of years of formal schooling attended by the respondent. According to Mansingh (1992) revealed that nearly one-third of the grapes growers (32.00%) possessed secondary education followed by 18.00 per cent who possessed collegiate education. A very meagre percentage (4.00%) of the grapes growers were illiterates; Ilayaraja (2001) confirmed that nearly two-fifth of the grapes growers (39.16%) had education upto secondary school level, followed by primary education (18.66%), middle school education (15.86%), collegiate (11.6%), illiterates (10.83%) and functionally literates (85.83%); Sukitha (2003) indicated that more than one-fourth (29.16%) of the grapes growers had education up to secondary level, followed by collegiate level education (10.00%) and 19.17 per cent had education up to middle school level; Ramani (2004) concluded that 28.33 per cent of the grapes growers had education upto secondary level, followed by an equal proportion (20.83%) of the respondents had education upto collegiate and primary level. Little more than sixteen per cent (16.68%) of the respondents had education upto middle level and 8.33 per cent of the respondents had education upto middle level. Around 9 per cent of the respondents were functionally literates and a meagre percentage of respondents (5.00%) were illiterate.

Occupational Status

Occupational status was operationalised as the profession in which an individual spends much of his time, money and resources for his livelihood to maintain himself and his family. It was assumed that those who had paid full attention to farming alone would be able to concentrate with undivided attention rather than those with subsidiary occupation. According to Varghese (1998) stated that majority of the respondents (73.33 per cent) were engaged in farming alone, whereas only a little more than one-fourth (26.67 per cent) of the respondents were engaged in occupation other than farming; According to Sriram (1997) more than three-fourths of the respondents had agriculture as their primary occupation; Ilayaraja (2001) found that 55.00 per cent of the grapes growers were found to have agriculture as their primary occupation, while 19.16 per cent of the respondents had farming plus wage earning as their occupation. He further added that a little above one-sixth (16.66%) of the respondents had farming plus service as their occupation; Sukitha (2003) indicated that farming was the major occupation for 54.17 per cent of grapes growers, 33.33 per cent of them had business along with farming, whereas 12.5 per cent were engaged in services in addition to farming; Nalini (2004) stated that 31.67% were engaged in farming alone, whereas more than one-fifth (21.67%) of the respondents were engaged in occupation other than farming; Ramani (2004) reported that farming was the major occupation for 95.00 per cent of the grapes growers. Only 5.00 per cent of the respondents were engaged in business in addition to farming.

Area under Grapes Cultivation

Area under grapes cultivation referred to the number of acres of cultivation a respondent possessed exclusively in grapes cultivation at the time of enquiry.

According to Ilayaraja (2001) found that majority of the grapes growers (74.66%) fell under medium level of farm size, followed by small farmers (22.00%) and big (3.34%) farmers; Ramani (2004) observed that majority of the grapes growers (74.17%) belonged to marginal to small farmers category. Only 25.83 per cent of the respondents belonged to big farmers category.

Farming Experience

Farming experience was operationalised as actual completed years of experience in farming. According to Mansingh (1992) reported that majority of the grapes growers had high level of experience in farming activities; Sukitha (2003) stated that nearly half (48.33%) of the respondents possessed less than 18 years of farming experience, whereas nearly one-third (30.00%) had medium level of farming experience. The rest of the respondents (21.67%) had high farming experience of more than 29 years; Ramani (2004) reported that most of the grapes growers (93.33%) had low to medium level of farming experience, whereas remaining 6.67 per cent of the respondents had high level of farming experience; Jebapreetha (2007) opined that majority of the respondents had high level of farming experience (77.50%) and more than one –fifth (22.50%) of the respondents had low level of farming experience.

Experience in Grapes Cultivation

Farming experience in grapes cultivation referred to the number of years of experience a respondent possessed exclusively in grapes cultivation at the time of enquiry. According to Thamarai Selvi (1989) found that 50.83 per cent of viticulturists possessed more than ten years of experience in farming; Ilayaraja (2001) observed that more than half of the grapes growers (52.50%) had medium level of experience in grapes cultivation, followed by high (27.50%) and low (20.00%) level; Sukitha (2003) revealed that 45.83 per cent of the respondents possessed more than 14 years of experience in grapes cultivation. This was followed by low (41.67%) and medium level (12.50%) of experience; Ramani (2004) reported that an overwhelming majority of the respondents (94.17%) possessed low to medium level of experience in grapes cultivation. Only 5.83 per cent of the respondents possessed high level of experience in grapes cultivation.

Annual Income through Grapes Cultivation

This was operationally referred to the total annual income of the grapes growers exclusively obtained from grapes cultivation, for the period of a year. According to Sukitha (2003) concluded that more than one-third (36.67%) of the grapes growers had moderate income of 2.5 to 5.0 lakhs, followed by high (32.50%) and low income levels (30.83%); Ramani (2004) observed that majority of the respondents (95.00%) earning low to medium level of annual income. Only 5.00 per cent of the respondents earn high level of annual income.

Farm Waste Disposal Behaviour

It was operationalised as the extent to which the farm wastes were disposed in line with eco preservation and conservation. Different modes of farm waste disposal were listed and respondents were asked to state the most commonly adopted method of disposing the farm waste. According to Ponnusamy *et al.* (1994) found that majority of the farmers were interested in preparing enriched paddy straw and enriched farm yard manure; Nirmaladevi (2000) inferred that there existed variations in the disposal of waste water and container. About 28.00 per cent of the farmers poured the wash water into irrigation canal, while 14.67 per cent poured it rightly into cotton field and 57.33 per cent stated that they used to pour the water into the field or irrigation canal. The empty containers were just thrown out by 10.00 per cent of the respondents, while 64.07 per cent reported that they used to sell the containers. However, nearly one-fourth of the respondents (23.33%) reported that they cleaned the containers and used for domestic purposes primarily for storing oil and transporting water; Arunachalam (2003) reported that majority of the respondents (92.00%) had safely disposed the remaining chemical wastes and plastic and aluminium containers after use of the inputs. Crop waste was disposed by in situ ploughing and animal waste was used for compost preparation by majority of the respondents. Most of the respondents (77.00%) burnt safely the dead animals and birds; Jebapreetha (2007) revealed that majority (77.50%) of the respondents had thrown the remaining chemical waste and waste water after washing the equipments, containers where chemicals were stored into the main field, 46.66 per cent of the respondents cleaned and used the plastic and aluminium containers for domestic purpose. More than half of the respondents (57.50%) had disposed the crop waste by in-situ ploughing and 55.00 per cent of the respondents had used the tree waste as fuel and 75.00 per cent used for domestic purpose.

Concern for Environment

It was operationalised as the degree of importance given by the farmer for preservation and conservation of our environment. Statements of importance of protecting and preserving our environment were prepared in consultation with local extension workers, crop scientists and progressive farmers. According to Gouranga (2002) opined that people living an Arnapurapur of Kamakhynagar block in the district of Dhenkanal, Orissa realised global warming and understood the importance of planting trees and to show their great concern on environment, they organized greenery club to plant trees and green vegetation in the wastelands of villages; Srinivasan (2003) expressed that people in Sempakudi village of Puddukottai district dugged a pond in the village wasteland to harvest maximum possible rainwater, with a purpose to recharge ground water without any help from government machinery and they collected money @ Rs. 1000/- each house for this purpose; Arunachalam (2003) stated that cent per cent of the respondents agreed that to plant more trees where ever possible to conserve our environment as their duty. Ninety nine per cent expressed their concern for conserving water as it is their precious resource. About 98.00 per cent of the respondents agreed that clean and healthier environment could be achieved by following organic farming practices. Almost an equal percentage of the respondents had shown their great concern on 'STL' (Soil testing lab) based fertilizer application to avoid pollution(91.00 %), minimum use of chemical inputs to avoid environmental hazards (91.50%) and preserving natural enemies while taking up chemical measures against crop pests (90.50%). Nearly 85.00 per cent of the respondents agreed that, they alone were responsible for global warming and further admitted that they have to take up proper ameliorative measures, while 83.00 per cent had indicated their concern positively on the environmental education for all; Ghosh *et al.* (2003) observed that farmers were concerned about three main harmful effects of soil erosion such as loss of soil, loss of water and loss of nutrients from their fields; Jebapreetha (2007) found that almost all the respondents had shown their greater concern for planting trees(90.84 %), conserving water (93.34%),preserving the natural enemies (91.67%), not polluting air (89.17%), having environmental education (87.50%), to go for minimum use of chemical inputs (88.34%), following STL recommendation (79.17%) and organic farming (70.00%) to have a clean and healthier environment.

Perception of Organic Manures

Perception is an act (or) power of perceiving (or) apprehending (or) combining the sensations into recognition of an object (or) stimulus. The perception of organic manure was operationalised as the power of perceiving manure in relation to eco-importance by the respondents. According to Varghese (1998) reported that majority (42.50%) of the respondents had medium level perception as eco-related effects of organic manures. One-third (33.33 %) of the respondents had high-level of perception, followed by low level (24.17%); Maheswari (2000) reported that 60.67 per cent of the farmers had a positive perception about organic manures; Chandra (2001) concluded that majority of the respondents (65.83%) had medium level of perception on organic manure followed by high level (28.34%) followed by 5.83 per cent had low level of perception on organic manure; Nalini (2004) inferred that more than one-third (35.00% and 34.17%) of the respondents had high and medium levels of perception on organic manures. The low level of perception was found with 30.83 per cent of the respondents.

Perception of Environmental Degradation

It was operationalised as the ability of the respondents to perceive the environment degradation. According to Varghese (1998) indicated that majority of the respondents (48.33%) had medium level of perception on environmental degradation. Little less than one-third (31.67%) of the respondents had high level of perception followed by 20.00 per cent of the respondents with low level of perception; Maheswari (2000) reported that 85.00 per cent of the respondents had a high perception on environmental degradation; Chandra (2001) indicated the majority of the respondents (51.67%) had medium to low level of perception on environmental degradation; Kanakasaba (2002) concluded that majority (75.83%) of the respondents had medium level of perception on environmental degradation, followed by high (12.50%) and low (11.67%) levels of perception on environment degradation; Nalini (2004) stated that more than half (53.33%) of the respondents had a high level of perception on environmental degradation, followed by medium and low levels (31.67% and 15.00%) respectively.

Perception of Health Hazards

It was operationalised as the ability of the respondents to perceive the harmful effect of pesticide on health of humans and animal. According to Kanakasaba (2002) reported that 55.00 per cent of the respondents had a medium level of perception about the health hazards posed by agricultural chemicals, while 30.83 per cent of the respondents had a high level of perception of the same, only 14.17 per cent had a low perception; Paneerselvam and Manuel (2004) indicated that forty per cent of the respondents had medium level of perception about the health hazards posed by agricultural chemicals, followed by high and low levels (39.17% and 20.00%) respectively.

Participation in Training

In this study, training undergone referred to the actual number of trainings attended by the respondents at the time of enquiry. According to Chandurkar (2004) said that the IPM(Integrated pest management) training and demonstrations have resulted in increased yield from 6.17 per cent to 42.14 per cent in areas covered under IPM demonstrations compared to non-IPM areas in rice; Nalini (2004) reported that 60 per cent of the respondents had not attended any training programme for the past three years; Ramani (2004) concluded that more than half of the grapes growers (67.50%) did not attend any training progamme. One training was attended by 28.33 per cent of the respondents and only 4.17 per cent of the respondents attended two trainings. None was found to have participated in more than two trainings.

Attitude of Farmers Towards Eco-friendly Agricultural Practices

Attitude is defined as a tendency to react positively (or) negatively to some person, object, situation, institution (or) event. According to Athimuthu (1990) found that almost equal percentage of the farmers (46.00 and 45.00%) had low and high attitude towards nutrient use technology. Only less than one-tenth

(9.00%) of them had medium level of attitude; Sriram (1997) concluded the majority of farmers (65.50%) had favourable attitude towards eco-friendly cultivation practices followed by most favourable (17.50%) and less favourable (17.00%) attitude; Noorjehan (1999) identified that majority of the respondents (89.00%) had favourable to more favourable attitude towards integrated pest management; Rahman and Mikuni (1999) revealed that half (50.00%) of the selected farmers had a less favourable attitude towards sustainable agriculture. Only 6.00 per cent of them expressed a highly favorable attitude and 44.00 per cent expressed a moderate attitude; Chandra (2001) indicated that majority of the respondents (55.00%) had favourable attitude towards eco-friendly cultivation practices followed by29.17 per cent with favourable attitude; Bhople and Borkar (2002) reported that majority of the farmers (83.33%) were found to be neutral in their feelings about biofertilizers. Nearly one-fourth of the farmers (24.67%) had favourable attitude towards bio-fertilizers. Only 12.00 per cent farmers had unfavourable in their reaction on biofertilizers; Nalini (2004) stated that nearly an equal number (44.16% and 41.67%) of respondents expressed more favourable and favourable attitude towards EAP (Eco-friendly agricultural practices). Only 14.17 per cent of the respondents expressed less favourable attitude.

Adoption of Recommended Grapes Growing Technologies

Adoption is operationalised as the adoption of practices as per recommendation or below the recommended level especially in the application of chemical fertilizers, insecticides, fungicides, and weedicides to prevent the environmental issues. According to Sainath (1982) revealed that out of six recommended practices in grapes cultivation only two practices *viz.*, manuring and weeding, were adopted by all the respondents, while practices like fertilization and plant protection were followed by 50.00 per cent of the respondents; Kumbar (1983) inferred that grapes growers did not show uniform pattern of overall adoption behaviour among themselves with reference to the selected recommended practices of grapes cultivation; Subbiah (1984) found that three -fourth (74.00 %) of the big farmers and two-third of small farmers were found under medium adoption level .The proportion of big and small farmers found under low and high adoption levels were more or less the same; Babu (1987) found that adoption pattern of grapes growers with respect to each of the specific practices were differed. The big farmers had higher adoption level than small farmers and similarly the small farmers had better adoption level than marginal farmers. In general, the adoption level of all the three categories was high; Kumar (1989) reported that there were more or less equal number of farmers in high (34.00%) and medium (36.00%) categories of overall adoption of improved grapes cultivation practices, followed by low adoption level (30.00%);

According to Mansingh (1992) indicated that cent per (100.00%) of the respondents were found to adopt the recommended practices in land preparation ,planting, training and pruning operations as such without any modification. Slightly more than half of the respondents (54.00 %) have not adopted the recommended spacing. All the farmers applied FYM (Farm Yard Manure) in less quantity against the recommended dose and applied nitrogenous fertilizers more than the recommended dose. The spray of insecticides and fungicides was more than the recommendation; Illayaraja (2001) revealed that more than fifty per cent of the grapes growers (57.50%) were found to be medium adopters, followed by low (23.34 and high 19.16%) adopters; Sukitha (2003) reported that majority (37.50%) of the grapes growers were seen in high adoption category, followed by low (33.33%) and medium (29.17%) level adoption behaviour or recommended grapes cultivation practices; Ramani (2004) stated that 37.50 per cent of the respondents had medium level of adoption, followed by low level (31.67%), high level (30.83%) of adoption possessed by the respondents.

Mismanagement of Practices

According to Ghodake *et al* (1973) from their study "an economics of pesticide use in cotton crop" concluded that the net returns from pesticides use were very high and optimum rates of pesticide application declined as percentage of crop damage increased and the economic optimum rates were substantially lower than the recommended rate; Marothia (1976) reported that in crops like maize, paddy and wheat, the level of pesticide use has increased inspite of increase in the prices of the same. The increase was attributed to the fact that the capital-intensive farmers had understood the economic significance of using pesticides in crop production and storage; Fernandez-Cornejo *et al.* (1998) observed that vegetable growers tend to be optimistic with regard to their output price forecasts and used more pesticides than the economic optimum level; Rahman *et al.* (1995) concluded that total pesticide consumption has doubled over the past six years in Bangladesh. Out of the total pesticide consumption organophosphorus compounds comprised 60.40 per cent, carbonates 29.00 per cent, organochlorines 8.00 per cent and others 3.40 per cent;

According to Soon (1996) reported that at least 50 per cent of farmers in Malaysia sprayed two to three times per week against the diamond back moth in cauliflower. In Honduras, on an average six to ten applications were made per crop season and Costa Rican farmers made 16 applications; Mahella and Jha (1997) opined that the state of pest infestation must be explicitly taken into account before recommending pesticide use, because increase in the level of infestation resulted in an increase in the optimum rate of pesticide use. Even in the years of low pest infestation, the returns to optimum use of pesticides were very high; Vasantha and Pochaiah (1998) reported that more than half of the vegetable growing farmers were found to be using higher tonnes of pesticides than recommended levels; Rajagopalan (2006) opined that agricultural pests have become a major problem primarily due to excessive use of chemical pesticides. To counter this problem, farmers are asked to apply more pesticides.

Causes for Mismanagement

According to Carlson (1970) observed that human judgements in foreseeing the occurrence of diseases influenced the quantum of pesticide use. Incorrect pesticide use resulted from an inappropriate view of the probability of disease development or misuse of disease forecasts; Malkhede and Pawasker (1973) reported that the use of pesticides and fertilizer in Amaravathi district increased considerably inspite of sharp rise in prices of the same. The availability of loans and inputs, yield prospects, awareness and knowledge of the cultivation were the influential factors for more pesticide use; Feder (1979) reported that the major motivation for pesticides application has the provision of some "insurance" against damage; that is the existence of uncertainty in the pesticide system by itself a factor leading to a higher and more frequent use of pesticides; Rao and Singh (1986) found that education, fertilizer expenditure, high yielding varieties and cost were the major factors influencing pesticide use among farmers. Among small farmers, those who grow high yielding varieties were more inclined to use pesticides. In the case of medium and large farmers, education was an important factor in pesticide use; Sasmal (1993) stated that inputs such as fertilizers, pesticides and labour had a significant impact on mean output in both the rainy and dry seasons. Pesticide use was found to be risky in the dry season and it's effect on production risk in the rainy season was in significant.

According to Nagaraja *et al.* (1994) reported that HYV(High yielding varieties) of brinjal production required intensive application of fertilizer and plant protection chemicals and their share in HYV of brinjal was high compared to local variety of brinjal; Gupta *et al* (2001) revealed that higher incidence of pesticide use were among farmers with high income, higher levels of education, large-size farms, predominance of export crops and with high prevalence of share cropping; Jeyanthi (2002) reported that higher pest incidence, ineffectiveness of pesticides to control pest, use of over dose by neighboring farmers and higher returns were the major reasons given by farmers for using over dose of pesticides; Nakov *et al.* (2002) reported that mistakes done in technology of grapes vine production: excessive use of chemicals(application of systemic fungicides with specific activity to certain pathogen) and some other non scientific driven activity on grapes ecosystem, have led to greater spread of pathogen, to outbreak of new ones and to soil pollution with pesticide and heavy metal residues; Boomiraj and Lourduraj

(2006) traced that the farmers rely mostly on the chemical pesticides because of the immediate and spectacular knockdown effects. Indiscriminate use of broad spectrum of pesticides resulted in outbreak of secondary pests, reduction in biodiversity of natural enemies, development of resistance to pesticides, pesticide induced resurgence, contamination of food and breakdown of pod web in the ecosystems; Kanwal (2006) reported the following reasons for excessive use of pesticides by vegetable growers. They were: for better control, to avoid risk of damage, on suggestions of dealers, lack of knowledge about recommendations, no faith in recommendation, resistance in pests, non-availability of subject matter specialists and lack of knowledge about compatibility of two pesticides.

Relationship of Characteristics of Respondents with Adoption of Recommended Grapes Growing Technologies

According to Illayaraja (2001) indicated that experience in grapes cultivation, economic motivation and scientific orientation had non-significant relation, whereas risk orientation had significant and positive relationship with adoption behavior of grapes growers; Sukitha (2003) confirmed that experience in grapes cultivation, socio-economic status, innovativeness, scientific orientation, mass media orientation and risk orientation had positive and significant association with adoption at one per cent level of probability; Ramani (2004) opined that area under grapes cultivation, farming experience, annual income through grapes cultivation, risk orientation, self confidence, information sources utilization, educational status and orientation with research station had shown a positive significant association with adoption of grapes growers.

Environmental Education

Environmental education is a way of creating knowledge, understanding, values, attitudes, skills, abilities and awareness among individuals and social groups about the environment and environmental protection. According to Environmental education refers to organized efforts to teach about how natural environments function and, particularly, how human beings can manage their behavior and ecosystems in order to live sustainably. The term is often used to imply education within the school system, from primary to post-secondary. However, it is sometimes used more broadly to include all efforts to educate the public and other audiences, including print materials, websites, media campaigns, etc. Related disciplines include outdoor education and experiential education; Environmental education is to create an awareness and understanding of the evolving social and physical environments as a whole, its natural, manmade, cultural, spiritual resources together with the rational use and conservation of these resources for development; Gangawane (1987) indicated that pesticide education was poor and farmers tend to use maximum doses of pesticides in order to eradicate the pest, which creates residual problems.

According to Birthal *et al.* (2000) concluded that reduction in pesticide use would occur through education of the farmers in pest management in particular and technology management in general; Balamurugan (2005) opined that environmental education in it's broadest sense encompasses public awareness that makes every individual to realize about environmental issues and help the learners to acquire awareness, knowledge, attitude, skill, critical evaluation and active participation to save the environment and humanity; Kumar (2005) expressed that environmental education would have a positive effect on the society and by gaining awareness, people would fight against pollution and protect the environment.

Farm Problems Encountered in Adoption of Recommended Grapes Growing Technologies

The constraints faced by the respondents in adoption of recommended practices were enquired and collected. According to Kumbar (1983) identified the reasons for non-adoption or partial adoption of the improved practices in grapes cultivation. They were lack of knowledge, lack of finance, lack of water in the well; Babu (1987) reported that majority of the grapes growers had expressed the constraints *viz.*, high cost of fertilizers, more diseases and pests incidence, lack of irrigation water and high cost of plant protection chemicals; Alagesan (1989) revealed the most important problems as perceived by the grapes growers were lack of high yielding grapes varieties, non-availability of quality rooted cuttings and lack of storage facility; Kumar (1989) revealed that the disease incidence, non availability of labourers, micro nutrient deficiency, lack of irrigation water, lack of regulated market and exploitation by middle men in marketing as the constraints of grapes growers; Rathakrishnan (1991) indicated lack of information support for grapes as the most important problem in grapes cultivation. Next important problem as perceived by the respondents were lack of technical competency with low level field functionaries, high cost of pandal material, lack of uniform colour development in bunches and inadequate irrigation facility; Chiprikar and Khuspe (1992) expressed the important problems faced by the grapes growers as non-availability of farm labourers in the season and poor market prices; Illayaraja (2001) stated lack of timely supply and high cost of fertilizers (81.66 %), lack of marketing facilities (69.66%), lack of irrigation facilities (36.67%) and high cost of plant protection chemicals(30.89%) were the constraints in the adoption of grapes technologies; Sukitha (2003) reported that majority (90-92%) of the grapes growers stated that poor keeping quality of berries and lack of cold storage facilities as their important problem /constraints.

Conclusion

Thus for continuous learning should be promoted for the grape growers on adopting the recommended dose of organic inputs and inorganic inputs in their field. Trainings could be given to grape growers to prepare organic manure themselves so that organic manures are available within the village in required quantity and at required time. Farming community should be educated about the positive impact of organic inputs on the environment and health of human beings though it has delayed response.

REFERENCES

Alagesan, V. (1989): Diagnostic Study on Communication Behavior of Viticulturists, AC&RI, TNAU, Coimbatore, pp: 48.

Alexandratos, N. (1998): World Agricultural Towards 2000, An FAO Study, *FAO / Belhaven Press*, Rome.

Ali, Farad. (2001): Pesticides – It is Safety above All, *Agriculture Today*, 4(8): 60.

Anil, K. Mali, J. S. Kurtadikar, D.W. Wandnerkar and P.W. Nemade. (2008): Studies on the Safety of Pesticide to Grapevine Meelybug Predator, *Journal of Pestology*, 32(1): 37-47.

Antle, John, M. and L. Pingali Prabhu. (1994): Pesticides Productivity and Farmers Health: A Philippine Case Dtudy, American *Journal of Agricultural Economics*, 76: 418-430.

Arora, Suwnitra and T. P. Trivedi. (2006): Pesticide and Environment in Today's Context, *Agriculture Today*, 9(2): 53-56.

Babu, Ramesh. (1987): A Study on Adoption Behaviour of Economic Performance of Grape Growers of Bangalore and Kolar district, University of Agricultural Sciences, Bangalore.

Babu, T. Ramesh, Mir Azam Sultan, K. Narasimba Reddy and D. Jagadishwar. (1999): Pesticides – Environmental Implications, *Indian Journal of Plant Protection*, 27 (1&2): 209-221.

Bakhetia, R. C. and A.S. Udean. (1998): Safe and Judicious Use of Pesticides, *Pesticides World*, 3(1): 19-27.

Balamurugan, B. (2005): Environmental Education for a Sustainable Future, *Kissan World*, 32(2): 26.

Bay, Dinabandhu. (2000): Pesticides and Health Risks, *Economic and Political Weekly*, 35(36): 381-383.

Bhatnayar, Ashok, N. S.Parihar, Alamelu Gupta and Banani Singh. (1997): Pesticide Residues in Farmgate Samples of Tomato, *Indian Journal of Plant Protection*, 25(1): 88-89.

Bindra, O. S. and R.L. Kalra. (1971): A Review of Work Done in India on Pesticide Residue, Symposium on Progress and Problems in Pesticide Residue Analysis, Punjab Agricultural University, Ludhiana.

Birthal S. Pratap, O. P.Sharma, Sant Kumar and A. Dhandapani. (2000): Pesticide Use in Rainfed Cotton: Frequency, Intensity and Determinants, *Agricultural Economics Research Review*, 13(2): 107-122.

Boomiraj, K. and A.Lourduraj. (2006): Effect of Organic Manures, Panchagavya and Herbal Leaf Extract Spray on Insect Incidence in Bhendi, *Journal of Ecobiology*, 18(3): 269-276.

Borkar, S.G. (2007): Diseases of Grapes their Forecasting and Control, *Pointer publishers*, Jaipur.

Braid, P. E. and T.F. Carthy. (1972): Proceedings Symposium an Fenitrothion, NRCL / UMRC No. 16073 : 62.

Brown, Chris. (2004): Apple a Day not always Good for Your Health; Pesticide Levels may be Threat According to Experts' Research, ***Pesticide Research Journal***, 8 (1): 45.

Cabras.P and E. Conte. (2001): Pesticide Residues in Grapes and Wine in Italy, *Food Additives & Contaminants*, 18 (10): 880 – 885.

Carlson, A. Gerald. (1970): A Decision Theoretic Approach to Crop Disease Prediction and Control, *American Journal of Agriculture Economics*, 52(2): 216.

Cesnik HB, Gregorcic A, and Cus F. (2008): Pesticide Residues in Grapes from Vineyards included in Integrated Pest Management in Slovenia, *Journal of Food Additives & Contaminants*, 25(4):438-43.

Chahal, K.K, A. S. Dhatt and B. S. Joia. (2006): Insecticide Residues in Market Samples of Mushroom in Punjab, *Journal of Pestology*, 30(3): 35-39.

Chandrasekaran, S, S. Kuttalam and A. Regupathy. (1997): Investigation of the Level of Contamination of Insecticide Residues in Ready to Market Vegetables in Tamil Nadu, *Vegetable Science*, 24(2): 136-139.

Chaudary, H. (1990): Studies on the Toxicity, bio-efficacy, Residues and Allied Problems of Some Insecticide against Pest of Soyabean, Rajastan Agricultural University, Bikaner.

Chechani, V. K. and H. C. L. Gupta. (2006): Residues of Ethion in / on Soyabean, *Journal of Pestology*, 30(5): 24-26.

Chechani, V. K. and H. C. L. Gupta. (2007): Extent of Residues of Cypermethrin in / on Soyabean, *Journal of Pestology*, 31(6): 32-35.

Chiprikar, B.P and T.S. Khuspe. (1992): A Study of Grape Growers with Special Reference to the Transfer of Grape Technology, *Maharastra Journal of Extension Education*, 6(2): 1234-1237.

Cohen M. (2007): Environmental Toxins and Health the Health Impact of Pesticides, School of Health Sciences, RMIT University, 1002.

Edward, C. A. (1982): Origin of Pollution of Aquatic System by Pesticides, Pesticide in Aquatic System Environment, *Plenum Press*, New York, pp: 11.

Feder, Gershan. (1979): Pesticides, Information and Pest Management under Uncertainty, *American Journal of Agricultural Economics*, 61(1): 97-103.

Fernandez-Cornejo. (1998): Environmental and Economic Consequences of Technology Adoption: IPM in Viticulture, *Journal of Agricultural Economics*, 18:145-155.

Fernandez-Cornejo, J. E. D, Beach, N. Uri and B. K. Goodwin., (1998): Testing the Rational Expectations Hypothesis using Survey Data from Vegetable Growers, *Economic Affairs*, CAB Abstract, 39(1): 9-22.

Fulekar, M. H. (2005): Climate Change–A Threat to Environment, *Indian Journal of Environmental Protection*, 25 (8): 718-722.

Gangawane, L. G. (1987): Rational Pesticide Use, *Pesticides*, 21(2): 11-14.

Ghodake, R. D. A. S. Sirahi and D. Jha. (1973): Economics of Pesticide Use in Cotton Crop, *Indian Journal of Agricultural Economics*, 23(4): 92-99.

Grace, Chitra A, V.R. Muraleedharan, T. Swaminathan and D. Veeraraghavan. (2006): Use of Pesticides & Its Impact on Human Health: A Case of Farmers in South India, *International Journal of Occupational and Environmental Health, Abel Publication Services*, Italy.

Gupta, H. K, Gupta .K and R. C. Sharma. (2005): Urban Air Quality in Regional Areas – Public Policy Challenge, *Indian Journal of Environmental Protection*, 25 (8): 691-701.

Gupta, P. N. M. Mathur, S. K. Rastogi, A. K. Srivastava, H. Chandra, B. S. Pangtey, P. N. Mahendra and R.S. Bharti. (1995): Socio-economic, Environmental and Health Aspects of Farm Workers Engaged in Mango Plantation, *Biomedical and Environmental Sciences*, 8(4): 301-309.

Gupta, Pratigya. (2001): Contamination of Mother's Milk with Pesticide Residues, *Pesticide Research Journal*, 13(2): 207-212.

Gupta, Susmita Das, Ntandu Mamingi and Graig Meisner. (2001): Pesticide Use in Brazil in the Era of Agroindustrialization and Globalization, *Environment and Development Economics*, 6(4): 459-482.

Guzzella,L A. De Paolis C. Bartone F. Pozzoni and G. Giuliano. (1996): Migration of Pesticide Residues from Agricultural Soil to Groundwater, *International Journal of Environmental Analytical Chemistry*, 65 (1) : 261 – 275.

Haverkort, B. (1997): An Introduction to LEISA, *Macmillan press*, The Netherlands.

Ilayaraja, N. M. (2001): A Study on the Knowledge Level and Adoption Behaviour of Grape Growers, Annammalai University, Annamalai Nagar.

Jain, K. L. and H. C.L.Gupta. (1999): Extent of Residues of Synthetic Pyrethroids in Cabbage Heads, *Indian Journal of Applied Entomology*, 13: 47-50.

Jelinek, C. F and A. F. Corneliussen. (1977): Entry of Toxic Chemicals through Food, Water and Air, *Environment Health Perspective*, 19: 83.

Jeyanthi, H. (2002): A Study on Economic and Environmental Impact of Pesticide Use in Vegetable Cultivation, AC & RI, TNAU, Madurai.

Jyotsna A. Patil, Arun J. Patil and Sanjay P. Govindwar . (2003): Biochemical Effects of Various Pesticides on Sprayers of Grape Gardens, *Indian Journal of Clinical Biochemistry*, 18(2): 96.

Kanjana, D and M. Kannathasan. (2007): Persistence, Degradation and Decontamination of Endosulfan and Carbofuran in Soils and Tomato, *Journal of Pestology*, 31(2): 20-23.

Kanwal, Mahindra. (2006): Reasons for the Excessive and Indiscriminate Use of Pesticides in Vegetable Cultivation, *Indian Journal of Social Research*, 47(3): 215-219.

Knight, L .Alan and George W.Norton. (1989): Economics of Agricultural Pesticides Resistance in Anthropods, *Annual Review of Entomology*, 34: 293-313.

Kumar ,P. (1989): A Study on Adoption Behavior and Information Consultancy Pattern of Grape Growers in Ranga Reddy District of Andhra Pradesh, University of Agricultural Sciences, Bangalore.

Kumar, Nisha. D.K. Shashi, A. Sharma and A. K. Sarkar. (2005): Monitoring of Pesticide Residue from Farmgate Samples of Vegetable Growing Areas Around Ranchi, *Indian Journal of Agriculture Chemistry*, 38(1, 2): 77-80.

Kumar, Ramesh. (2005): Protecting Environment through Environment Education, *Kissan World*, 32(2): 7.

Kumar, Surender and P. R. Yadav. (1998): Insect Pest Population Fluctuation on Early Season Cauliflower Crop under Haryana Agro Climatic Conditions, *Indian Journal of Plant Protection*, 26(2): 145-148.

Kumari , Beena, V. K. Madan and T. S. Kathpal. (2006): Monitoring of Pesticide Residues in Fruits, *Journal of Environmental Monitoring and Assessment*, 123(3-10): 407-412.

Kumbar, S. V. (1983): A Study on Adoption Behaviour and Consultancy Pattern of Grape Growers of Bjiapur District in Karnataka State, University of Agricultural Sciences, Bangalore.

Lakshminarayan, V and P. Krishna Menon. (1975): Screening of Hyderabad Market Samples of Food Stuff for Organochlorine Insecticide Residues, *Indian Journal of Plant Protection*, 3: 208.

Lalik, R. and S. B. Pandeya. (2005): Agricultural Technologies and Environment, *Agriculture Today*, 8 (9): 39-40.

Lofquist, Bruce. (2002): Home Hazards: Residential Pesticides Pose Threats to Children's Health, Pesticide Research Journal, 4 (1):36-41.

Mahella, Y. P. and Jha. (1977): Economics of Pesticide Use in Cotton Production, *Indian Journal of Agricultural Economics*, 32(1): 120-136.

Mahindra, Rabinderijit and Nardeep Kaur. (2004): Extent of Awareness of Farm Women Regarding Pesticide Residues in Cereals, Vegetables, Milk and Milk Products, *Agricultural Extension Review*, 15(4): 16-21.

Maliwal,G.L. (2005): Crop Production With Waste Water. *Agrotech Publishing Academy*, New Delhi.

Malkhede and D. G. Pawashkar. (1973): Importance of Price of Inputs in Determining the Levels of Their Use in Four Sample Villages of Amaravathi District, *Indian Journal of Agricultural Economics*, 29(4): 205.

Manoj,P. (2006): Organic Farming Helps bring Pesticide-free Grapes to Bangalore, *The Hindu*, 8th September 2006, pp: 6.

Mansingh,M, Paul. (1992): Reinvention and Discontinuance of Recommended Practices in Grapes and Sugarcane, AC& RI, TNAU, Coimbatore.

Marothia, D. K. (1976): Impact of Increase in Input Price on Production and Profitability of Major Crops of Tarai, *Indian Journal of Agricultural Economics*, 31(3): 81-85.

Miles, Janelle. (2006): Pesticides may Increase Risk of Motor Neuron Disease, Pesticide Research Journal, 12(2): 21-25.

Mohapatra, S. P. V.T.Gajbhiye and N. P. Agnihorti. (1994): Organophosphorus Insecticide in the Aquatic Environment of a Rural Area, 6(2): 157.

Mohideen, Peer, A. (2005): Hazards of Pesticides, *Kissan World*, 32(8): 610-62.

Murthi, P. V. V. (1998): CETPS Fail to Convince Farmers, *The Hindu*, Sept. 10, pp: 3.

Murugesan, A., Ramu .A and N. Kannan. (2005): Characterization of Ground Water Quality in Madurai Region, *Indian Journal of Environmental Protection*, 25 (10): 885- 892.

Nagaraja, G.N. M.S. Nataraju and T. C. Narayana Swamy. (1994): Technological Change and Factor Shares in Brinjal Production, *Agricultural Banker*, 18(3): 8-10.

Naidu. (2000): Central Programmes Likely an Eco-friendly Farming Practices, *The Hindu*, November 2, pp: 16.

Nakov, B. K, M.B.Navoka and M.A.A.Rehab. (2002): Long-Term Assessment of Pollution Problem in Grapes Cenosys, *Journal of Environment Protection and Ecology*, 3 (4): 890-895

Paneerselvam, P. and Manuel. R., Issac. (2004): Sustaining Agriculture through Green Manuring, *The Hindu*, Feb.5, pp: 6.

Parate, Pradeep. (2006): Indian Export Scenario for Grapes, College of Agricultural Banking Calling (Jan-Mar): 43-44.

Pariyar, Chitramal. (2006): Agricultural and its Impact on Ecological Balance, *Agricultural Today*, 9(10): 48-49.

Paroda, R. S. (1995): Sustainable Growth: Major Planks of Strategy, The Hindu Survey of Indian Agriculture, pp: 21.

Pokharkar, D. S. N. S. Kulkarni and P. R. Palande. (2007): Toxicity of Pesticides to Australian Leady Bird Beetie, *Journal of Pestology*, 31(6): 39-42.

Prasad, Devendra, Prem Chand and B. P. Jain. (2004): Role of Insecticides in Environment Pollution, Recent Researches in Ecology, Environment and Pollution, Vol. 5, *Today and Tomarrow's Printers and Publishers*, New Delhi, pp: 193-201.

Rahman, M. S. M. A.Malek and M. A. Matin. (1995): Trend of Pesticide Usage of Bangladesh, *Science of the Total Environment*, 159(1): 33-29.

RajaGopalan, R. (2006): Environmental Education, *Oxford University Press,* USA.

Ramani, R. 2004. Yield Gap Analysis and Constraints in Grape Cultivation, AC&RI, TNAU, Madurai.

Ramesh, D. (1994): Farmers Awareness and Knowledge Level about Environmental Pollution, Annamalai University, Annamalai Nagar.

Rao, A. N. and J. J. Singh. (1986): Factors Discriminating Pesticides Use, *Agricultural Situation in India,* 40(112): 1085-1089.

Rathakrishnan, T. (1991): Information Sources and Adoption of Practices Among Grape Growers, AC& RI, TNAU, Coimbatore.

Safiatou Berthe Dem, Jean M. Cobb, Donald E. Mullins. (2007): Pesticide Residues in Soil and Water from Four Cotton Growing Areas of Mali in West Africa, *Journal of Agricultural Food and Environmental Sciences,* 1 (1): 78.

Sainath, S. (1982): A Study on Adoption Behaviour and Motivational Pattern of Grape Cultivators in Bangalore District of Karnataka state, University of Agricultural Sciences, Bangalore.

Sasmal, J. (1993): Considerations of Risk in the Production of High Yielding Variety Paddy: A Generalized Stochastic Formulation for Production Function Estimation, *Indian Journal of Agricultural Economics,* 48(4): 694-701.

Seshabala, P and P. Chandrasekhar Reddy. (2007): Heavy Metal Uptake by Vegetable Crop, *Journal of Current World Environment,* 2(2): 229-232.

Shah, P.G, M. F. Raj, B. A. Patel, B. K. Patel, K. D.Diwan, J. A. Patel and J. G. Talati. (2000): Pesticide Contamination Status in Farm Gate Vegetables in Gujarat, *Pesticide Research Journal,* 12(2): 195-199.

Siddiqui, M. K. J, T. D. Seth and M. C. Saxena. (1981): Organochlorine Pesticides in Edible Oils, *Pest. Annual*: 108 -110.

Singaravel, R. D. Elayaraja and V. Prasath. (2007): Quality of Irrigation Water in Coastal Areas of Cuddalore and Nagapattinam District, *Journal of Ecobiology:* 20(3): 225-228.

Singh, Banani, Alamelu Gupta, Ashok Bhatnayar and N. S. Parihar. (1999): Monitoring of Pesticide Residues in Farmgate Samples of Chilli, *Pesticide Research Journal,* 11(2): 207-209.

Singh, K. K., Patrin, M. L. and H.C. Sharma. (2000): Environmental Protection and Sustainable Agriculture, *Intensive Agriculture,* 38 (1-2): 12-16.

Singh, Naveen Kumar and D. S. Kadam. (2007): A Study of Fluoride in Ground Waters of Karera Block, *Journal of Current World Environment,* 2(1): 97-98.

Soon, Lim Guan. (1996): Integrated Pest Management in Developing Countries, *CAB International,* 61-75.

Steven, J. T, and L. G. Dipasquale. (1979): Pesticide, *Bull Environment Contamination,* 21: 304.

Strect, J. C. (1981): Pesticide and the Immune System, *Immunologic Considerations in Toxicology,* 1: 45.

Subbiah, M. (1984): Comparative Study on Information Need and Adoption Behavior of Big and Small Farmers Growing Grapes, AC&RI, TNAU, Madurai.

Subramani, M. R. (2003): Government to Test Pesticide Residue in Grapes for Export at Farm Level, *The Hindu,* December 30, pp: 4.

Subramaniam, Kallidass and RD. Jebakumar Solomon. (2006): Organochlorine Pesticides BHC and DDE in Human Blood in and Around Madurai, India, *Indian Journal of Clinical Biochemistry,* 21 (2): 169-172.

Sukitha, R. (2003): An analysis of Technological Utilization by Grape Growers, AC&RI, TNAU, Madurai.

Tripathi, P. S. and O. P. Singh. (2005): Forest Resources and Community Development, *Indian Journal of Development Research and Social Action*, 1(1): 84-85.

Vasantha, R and Pochiah Maraty. (1998): Extent of Use of Pesticides by Vegetable Growing Farmers, *Journal of Extension Education*, 9(4): 2235-2239.

Venkateswarlu, Padala, K. Rama Mohan, Ch. Ravi Kumar and K. Seshaiah. (2007): Monitoring of Multi-class Pesticide Residues in Fresh Grape Samples Using Liquid Chromatography with Electrospray Tandem Mass Spectrometry, *Journal of Food Chemistry*, 105(4):1760-1766.

Verma, Gyarti and K. K. Singh. (2000): Organophosphate Pesticides and Their Environmental Impact, *Pestcides information*, 25(3): 6-10.

Farming and Development : *Technological Perspectives*
***Edited by:* Dr. Pawan Kumar 'Bharti' & Dr. Jaswant Ray**
ISBN: 978-93-88854-08-5
***Edition:* 2019**
***Published by:* Discovery Publishing House Pvt. Ltd., New Delhi (India)**

Pages 35-45

3 Farm Mechanization and Machinery for Conservation Agriculture

[1]Amit Namdeo

Conservation Agriculture

A principal component of conservation agriculture is the reduction of soil manipulation to maximise the vegetative soil cover that will protect the soil surface. Tillage can be reduced with the use of rippers. Even greater reductions in energy needs can be made with direct sowing into the stubble of the previous crop, and options exist for this to be done by hand, Animal Power, or tractor. The practice of conservation agriculture aims to conserve, improve, and make more efficient use of natural resources through integrated management of available soil, water and biological resources combined with external inputs. In addition to reducing farm power requirements, it contributes to environmental protection as well as to enhanced and sustained agricultural production. It can be thought of as resource-efficient/ resource-effective agriculture. Conservation agriculture is an alternative to traditional land use and management. It is a practical method to reduce soil erosion, restore organic matter, and conserve soil moisture and soil fertility. The method is based on the following:

- Maintaining a permanent or semi-permanent organic soil cover to protect the soil physically from sun, rain and wind and to feed soil biota;
- Zero tillage (or minimum tillage). The principle is to eliminate mechanical tillage in order not to disturb the activities of soil micro-organisms and soil fauna;
- Crop rotations to reduce disease and pest problems, to explore different soil strata for water and nutrients, and for biological tillage (e.g. to break hardpans).

Farm Mechanization

Farm mechanization is the process of using agricultural machinery to mechanize the work of agriculture, greatly increasing farm worker productivity. The effective mechanization contributes to increase production in two major ways: firstly the timeliness of operation and secondly the good

[1] Irrigation Colony, Kailash Nagar, Rajnandgaon (Chhattisgarh) 491441, India

quality of work. The requirement of power for certain operations like seedbed preparation, cultivation and harvesting becomes so great that the existing human and animal power in the country appears to be inadequate. As a result, the operations are either partially done or sometimes completely neglected, resulting in low yield due to poor growth or untimely harvesting or both.

Scope of Mechanization

It is quite true that the Indian farmers have the lowest earnings per capita because of the low yield per hectare they get from their holdings. One of the few important means of increasing farm production per hectare is to mechanize it. Mechanization in India may have to be done at various levels. Broadly, it can be done in three different ways:

- By introducing the improved agricultural implements on small size holdings to be operated by bullocks.
- By using the small tractors, tractor-drawn machines and power tillers on medium holdings to supplement existing sources.
- By using the large size tractors and machines on the remaining holdings to supplement animal power source.

Farm Machinery for Conservation Agriculture

- Minimum tillage implements
- Direct seeding implements
- Cover crop and weed management implements

Minimum Tillage Machineries

Minimum tillage is a soil conservation system like Strip-till with the goal of minimum soil manipulation necessary for a successful crop production. It is a tillage method that does not turn the soil over. It is contrary to intensive tillage, which changes the soil structure using ploughs, chisels and subsoilers.

The plough in its different shapes as traditional plough or as mouldboard plough is probably the most popular land preparation tool that is used in both developing and developed countries. There is no other tool that symbolizes agricultural development, like the plough. Tillage tools might still be necessary for some specialized operations even under Conservation Agriculture.

The plough is mainly used for primary tillage: opening up the soil with the aim of loosening it for good root penetration and cutting and burying weeds. The plough can be pulled by one pair of bullock. Disadvantages of the plough include:

- At the beginning of the rainy season strong animals are needed to draw the plough while at that time most animals are weak.

- Repeated ploughing at the same depth can create plough pan or compacted layer.
- Turning the soil upside-down will result in loss of soil moisture through evaporation

The design of the mouldboard, like the size and form, determines the quantity of crop residues that is left on the surface and the part that is mixed into the soil. The bigger and more curved the mouldboard the higher the amount of the residues that is inverted in the soil and thus fewer residues that are left on the surface. As a first step to convert from conventional plough based farming towards conservation agriculture, farmers might opt for tined implements like chisel or cultivator.

Chisels or rippers are sharply pointed, metal tines that can be attached to the ordinary plough beam. Usually, farmers who want to avoid ploughing in minimum or reduced land preparation activities use chisels.

Fig. 3.1: Animal drawn ripper

Subsoilers are used to break up hard or compacted soil layers, with the aim to improve water.

Infiltration and root penetration. It can be attached to the ordinary plough beam. It can also be used to break up dry soil. The point is brought right under the compacted layer and can be used up to soil depths of 25-60 cm. With animal traction the maximum working depth of a chisel is around 30 cm.

Fig. 3.2

Direct Seeding Implements

Direct seeding is practiced in a lot of places in the tropical world, although the terminology is not used as such.

Manual Direct Seeder or Hand Jab Planter

In order to speed up the process of planting, hand jab planters have been developed. It is a hand-held tool that allows the farmer to plant from a standing position and faster than with other hand tools (average 2 days per hectare). The tool comprises two long levers joined with a hinge to form a V with a pointed tip. The metal pointed tip is pushed into the soil. By closing the levers the tip is opened to release the seed and fertilizer into the soil. At the same time new seed and fertilizer is charged into the metering mechanism. The planter is pushed into the soil at every step, allowing a regular spacing.

There are two types of jab planters: with broad tip and with narrow pointed tip.The former type is used on prepared land, for example when the planting line is ripped. The second one with the narrow pointed tips is designed for manual no-till planting and thus more recommended for conservation agriculture. One of the modifications to the planter is a second hopper, opposite the seed hopper, for fertilizer. This allows the farmer to fertilize and plant at the same time. If the jab planter is provided with a second hopper to apply fertilizer and seeds in one operation, it has two separate delivery tubes and points to make sure the seed and fertilizer are not deposited too close to each other.

Fig. 3.3

Direct seeders have five working elements:

- **A disc to cut through the surface mulch and open a slot in the soil.** The efficiency of the disc that cuts the (cover) crop residues depends on various factors:
- Soil conditions: texture, resistance to penetration, humidity and porosity.
- Straw and residue conditions: resistance to cutting, humidity, quantity and management.
- Seeder: weight and dynamics.
- Disc: size, shape and profile.

For good results it is recommended:

- To work during the warmest hours of the day (after 10 in the morning). Work when the straw is either green or completely dried, never when it is only wilted.
- Operate when soil moisture is at the point of soils being friable.
- When using animal traction, never try to seed when more than 5 tons of dry matter per hectare is left on the surface.

Inefficient cutting leads to an accumulation of residues between the different parts of the seeder and results in seed and fertilizer placement problems, i.e. irregular spacing or complete absence of seeds.

The soil needs to be firm enough to facilitate cutting through the residues, otherwise these will be pressed into the soil, resulting in hairpinning and bad soil contact for the seed. Blockage of the equipment could also result from incomplete residue cutting on soft soils. The cutting discs have either smooth edges that facilitate penetration into the soil or wavy or fluted edges if more soil movement is desired, for instance when Fusarium (= a large genus of filamentous fungi widely distributed in soil and in association with plants) infestation is expected and a drier soil is needed, or to improve disc rotation and avoid blockage.

A furrow opener (= a tool that makes a channel or flute in the ground) to place the fertilizer or the seed

Furrow openers for seed and fertilizer on animal traction or micro-tractor planters are usually a chisel tine (= long, straight piece of metal with a flat end) or hoe, double discs or by rolling punch type injection. Usually the furrow opener is placed just before or on the tip of the tubes that drop the fertilizer and the seeds.

The performance of the furrow opener depends on its geometric characteristics; the forward speed; the texture and density of the soil; the quantity of residues; and the vertical loading placed on it by the seeder.

It can take the form of:

- **A chisel tine:** commonly used in soils that have a higher resistance to penetration, but results in more problems with clogging up the implement with residues, and cannot be used in areas with stones, trunks or a lot of roots. Chisels are preferred for animal drawn implements as they require less weight due to the better penetration characteristics.
- **Double discs**, either the same diameter or not and offset at an angle forming a "V" to each other. The additional effect is that residues that may not have been very well cut by the main cutting disc, are cut by these discs resulting in less obstruction of the implement. The implement has less capacity to penetrate the soil, especially in clay soils (Ribeira et al., 1999). Discs of different diameter and offset axles have better self-cleaning and penetration characteristics than those of similar diameter. If double disc openers are used at all, then offset double discs of different diameter are therefore the preferred option for animal traction planters.

The following are the most common furrow-types created by animal traction direct planters

V-shaped Slots

In conservation agriculture, V-shaped slots are almost always created by twin discs which touch at the leading edge and are angled outwards at the rear. The angle of the V is usually about 10 degrees. Each of the angled discs pushes roughly an equal amount of soil sideways when both discs are at the same angle to the vertical. The biggest advantage of vertical double discs is their ability to handle surface residues without blockage. The construction is relatively simple and maintenance free.

When the front edges of the two discs leave a gap open at ground level, this can cause problems with the entry of residues and soil. This can be avoided through:

- Placing a third disc ahead of, or in between the two angled discs, which cuts the residues; or;
- Positioning one of the two discs forward of the other as to present a single cutting edge; or;
- Replacing one of the two discs by a smaller one; the larger disc becomes the leading edge to cut the residues.

U-shaped Slots

U-shaped slots are in animal traction and micro-tractor planters usually formed by the following furrow opener types:

- Hoe or chisel openers (= see description above)
- Power tiller openers

All of these designs produce some loose soil on the surface near the slot that can be used to cover the slot again. Hoe and chisel type openers burst the soil upwards; power tiller openers chop the soil with a set of rotating blades; and furrow openers scoop the soil out from the slot zone.

Hoe Type Openers

Hoe type openers refer to any shaped tine or chisel, which is designed to vertically penetrate the soil. Seed is delivered either down the inside of the hollow tine itself or down a tube attached to it, which is usually open at the back. The biggest disadvantage of hoe openers is the fact that they do not handle even modest levels of residues without blockage, unless a leading disc is placed ahead of the hoe opener to cut the residues.

Advantages of Hoe Openers:

- Low cost.
- They penetrate the soil better than discs, requiring less weight of the implement. This makes them the best option for animal traction.
- They do not tuck residues into the slot, but 'brush' them sideways.
- They do not create smear surfaces at the sides of moist planting slots and so create a better seedbed.

Disadvantages:

- Problems with stones and other obstacles.
- Requires a good cutting disc for long residues.
- Considerable soil movement depending on shape and width.

The Rolling Punch Injection

The rolling punch injection is another form of furrow opener. It handles residues quite well, but tends to clog when used in sticky soils. Placing seed and fertilizers For annual crops, it is recommended that fertilizer should be placed about 5 cm to the side and beneath the seeds. In a direct seeder this would mean that the opening device for fertilizer is placed outside the line of work for the seeding slot. However, in animal drawn direct seeders the fertilizer is placed under the seed, but in the same line. (Picture9) shows detail of the inside of the seed hopper (=A funnel-shaped container in which materials, such as grain or coal, are stored) of a direct planter, showing the seed plate and expeller to distribute the seeds. Seed plates inside the hoppers (=see the description above) control the plant density in the field. They are rotated by a transmission from one of the wheels either with a chain or gear. The distance between the soil and the delivery tube inlet defines the precision of planting: if the distance is bigger, the chance is greater of the seeds deviating from the desired plant spacing.

Seed plates in animal traction planters can be custom made by the planter-manufacturer. To reduce seed damage, the diameter of the plate should be large enough, so that the revolution speed of the plate is not too high. Animal traction planters with small metering discs should only be used with oxen and not with horses, as horses have higher forward speeds. Most modern animal traction planters now use standard discs designed for tractor planters, which can cope with the speed of any draught animal. For many years, scientists have thought that the best cover for seeds is loose soil. This thinking has evolved from situations with tilled seedbeds. However, especially under dry conditions, it can be observed that seeds under mulch cover germinate better than those covered by loose soil. Since under tilled conditions (loose soil) the macro-pore (=A pore in soil of a large enough size so that water is not held in it by capillary attraction) system in the vicinity of the seeds is completely destroyed the soil moisture equilibrium and the capillarity is disturbed. In undisturbed soil, the soil humidity equilibrium is intact providing optimal exchange of moisture between soil particles and pores. This allows the capillary supply of soil water to the soil surface while reducing the evaporation loss with the mulch cover.

In conservation agriculture, soil moisture loss takes place in the slot, and depending on the type of slot more or less moisture is lost. Further details of the relative moisture-conserving benefits of the different types of slot can be found in Baker et al. 1999. The inverted T-slot traps water vapour within the slot, which germinates the seed. Pressing on the seeds in V- and U-shaped slots before covering the seeds improves their performance, especially in dry soils. 1. Press wheels to close the slot in order to secure a good contact between soil and seed. The wheels at the back of the implement serve to press humid soil or crop residues on the slot in order to place the seed into close contact with the soil. Some seeders lack this wheel and in that case it is the operators of the planter who put the seeds into contact with the soil, as they walk on the slot. Surface residues are an important resource for promoting seedling emergence from dry soils and it is possible to obtain more effective seedling emergence from a dry soil by direct seeding than by tillage, provided the correct technique and equipment are used. The animal traction prototype seeders were originally made to plant one row at a time, but planters are now manufactured that can seed more rows. Multi-row versions might even provide an operator's seat.

Cover Crop and Residue Management in Conservation Agriculture

Conservation agriculture practices require a critical level of crop residues and cover crops to maintain or enhance soil chemical, physical and biological properties and prevent land degradation. In many areas of the world, crops and livestock compete for the same resources, and require proper management to meet conservation agriculture objectives.

Distribution of Residue on the Plant

In conservation agriculture, residues should be manipulated from harvest onwards. It depends on the following cover crop whether or not the residues should be distributed equally over the field or left intact so climbing cover crops like mucuna can use the maize stalks for support.An equal distribution of residues provides homogenous temperature and humidity conditions. If residues are not distributed more or less equally on the soil surface, this may cause the following problems:

- Bad placement of the seeds at sowing, resulting in an uneven germination.
- A cold and wet seed environment favours the development of pests and diseases.
- Allelopathy (=is a biological phenomenon by which an organism produces one or more biochemical that influence the growth, survival, and reproduction of other organisms) may be encouraged.

Timing Issues

It is important to choose the precise moment at which the vegetative cover is controlled, because most of the species used can regenerate if their growth is interrupted prematurely. Alternatively, seeds of the cover crop can germinate if the plants are allowed to mature, as may happen with oats, rye, chickpea, vetches and forage radish. There are, however, species and rotations where cover crops are purposely brought to maturity to establish a seed bank which will allow the cover crop to grow automatically once the cash crop is harvested.

The best moment to control the majority of cover crop species is at the full flowering stage when they have accumulated maximum biomass. In the case of legumes, the pods from the first flowering should be already formed but not yet mature. Vetches should have some mature pods. Oats and rye can be best managed at the milk stage. Horse radish can be slashed at any growth stage, but in systems of direct sowing and minimum tillage, seeds should be green and physiologically immature to avoid the germination of new plants. Both sunn-hemp and pigeon pea need to be controlled before flowering due to a high re-growth rate and excessive wood development in the stems.

The most adequate way to manage the cover crops depends on the objective of the cover crop and the possibilities of the farmer. If the requirement is for the dead mulch to cover the soil for as long as possible, the best way to manage the biomass is by using a knife-roller, chain, sledge (= a land vehicle with a smooth underside or possessing a separate body supported by two or more smooth, relatively narrow, longitudinal runners that travels by sliding across a surface) or herbicides.Cover crops can help to improve the resilience of the crop system against weather variability and climate hazards and minimize soil nutrient losses. This in the long run will benefit the soil quality and hence, all the aspects of farmer's livelihoods related to better crop yields. Adequate cover crop practices help to buffer the effect of erratic rainfall and mitigate moisture evaporation during droughts. Also helps water infiltration and increases water holding capacity, avoiding soil losses due to erosion and runoff.

Multi-Crop Zero Till Planter

Due to fragmented and small land holdings and variable farmer typology, it is neither affordable not advisable to purchase many machines for the planting of different crops by the same farmer. The multi-crop planter can plant different crops with variable seed size, seed rate, depth, spacing etc., providing simple solution to this. In addition to adjustments for row spacing, depth, gears for power transition to seed and fertilizer metering systems, the multi-crop planters have precise seed metering system using inclined rotary plates with variable grove number and size for different seed size and spacing for various crops. This provides flexibility for use of these planters for direct drilling of different crops with precise rate and spacing using the same planter which does not exist in fluted roller metering drills. Hence, the same multi-crop planter can be used for planting different crops by simply changing the inclined plates. The planter can also be used to make the beds and simultaneously sowing the crop just by mounting the shovels and shapers which can be easily accomplished due to the given provision in the machine. The planter has the provision of drilling both seed and fertilizer in one go. Also, as seed priming is very important for good germination and optimum plant population, the multi-crop planters provides opportunity to use primed seeds which is not possible in flutted roller metering drills.

1. Frame, 2. Furrow openers, 3. Tyres, 4. Fertilizer box, 5. Seed box, 6. Chain and gear drives, 7. Drive wheel, B. Depth control wheel, 9. Fertilizer delivery pipe, 10. Seed pipe, 11. Fertilizer rate adjusting nut, 12. Seed rate adjusting strip

Fig. 3.4

REFERENCES

Baker CJ, Saxton KE, Ritchie WR, Chamen WCT, Reicosky DC, Ribeiro MFS, Justice SE, Hobbs PR (2007) No-tillage Seeding in Conservation Agriculture, 2nd edn. FAO, Rome.

Calegari A, Darolt MR, Ferro M (1998) Towards Sustainable Agriculture with a No-tillage System. Adv Geo Ecol 31:1205–1209.

FAO (Food and Agriculture Organization of the United Nations) (2014) Conservation Agriculture. Rome (Agriculture and Consumer Protection Department) http://www.fao.org/ag/ca/6c.html. Accessed 29 June 2014

FAO. Mechanization for Rural Development. A Review of Patterns and Progress from around the World; Food and Agriculture Organization of the United Nations: Rome, Italy, 2013; p. 336.

FAO. Testing and Evaluation of Agricultural Machinery and Equipment: Principles and Practices; FAO Agricultural Services Bulletin 110; Food and Agriculture Organization of the United Nations: Rome, Italy, 1994; p. 102.

Farming and Development : *Technological Perspectives* **Pages 46-83**
Edited by: **Dr. Pawan Kumar 'Bharti' & Dr. Jaswant Ray**
ISBN: 978-93-88854-08-5
Edition: **2019**
Published by: **Discovery Publishing House Pvt. Ltd., New Delhi (India)**

4

Poultry in Integrated Farming Systems

[1]Alok Kumar Patra and [2]Tapas Kumar Raul

ABSTRACT

Poultry farming is an important component in any farming system. It plays a very vital role in imparting sustainability to the integrated farming system through organic manures. Poultry farming generates employment, especially for women in backyard poultry rearing. Thus, it provides more income and employment to ensure sustainable development of farm families. Much attention is being given for the development of poultry farming in India and with improved scientific management practices poultry has now become a popular rural enterprise in different states of the country. To bridge the gap between the demand and supply of eggs and meat poultry production both at commercial farming as well as in integrated approach with other enterprises can be encouraged. In this chapter an attempt has been made to enumerate the benefits of integrating poultry in farming systems and management of various poultry birds like chicken, duck, guinea fowl, quail, turkey, pigeon and emu.

INTRODUCTION

'Farming' is a process of harnessing solar energy in the form of economic plant and animal products. 'System' implies a set of interrelated practices and processes organised into functional entity, i.e. an arrangement of components or parts that interact according to some process and transforms inputs into outputs (Fresco and Westphal, 1988).

The International Organisation of Biological Control describes integrated farming as a farming system where high quality food, feed, fibre and renewable

1 Professor (Agronomy), All India Coordinated Research Project on Integrated Farming Systems, Orissa University of Agriculture and Technology, Bhubaneswar-751003, Odisha, India

2 Research Scholar, Department of Veterinary Parasitology, College of Veterinary Science and Animal Husbandry, Orissa University of Agriculture and Technology, Bhubaneswar-751003, Odisha, India

energy are produced by using resources such as soil, water, air and nature as well as regulating factors to farm sustainably and with as little polluting inputs as possible. Integrated farming system (IFS) is a commonly and broadly used word to explain a more integrated approach to farming as compared to monoculture approaches. In this system an inter-related set of enterprises are maintained and by-products or wastes from one production system becomes an input for another production system, which reduces cost and improves production and/or income. Thus, IFS works as a system of systems (Soni *et al.*, 2014). FAO (1977) stated that 'there is no waste', and 'waste is only a misplaced resource which can become a valuable material for another product' in IFS.

Different scientists have defined a farming system differently. However, many definitions, in general, convey the same meaning that it is the strategy to achieve profitable and sustained agricultural production to meet the diversified needs of farming community through efficient use of farm resources without degrading the natural resource base and environmental quality. Farming system is a decision making unit comprising the farm household, cropping and livestock system that transform land, capital and labour into useful products that can be consumed or sold (Fresco and Westphal, 1988).

Farming system represents an appropriate combination of farm enterprises (cropping systems, horticulture, livestock, fishery, forestry, and apiculture) and the means available to the farmer to raise them for profitability. It interacts adequately with environment without dislocating the ecological and socioeconomic balance on one hand and attempts to meet the national goals on the other (Jayanthi *et al.*, 2002). Thus, integrated farming is a system which tries to imitate the nature's principle, where not only crops but, varied types of plants, animals, birds, fish and other aquatic flora and fauna are utilized for production. These are combined in such a way and proportion that each element helps the other; the waste of one is recycled as resource for the other through 'low external input and sustainable agriculture' (LEISA) techniques (Das, 2013). The rationale of IFS is to minimize the wastes from the various subsystems on the farm and thus it improves employment opportunities, nutritional security and income of the rural people (Panke *et al.*, 2010).

WHY INTEGRATED FARMING SYSTEMS?

Farming systems approach introduces a change in farming techniques for higher production from the farm as a whole with the integration of all the enterprises. The farm products other than the economic products, for which crops are grown, can be better utilized for productive purposes in the farming systems approach. A judicious mix of cropping system with associated enterprises like dairy, poultry, fishery, apiary, sericulture, piggery, etc. suited to the given agroclimatic conditions and socioeconomic status of farmers would bring prosperity to farmer (Panda, 2004).

Integrated farming system has the advantages of increasing economic yield per unit area per unit time, profitability, sustainability and provides balanced nutritious food for the farmers, pollution free environment and provide opportunity for effective recycling of one product as input to other component, money round the year and solve the energy, fodder, fuel and timber crisis, avoids degradation of forests and enhance the employment generation, increase input use efficiency and finally improve the livelihood of the farming community (Suba Reddy and Ramakrishna, 2005). Thus the IFS is part of the strategy to ensure sustainable use of the natural resources for the benefit of present and future generations. The major benefits of integrated farming system can be summarised as below.

1. **Productivity:** IFS improves space utilization and increase productivity per unit area. Thus it provides an opportunity to increase economic yield per unit area per unit time by virtue of intensification of crop and allied enterprises.
2. **Profitability:** In IFS waste materials of one component are uses as inputs of another component at the least cost. Thus cost of production is reduced and interference of middleman in procuring most of the inputs is eliminated. Therefore, return per rupee invested or benefit to cost ratio in the farming is increased.
3. **Sustainability:** In integrated farming systems, organic supplementation through effective utilisation of by-products of linked components as a measure is possible and this provides opportunity to promote soil health and to sustain the potentiality of the soil for much longer periods.
4. **Balanced food:** In IFS, components of different nature are linked enabling production of different sources of nutrition, namely, protein, carbohydrates, fats, minerals, vitamins, etc from the same unit. It provides opportunity to mitigate malnutrition problem of the farm family.
5. **Pollution abatement:** In crop based activity, some of the organics are left as waste materials which in turn pollute the environment on decomposition. Application of huge quantities of fertilisers, pesticides, herbicides, insecticides, etc. pollutes soil, water and air. Much of the wastes could be converted/ recycled to some other forms of economic/ ecological/social value, under the integrated farming system. Integrated farming will also help in environmental protection through effective recycling of waste from animal activities like piggery, poultry and pigeon rearing.
6. **Recycling:** Effective recycling of waste materials (crop residues and livestock wastes) is possible in IFS. Therefore, there is less reliance to outside inputs like fertilizers, agrochemicals, feeds, energy, etc.

7. **Income rounds the year:** IFS provides diversified products. It provides flow of money to the farmer round the year due to integration of enterprises like crops, birds, animals, mushroom, honey, fish, etc. Thus it provides opportunities as crop insurance cover as money round the year is obtained from different farm produces. There is higher net return to land and labour resources of the farming family.
8. **Adoption of new technology:** Resources farmer (big farmer) fully utilise technology. On the other hand money flow in IFS round the year gives an inducement to the small/ marginal farmers to go for the adoption technologies.IFS promotes technology infusion through Research and Development (R&D) integrated with indigenous/traditional knowledge.
9. **Saving energy:** IFS provides an opportunity to identify an alternative source to the fossil energy. Effective recycling technique of the organic wastes available in the system can be utilised to generate biogas.
10. **Meeting fodder crisis:** Every piece of land area is effectively utilized. Plantation of perennial legume fodder trees on field borders and farm boundary will greatly relieve the problem of non-availability of quality fodder to the farm animals. This practice also improves soil fertility through atmospheric nitrogen fixation. Cultivation of fodder crops as intercropping and as border cropping will also result in the availability of adequate nutritious fodder for animal components like milch cow, goat / sheep, pig and rabbit.
11. **Solving fuel and timber crisis:** The production level of fuel and industrial wood can be enhanced by integrating suitable perennial tree species in farming system (agroforestry) without affecting the crop productivity. This will also greatly reduce pressure on forest resource, thus it preserves the natural ecosystem.
12. **Employment generation:** Integrating crop with livestock enterprises would increase the labour requirement significantly and would help in reducing the problems of unemployment to a great extent. IFS provides enough scope to employ family labour round the year.
13. **Agro-industries:** Integrated farming also provides opportunities for agri-oriented industries, tourism and related tourism based activities. When produce of any component of the IFS is increased to commercial level there will be surplus for value addition, leading to development of allied agro-industries.
14. **Increasing input efficiency:** IFS provides good scope to use inputs in different components with greater efficiency and benefit cost ratio.
15. **Improving/ maintaining soil health:** IFS improves soil fertility and soil physical structure through practice of appropriate crop rotation, cover crop, green manuring, composting farm organic wastes and recycling

crop residues. Soil erosion can also be checked by agroforestry and proper cultivation of each part of land by integrated farming.

16. **Reduction of pests:** Adoption of appropriate crop rotation in the farming system can reduce the infestation of weeds, insect pests and diseases.

COMPONENTS OF IFS

Farmers make decisions about what to grow, what animals to keep, the level and type of inputs and the methods they will use. Their decisions are based upon a range of social, economic and environmental factors. The farmers' attitudes and level of knowledge are also important. However, the selection of enterprises must be based on cardinal principle of minimising the competition and maximising the complementarities between the enterprises (Annadurai *et. al.,* 1994). The important factors that govern choice of IFS modules include climatic conditions, soil type, farmers' preferences, size of the farm, knowledge, skill and technology, storage, transport and marketing, resource mobilizing power, credit facilities available, socioeconomic conditions, customs, sentiments and believes, etc.

Integrated farming system is a resource management strategy to achieve economic and sustained agricultural production to meet diverse requirements of farm household while preserving the resource base and maintaining high environmental quality. The entire philosophy of farming system revolves around better utilization of time, money, resources and family labour. Integrated farming system is focused around a few selected, inter-dependent,

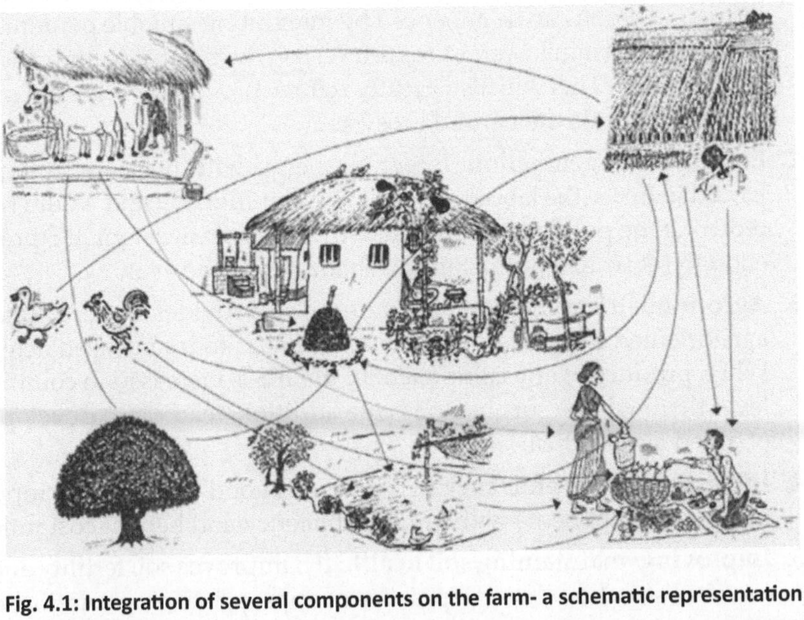

Fig. 4.1: Integration of several components on the farm- a schematic representation

(**Source:** http://www.agriculturesnetwork.org/magazines/india/family-farming/integrated-farming)

inter-related and often inter-linking production systems based on few crops, animal and related subsidiary enterprises. It involves the utilization of primary and/ or secondary produce of one system as raw material for other system, thus making the entire system mutually interdependent as one whole unit. There is a need for effective linkages and complementarities of various components to develop holistic farming system. Important components of the farming system include field crops, vegetable crops, fruit crops, floriculture, livestock (cow, buffalo, sheep, goat, pig, etc), pisciculture, poultry, duckery, agroforestry, bee keeping, mushroom cultivation, bio-gas, vermicompost, etc.

This farming system seems to answer the problems of increasing food production, increasing net farm income, improving nutritional status, promoting natural resource management, sustainable use of land, water and biota. Integration of poultry with IFS might be an economically viable and productive system for both rural farmers and commercial entrepreneurs.

BENEFITS OF POULTRY FARMING

Generally, poultry farming means, raising various types of domestic birds for the purpose of producing foods like eggs and meat. In this context, animal husbandry sector plays a major role in alleviating protein deficiency and sustainability of rural economy. Rural poultry is a good occupation for the rural masses for economic sustainability and nutritional security. Many developing countries have adopted poultry as a microenterprise with women empowerment as a model for rural economic sustainability. The most common and widely raised poultry birds are chicken and ducks. The other popular poultry birds for farming in India include turkey, quail, guinea fowl and pigeon.

1. The poultry farming does not require high capital for starting. Most of the poultry birds are not costly enough to start raising. It requires less investment compared to rearing other livestock. Farming with about 100 chickens requires only around 10,000/- on fixed capital. Thus small and marginal farmers and even agricultural landless labourers can start poultry farming on a small scale. It can be well suited to many other components in an in integrated farming system.
2. Poultry farming does not require a big space unless it is started commercially. Some birds can easily be raised on backyard with one or numerous coops or cages.
3. Poultry farming ensures high return of investment within a very short period. Some poultry birds like broiler chickens take shorter duration of time to mature and generating profit. Chicken start laying eggs in 10 to 12 weeks and broilers can be sold for meat between 6 and 10 weeks. The interval between generations is very small and hence, production can be phenomenally increased within a short period.

4. Poultry is capable of utilizing large quantities of farm by-products like bran, substandard grains, vegetables, fruits, etc. which normally go as waste. Broilers intake of feed is comparatively very low while it produces maximum possible amount of food for humans.
5. Poultry farming is a continuous source of income. It is not seasonal and can produce income for the entire year. Meat, eggs and manure of poultry birds are all saleable and income generating.
6. Poultry farming requires very little water for both drinking and cleaning. One litre of water is sufficient for 5 birds for a day.
7. Poultry farm structures do not require high maintenance. Diseases and illness in poultry can be minimised by following proper hygiene and care. Diseases are less in some poultry birds like quails, turkeys, etc.
8. Poultry droppings are rich in nitrogen and organic material and hence, are considered valuable as fertilizers.
9. Poultry offers full time or part-time employment opportunity to farmers. Unemployed educated youth can easily create an income and employment opportunity for them by raising poultry. Women and students can also do this business along with their daily activities.
10. Poultry provides fresh and nutritious food and has a huge global demand. Poultry products like egg and meat have high nutritional value. Among all edible meat, broiler meat has the least fat content. Poultry meat contains more protein and essential amino acids than other meats and is low in its cholesterol content. Poultry products are not much expensive and most of the people can afford those.
11. Poultry feathers are also used for making pillows and fancy articles.
12. Marketing poultry products is very easy. There is an established market for poultry products in both urban and rural areas. So poultry products can easily be sold in the nearest local market.

Poultry is a remunerative and popular component in an integrated farming system. Net return from poultry component mostly depends on feed quality and feed formulation system. For proper growth and desired production, all types of poultry birds need some essential nutrients. Most of these essential nutrients come from the natural sources. Pasture, grains and seeds, bugs and insects, sunshine, gravel etc. meet up the demands of necessary nutrients.

CHICKEN FARMING

Nowadays, chicken (*Gallus gallusdomesticus*) farming is considered the synonym of poultry farming in India because it dominates the poultry market both in meat and egg production. The largest number of chicken population in India is found in Andhra Pradesh, Telengana, Tamil Nadu, Maharashtra, West Bengal, Karnataka, Bihar, Odisha, Kerala, Assam, Uttar Pradesh and Punjab. Chick eggs come second only to mother's milk in terms of nutritive value. As per the ICMR recommendations, the annual average per capita egg consumption should be 180 and meat 11 kg. Besides subsidiary income generation, rural backyard chicken provides nutrition supplementation in the form of valuable animal protein and empowers women. Backyard chicken farming can suitably be integrated to any farming system.

Backyard Chicken Farming

As the name indicates the birds are reared in the backyard of the homestead. Backyard chicken rearing requires hardly any infrastructure setup. Backyard rearing is mostly seen in villages but some houses in the urban areas also rear chicken in the backyard. The birds are provided with lots of kitchen waste and food leftovers. They scavenge and eat termites, ants, earthworm and insects. During the dry seasons, the birds may additionally be provided with rice bran or wheat bran mixed with the rice starch and other vegetables. Besides targeted egg and meat production, it is a potent tool for up-liftment of the rural poor. It has a very positive impact to improve the socio-economic factors of the socio economically backward people. Backyard chicken production can cater to the nutritional requirements of the family as well as cater to a niche market, thus providing a source of subsistence income. Backyard chicken can be taken up by every household as a subsidiary occupation, as a source of additional income or to cater to the egg and meat requirements of the family by taking up coloured bird units ranging from 10-20 birds per family in their backyards. Such units require very little hand feeding and can give a fairly handsome return with bare minimum night shelter.

Semi-intensive system may be adopted where the amount of free space available is limited, but it is necessary to allow 10-20 m^2 area per bird of outside run. In the semi-intensive system of rearing, feed and water are placed in the outside run or yard. The floor in the run can be cemented with addition of litter over the cemented floor or it could just be a sand floor. The run is fenced by using wire, bamboo or any other local material. The birds are driven to the pen during dusk, and they are well protected during the night. At daytime the birds are let out into the yard or run and stay there till the evening. The yard and the pen must be cleaned regularly once the birds are out of them. Under the semi-intensive system of rearing birds are provided with feed and clean potable water. The feed could be a well balance mash or pellet, or it could be the remains of household waste, vegetable waste mixed with some cheap grains and by products of grains.

Native chicken have undergone natural selection and are best adapted for the local climatic conditions, they can survive on kitchen and agricultural wastes and survives well on scavenging and left over feed. They are hardy and resistant to many diseases. They survive well from predators. Native hens are good brooders and have good mothering ability. But native chicken are low on productivity, so to increase productivity improved varieties of chicken need to be reared.

There is a wide a variety of chicken breeds, developed for egg production, meat production, and/or good looks. While many breeds are adaptable to a backyard setting, certain breeds are better than others for backyard conditions. Improved varieties like, Cauvery, Kalinga Brown, Nirbheek, Gramapriya, Blackrock and Vanaraja due to their moderate body weight and high egg yielding capacity are more preferred under semi-intensive farm conditions in rural areas. The feather colour of all the rural type birds are multiple coloured and mostly brown eggers. They have the better immune capacity and thereby strength of survivability is maximum. Because of moderate body weight the birds can escape from predators.

Rural chicks need brooding care during the initial 6 weeks of age. After 6 weeks, they can be let free for scavenging in the backyard. The excess males can be reared separately and marketed for meat purpose. The birds need to be initially trained to return to the nest in the evening for night shelter for security and safety reasons. The night shelter should have good ventilation and protection from predators and plenty of clean water should be made available.

Advantages of Rearing Indigenous Birds Over Exotic Birds

- Acceptability of the coloured desi bird by the landless labourers or marginal farmers.
- Use of broodiness for hatching the chicks.
- Capability of self-defence from predators due to its alertness, light body weight longer shank length, camouflagic characters and aggressiveness.
- Can thrive well under adverse environments like poor housing, poor management and poor feeding.
- Indigenous birds are comparatively disease resistant to protozoon and ecto-parasites.
- Have better adaptability to extreme climatic conditions prevailing in the country.
- They are comparatively hardier and need less health care than exotic birds.
- The meat from native fowl has significantly higher amino acid contents (arginine and lysine) than meat from exotic birds and is widely preferred especially because of their pigmentation, taste, leanness and suitability for special dishes and often fetches higher prices.
- The brown-shelled eggs of native fowl are rich in threonine and valine than farm eggs, have good flavour and fetch premium price.

Indian Breeds of Chicken

Aseel: 'Aseel' is well known for its pugnacity, high stamina, majestic gait and dogged fighting qualities. The name Aseel appears to have been given to this indigenous breed because of its inherent qualities of fighting. Andhra Pradesh is said to be the home of this important breed. The best specimen of this breed, although rare, is encountered with the fanciers and the people engaged in cock-fighting show throughout the country. The standard weight varies from 3 to 4 kg for cocks and 2 to 3 kg for hens. The bird attains sexual maturity at 196 days. A hen lays about 92 eggs in a year and average weight of an egg is 50 g.

Kadaknath: This breed is otherwise known as 'Kalamasi' which means 'fowl with black flesh' and is native of Madhya Pradesh. The colour of the day old chicks is bluish to black with irregular dark stripes over the back. The skin, beak, shank, toes and soles of feet of males and females are dark gray colour. Even the comb, wattles and tongue also show a purplish hue. The shining blue tinge of the earlobes adds to its unique features. The peculiarity of this breed is that most of the internal organs show the characteristic black pigmentation which is more pronounced in trachea, thoracic and abdominal air sacs, gonads, elastic arteries, at the base of the heart and mesentery. Varying degree of blackish colouration is also found in the skeletal muscles, tendons, nerves, brain and bone marrow. The black colour of muscles and tissues is due to the deposition of melanin pigment, a genetic condition called 'Fibromelanosis'. Body weight of a bird at 20 weeks is 920 g. The bird attains sexual maturity at 180 days. A hen lays about 105 eggs in a year and average weight of an egg is 50 g.

Naked neck: 'Naked neck' is relatively larger inbuilt with long cylindrical neck. As the name indicates, neck of the birds is fully naked or only a tuft of feathers is seen on the front of the neck above crop. The resulting bare skin becomes reddish particularly in males as they approach sexual maturity. General body feathering is also reduced. Due to the reduced feathering, the birds are capable to tolerate the tropical stress. It lays the biggest size eggs among all the Indian native breeds of chicken.

Table 4.1: Indian Breeds of Chicken

Breed	Home Tract
Ankaleshwar	Gujarat
Aseel	Chhattisgarh, Odisha, Telengana and Andhra Pradesh
Busra	Gujarat and Maharashtra
Chittagong	Meghalaya and Tripura
Daothigir, Miri	Assam
Ghagus	Karnataka, Telengana and Andhra Pradesh
Harringhata Black	West Bengal

Kadaknath	Madhya Pradesh
Danki, Kalasthi	Telengana and Andhra Pradesh
Kashmir Favorolla	Jammu and Kashmir
Nicobari	Andaman & Nicobar
Punjab Brown	Punjab and Haryana
Tellichery	Kerala
Mewari	Rajasthan

Improved Varieties of Chicken

Vanaraja: 'Vanaraja' is a dual-purpose variety for free range farming in rural and tribal areas. It can be reared in backyards on natural, scavenged food with minimal supplementation. It produces eggs and meat based on rearing and feeding practices. Important features of this breed are multi-color feather pattern, immunity to disease, perform with less nutrition, grow faster and produce more eggs, produce brown eggs like local hens. Males weigh about 1.2 to 1.5 kg at 10 wks and females lay about 120-140 eggs per year. This variety is best suited to the agro-climatic zones of Telangana and Andhra Pradesh.

Gramapriya: 'Gramapriya' is a layer type variety developed for free range farming in rural areas. It starts laying eggs at an age of 175 days. The bird has the production potential of 230-240 eggs in a year and can lay 160-180 eggs in free-range conditions with minimum supplementary feeding. The males weigh around 1.2 to 1.5 kg at 15 weeks of age. The bird has coloured plumage and lays bigger (57-59 g) and brown eggs. It is hardy and has immunity to disease.

Giriraja: 'Giriraja' breed of chicken is suited for mixed and backyard farming. Females lay 130-150 eggs per year, with each egg weighing 52-55 g. The eggs have a good hatchability (80-85 per cent), and enable farmers to raise their own stock. Their shells are brown in colour and thicker than that of other commercial eggs. The bird's exhibit better growth compared to local varieties, they can be raised as free-roaming birds and can be fed with locally available materials. Being good scavengers, they feed on a variety of insects and green foliage. They can also be fed on farm and kitchen waste. The birds are resistant to many diseases. For backyard rearing, a flock of five hens and one cock is ideal.

Swarnadhara: 'Swarnadhara' is a hardy bird having high egg production potential along with better growth compared to other local varieties and are suited for mixed and backyard farming. The bird can be reared for both eggs and meat. Hens attain a body weight of about 3 kg and the cocks about 4 kg by 23rd week. They lay about 180-190 eggs in a year. Each egg weighs about 55-60 g. The eggs have good hatchability (80-85 per cent) and enable the farmers to raise their own stock. The eggshell is brown in colour and thicker than that of other commercial eggs and does not break easily. The eggs can be stored for 8-10 days at room temperature during summer and during winter for about 15 days. The birds are only layers and not brooders. The eggs have to be hatched by local brooder hens. For backyard rearing, a flock of five hens and one cock can be ideally grown. They can be raised as free roaming birds and can be fed with locally available materials, being good scavengers; they feed on a variety of insects and green foliage. They can also be fed on farm and kitchen wastes. The birds have a high longevity, they are sturdy and resistant to major infections and diseases.

Gramalakshmi and Gramasree: These two varieties have a high production potential along with better growth rate suited for mixed and backyard farming. 'Gramalakshmi' birds are white in colour with black speckles throughout the body while 'Gramasree' birds are dark brown with a sprinkling of black, and grey on different parts of the body. The hens attain a body weight of 1.4 kg in five months and start laying eggs after 160 days. The males attain a body weight of 1.5 kg in three months and are popular for their meat, which is low in fat content compared with present day broilers. Both the varieties lay about 200 eggs in a year with each egg weighing about 50 g. The eggshell is brown in colour and thicker than that of other commercial eggs and does not break easily. The birds are hardy and require little care and can be reared in the open. They can be fed on farm and kitchen waste. The birds are usually kept in the ratio of one cock for 10 hens. These varieties are only layers and cannot hatch the eggs. For hatching purposes local hens are to be used.

Srinidhi: 'Srinidhi' is a dual purpose variety for rural chicken production. The bird has coloured plumage and lays bigger (57-59 g) and brown eggs. The bird is early maturing (175 days) and annual average egg production is 150. The survivability is more than 95%. It is hardy and liveability is high. The rural and tribal farmers of many states are being profited by this variety.

Jharsim: 'Jharsim' is a dual purpose chicken variety suitable for Jharkhand state. These birds have attractive multi-colour plumage; perform better on low level of nutrition, faster growth, optimum egg production and better adaptability to agro climatic conditions of Jharkhand. The birds weigh 400-500 g at 6 weeks and 1600-1800 g at maturity under backyard system. The age at first egg laying is 175-180 days and egg weight is 52-55g at 40 weeks of age. The birds have the potential to lay 165-170 eggs per year under backyard system. This variety can provide higher supplementary income and nutrition through both egg and meat to rural people.

Kamrupa: 'Kamrupa' is a multi-coloured dual purpose variety for free range farming suitable for Assam. This variety has coloured plumage, mediocre body weight and longer shanks with optimum egg production. Under backyard system, the body weight at 8 and 20 weeks is 500-650 g and 1300-1500 g, respectively. The male birds weigh 1800-2200 g at 40 weeks of age. The annual egg production is 118-130 eggs with an egg weight of 52 g.

Pratapdhan: 'Pratapdhan' is a dual purpose chicken variety to cater to the needs of rural chicken growers of Rajasthan. Birds have longer shank length which helps in self protection from predators in backyard areas and has capacity to survive on low nutrition and harsh climatic conditions. It lays brown eggs weighing around 50 g and has broody characteristic to some extent. It has fast growth rate with average adult body weight at 20 weeks of age ranged from 1478 to 3020 g in males and 1283 to 2736 g in females. The age at sexual maturity was 170 days. 'Pratapdhan' produces about 160 eggs annually.

Krishibro: This variety is multi-coloured, hardy, well adapted and is for meat purpose. It attains body weight by 6 weeks of age with less than 2.2 feed conversion ratio. The survivability of this bird upto 6 weeks of age is around 97%. These birds have attractive colour plumage and are well adapted to tropical weather conditions. The commercial 'Krishibro' has highly resistance against the common poultry diseases like ranikhet and infectious bursal diseases.

Chicken Housing and Management

Good and suitable housing play a vital role in raising chickens. Birds can be raised in both free range and indoor production systems. In case indoor production system, it is very crucial to manage the environment. Chickens need accurate management and environment for better production. Sufficient space should always be kept in the houses so that birds can live, grow and produce happily. Poultry house should never be overcrowded. A minimum 3-5 square feet floor space is required per bird, including outdoor space. The house should be well ventilated and sufficient flow of fresh air and light inside the house should be ensured. The house and equipment are to be cleaned on a regular basis and the house should be sterilized before bringing new chicks. Care must be taken for suitable drainage system inside the house for cleaning it properly. Predators and harmful animals should be kept away from the shelter. The main predators are rats, owls, hawks, stray dogs and cats.

A quality coop is essential to backyard chicken production. Layers need nest boxes, one per 4-5 birds. Coops must provide protection from the weather. There should be a well-insulated area with a light bulb or heat lamp for the winter months as well as ventilation for fresh air. An enclosed space for them to stay at night is essential to their protection. The housing system must have to be weather proof. Weather proof housing system keeps the birds safe from the adverse weather conditions such as cold, rain, wind, hot sun etc. The chicken housing system should have the facilities of providing warmth, particularly during brooding period and winter season.

Well ventilation inside poultry housing system plays a very vital role to control the indoor environment. It removes moisture, heat, gas etc. and brings fresh air inside the chicken house. The chicken houses should be provided with wide windows and side curtains to ensure the entrance of fresh air to make the house cold during summer season. A pair of vent in the roof of the house will help to remove the hot air. A roof of at least six feet height from the floor is suitable for this purpose.

Light is also a very important element for chicken farming as birds are very sensitive to light. Light helps the birds to be productive, finding food and simulating them for reproduction. Besides light, the poultry birds also need dark period for keeping good health and producing melatonin hormone, which is very important for immune function. Birds require 8 hours of darkness period and 16 hours presence of light. Darkness is helpful for some fast growing broiler species, and helps them for reducing leg disorders and builds their body frame. However, young chicks require 24 hours light daily after hatching for finding food and water pot.

For successful chicken farming and getting desired production, litter management is very important. Usually the litter is used for covering the floor of housing system which may be made of concrete, wood or earth. Litter absorbs the moisture of closet and dilutes the manure. It also works as the bed for the poultry birds. Rice hulls, hay and straw and soft wood shavings are the common materials used as litter in chicken house floors. A good litter contain about 20% to 30% moisture and depth about 5 to 8 cm. High moisture in litter is very harmful for chicken health. Wet litter causes some problem like sores, and blister on birds and produce ammonia gas which hampers the respiratory system of birds. Aluminum sulfate or hydrated lime may be used to reduce ammonia gas from the litter. After disposal of all birds the used litter from house floor should be removed. This litter can be used as good manure in the agricultural land for crop production. Dry poultry manure contains about 3.5% nitrogen, 2.0% phosphorus and 1.5% potassium.

Effect of Climate on Chickens

Hot weather can have a severe impact on performance of chicken. The climate in chicken houses influences the health of the birds. Respiratory, digestive and behavioural disorders are more likely to occur in houses in which the climatic conditions are not up to standard. Production efficiency can be affected long before the temperature reaches a level at which survival becomes a concern.

Table 4.2: Effect of Ambient Temperature on Adult Birds

Temperature range (in degree Celsius)	Effect on adult poultry birds
13 - 24	Thermal neutral zone. The temperature range in which the bird does not need to alter its basic metabolic rate or behaviour to maintain its body temperature.
19 - 24	Ideal temperature range.
24 - 30	A slight reduction in feed consumption can be expected, but if nutrient intake is adequate, production efficiency is good. Egg size may be reduced and shell quality may suffer as temperatures reach the top of this range.
30 - 33	Feed consumption falls further. Weight gains are lower. Egg size and shell quality deteriorate. Egg production usually suffers. Cooling procedures should be started before this temperature range is reached.
33 - 35	Feed consumption continues to drop. There is some danger of heat prostration among layers, especially the heavier birds and those in full production. At these temperatures, cooling procedures must be carried out.
35 - 38	Heat prostration is probable. Emergency measures may be needed. Egg production and feed consumption are severely reduced. Water consumption is very high.
> 38	Emergency measures are needed to cool birds. Survival is the concern at these temperatures.

(**Source:** Anderson and Carter, 2007)

The layers are warm blooded with a body temperature of 41 - 42.2° C. Body temperature is kept quite constant and is regulated by part of the chicken brain. It takes some time before heat regulating mechanisms start functioning in newborn chicks and therefore they need a higher ambient temperature than adult birds do. Furthermore, the ratio between the surface area and weight of young chicks is unfavourable and they do not have any fat reserves. The comfort zone is defined as the temperature zone in which the birds are able to keep their body temperature constant with minimum effort. Behaviour of birds will change when temperatures rise to above or decrease to below the comfort zone.

The thermo-neutral zone is defined as the temperature zone in which the birds are able to keep their body temperature constant with the help of physical heat regulation. The lowest temperature in the thermo-neutral zone is called the lowest critical temperature. If temperatures fall to under this temperature the bird will start to use feed energy to warm itself and will consequently consume more feed. The highest temperature in the thermo-neutral zone is called the highest critical temperature. If the temperature rises above this temperature the birds can no longer dissipate their heat. They will start to consume less feed and production will drop as a result. The highest and lowest critical temperature of a bird depends on its age and bodyweight, housing system, feeding level, relative humidity and air velocity. The critical temperature for layers is 20°C. For every 1°C lower than 20°C, the birds require an extra 1.5 g of feed per day. The most efficient temperature for layers lies between 20 and 24°C. When temperature rises above 24°C, shell quality and egg weight will reduce. The critical temperature for broilers and rearing birds is highly dependent on age.

Relative humidity in poultry houses is measured to determine its impact on respiratory disorders. If the relative humidity is too high, condensation may accumulate in the house which leads to wet litter. This has a direct effect on the growth of microorganisms. Humidity is controlled by the intense heating or cooling of air inside the house in response to the temperature outside the house. The ideal relative humidity for poultry is 60 - 80%.

Table 4.3: Recommended Temperature and Relative Humidity for the Birds

Age of the bird (in days)	Recommended ambient temperature (°C)	Recommended relative humidity (%)
1	33	50
7	31.5	50
14	28.5	60
21	28.5	65
28	26	70
42	23	85

(**Source:** Hulzebosch, 2006)

Chicken Feed Management

Rural chicks need brooding care during the initial 6 weeks of age. After 6 weeks, they can be let free for scavenging in the backyard. For healthy life, proper growth, maximum production and suitable breeding, all types of poultry birds need some essential nutrients. Most of these essential nutrients come from the natural sources. Chickens are omnivorous. They eat grains, fruits, and vegetables as well as insects. Chickens should typically be fed a prepared feed that is balanced for vitamins, minerals, and protein. A healthy laying hen diet should also contain crushed oyster shell for egg production, and grit for digestion. Birds also love fruit and vegetable scraps from the kitchen and garden, as well as bread. Feed consumption may increase in the winter, and decrease in the heat of the summer. A critical part of a chicken's diet is continual access to clean, fresh water. This is especially true in the summer as they cool themselves by panting.

During the first day, feed may be sprinkled or provided in the trays for encouraging the new born chicks to pick up feed. From day two onwards feed is provided in trough type of feeders. As the chicks grow bigger suitable feeders are used. The feeders should be at proper height for the birds to eat properly. As chicks grow the feeder should be lifted up by adjusting their height to the back level of the bird. The level of feed in feeder has a direct correlation with feed wastage. As a thumb rule, 10 percent feed is wasted if the feeders are two thirds full compared to 3 percent wastage if they are half full and only 1 percent if they are one third full. Therefore, feed should be offered more frequently with small quantity at each time and helps to gain weight more uniformly. During first week, frequent feeding of small quantity should be practiced to stimulate feed consumption.

Clean and fresh water should be provided to the chicks. Water may be provided using troughs, bell shaped drinkers and caps. With these drinkers 2 cm of water space per bird is recommended. Water should be provided before the chicks are released under the brooders. Height of the drinkers needs to be adjusted according to the chick height. One chick drinker is enough for 100 chicks up to 2 weeks of age and regular bell drinker is sufficient for 50 birds from third week onwards.

The most expensive poultry feed element is protein. There are two types of protein source are available, animal and vegetable protein. Animal protein is a great source of adding required protein in poultry feed. The animal protein means, that comes from animals sources such as meat, meat meal, milk, liver etc. This type of protein is very helpful for proper growth and better egg production, than vegetable protein. Carbohydrate is essential for a starved flock. This poultry feed materials can be found in grains and grainy products. Carbohydrate provides energy to the birds and keeps them productive. Proper ratio of fat in poultry feed is also very essential. Usually fat is available in almost all types of feed elements. But an excess amount of fat that comes from fish products, fish oil or meat can causes digestive problem and lead to various poultry disease. Calcium carbonate helps to formulate the egg shell. Calcium and phosphorous make the major part of poultry bird's bone. But excess amount of phosphorous in poultry feed lead to crooked bones and slipped tendons in chickens and poultry birds. Salt is also a reliable source of essential minerals.

Any vitamin deficiency in poultry feed rations can hinder the natural growth of young poultry birds. Vitamin A comes from green feed ingredients, yellow corn and fish oils. It is essential to protect the poultry birds against colds and infections. Vitamin D helps to prevent leg weakness and rickets. It is found in synthetic products and also available in sea fishes. Vitamin D is a must added elements in poultry feed. Vitamin B complex is available in milk, green feed, liver, synthetic riboflavin etc. It helps to increase the growth of chickens. It also helps to prevent curled-toe paralysis in young chickens. While preparing poultry feed, adequate amount of Vitamin B Complex should be added in the poultry feed mixture.

Sanitation and Chicken Health

An important element to bird health is sanitation. In order to maintain a clean, healthy environment, the coop and outdoor area should be cleaned out weekly or as needed to control manure and odour build up. Feeders and waterers should be regularly cleaned and disinfected. It is important that at least once a year, a thorough cleaning is done on the coop and yard. Also cleaning before introducing new birds to the area will limit the spread of disease. Inhalation of dried chicken manure can be harmful to humans.

Healthy birds will be active and alert with bright eyes. Chickens raised in backyard settings generally stay healthy and are not easily susceptible to diseases. The easiest way to find disease in chickens is to know what a healthy bird looks like. When a chicken is not acting normal, for instance if she does not run to the food as usual or she wheezes or sneezes, an investigation should be carried out to know what is wrong with the bird.

The birds must be vaccinated against Marek's and Ranikhet diseases. Birds should be dewormed starting from 7th week and repeated at 3-4 months intervals so as to give a total of 4 deworming. Piperazine compounds, albendazole, mebendazole etc. can be used against round worms. While medicating through drinking water, it should be done by mixing the required quantity of medicine in the quantity of water that chicks normally consume in 4 hours' time. One hundred chicks of 6 week-old consume approximately 6 litres water per day. Additional water should be given only when all the medicated water is consumed by the chicks.

Diseases of Chicken

Various types of poultry diseases can cause serious loss in the poultry farming. Diseases occur due to lack of proper care and management, inadequate nutritious feeding and some other factors. However, serious illness is unlikely in a backyard flock, especially if the chickens are vaccinated. Antibiotics do not help viruses in birds. Proper nutrition and keeping the birds healthy at all times will help avoid most chicken diseases and symptoms. Preventative measures for most of the chicken diseases are always better than curative measures.

Infectious Bronchitis is a common chicken sickness in backyard flocks. Its severity ranges from mild to severe. Most flocks are exposed to it from wildlife and develop a certain resistance to it. The best way to prevent disease in any livestock is to keep their immune system as healthy as possible. Symptoms include marked decrease in eating and drinking, discharge from the nostrils and eyes, gasping, coughing, breathing sounds, decreased egg laying, misshaped eggs and soft-shelled. A heat lamp should be used on the affected birds to keep them warm and antibiotic treatment can be given.

Fowl Pox is another common chicken sickness in backyard flocks. This disease has fewer fatalities. Symptoms include white blister-like lesions appearing more noticeably on the combs and wattles and in extreme cases, these are found on the legs and body. Like chicken pox in a human, they develop scabs which will heal and fall off in about three weeks. On the rare occasion, the pox can also be in the chicken's mouth and throat which may cause breathing problems. This is the usual cause of death from this disease. Vaccine is available for this disease and recovered birds are immune and do not carry the disease.

Symptoms of infectious coryza, a bacterial disease include facial puffiness, discharge from eyes and nose, sneezing and coughing, difficult and laboured breathing, staggering, reduced or no eating and drinking, reduced or no egg laying, wheezing and raspy breathing. An antibiotic for this disease is available but may not fully control the disease. Birds should be destroyed as they remain carriers for life.

Marek's disease is more common in younger birds that are usually under the age of 20 weeks and it is very easy for them to catch. It is a virus which means it is super easy to transmit from bird to bird. The disease causes tumours externally and internally; paralysis; iris of eye turns gray and does not react to light. If a chick gets this disease it needs to be put down because it will remain a carrier of the disease for life if it survives. However, there is a vaccine and it is usually given to day old chicks.

Chicken-Fish Farming

Chicken excreta are an excellent feed for fish as it contains highly soluble organic salts, more N and P as compared to other livestock manure. Thus, growing chicken for meat or eggs can be integrated with fish culture to reduce costs on fertilizers and feeds in fish culture and maximize benefits. Chicken can be raised over or adjacent to the ponds and the poultry excreta recycled to fertilize the fishponds. Raising chickens over the pond has certain advantages; it maximizes the use of space, saves labour in transporting manure to the ponds and the poultry house is more hygienic. No significant differences have been observed on the chickens' growth or egg laying when they are raised over the ponds or on land. In case of the former, the pond dykes can also be utilized for raising vegetables and short duration fruit crops like papaya, pineapple, banana, lemons, etc.

For the first 14 days, chicks need to be raised separately in a brooder (not on the shelters over the pond), as they need higher temperature of 28-33°C. Each chick during this period needs a space of about 7.5 × 7.5 cm. To maintain the required temperature range, an electric lamp can be hung above the chicks kept in a bamboo fence.

Broilers: 30-50 broilers could be raised on a 1000 m^2 pond. The chicken house can be constructed over the pond at least 0.5 m above maximum pond water level, or on the embankment. 50 birds require 75 ft^2 space. The house can be made of bamboo or any other locally available cheap materials. Roof can be covered with hay or similar material. Enough cross ventilation should be maintained to keep cool during hot days. Floors are to be constructed with bamboo slats, with 1 cm gap, to allow excreta to fall into pond, but not wide enough for the chicken's feet to get caught in between and injured. Feed with starter mash for 1-4 weeks and with finisher mash for 5-8 weeks, given as much as they can consume. A 100-kg starter mash requires 50 kg crushed wheat, 14.5 kg rice bran, 16 kg sesame oil cake, 19 kg fishmeal and 0.5 kg salt. A 100 kg finisher mash requires 50 kg crushed wheat, 17 kg rice bran, 15 kg sesame oil cake, 16 kg fish meal, 1.5 kg bone meal and 0.5 kg salt. In both cases, vitamin premix is added at the rate of 250 g/100 kg of feed. Water should be provided at all times. Broilers reach market size of 1.5-1.8 kg in 7-8 weeks and it is possible to raise five to six batches in a year.

Chicken layers: 30-50 layers can be raised over a pond of 1000 m^2. Housing can be constructed on pond or on embankment. 50 birds require 150 ft^2 space. For the first 16 weeks, feed is given at the rate of 80-110 g/bird/day and from 17th week onwards, 110-120 g/bird/day. Temperature in the poultry house should always be above 20-22°C. When the temperature goes below this level, two 200-watt electric bulbs can be hung for every 50 chickens. Layers start laying after 22 weeks and 250-280 eggs/bird/year could be obtained. Egg laying becomes uneconomical after chickens reach the age of 18 months, when they need to be replaced.

DUCK FARMING

Ducks form about 10% of the total poultry population and contribute about 6-7% of total eggs produced in the country. Ducks are mostly concentrated in the eastern and southern states of the country.

Advantages of Duck Farming

1. Ducks lay more egg per bird per year than chicken.
2. The size of the duck egg is larger than hen egg by about 15 to 20 g.
3. Ducks require lesser attention and thrive well in scavenging conditions.
4. Ducks supplements their feed by foraging. They eat fallen grains in paddy fields, insects, snails, earthworms, small fishes and other aquatic materials.
5. From commercial point of view, ducks have a longer profitable life. They lay well even in second year.

6. Ducks do not require any elaborate houses like chicken
7. Ducks are quite hardy, more easily brooded and more resistant to common avian diseases.
8. Marshy river side, wet land and barren moors upon which chicken or no other type of stock will flourish, are excellent quarters for duck farming.
9. Ducks lay 95-98% of their eggs in the morning before 9.00 AM. Thus it saves lot of time and labour of the grower for collecting eggs.
10. Ducks are suitable for integrated farming systems such as duck-cum-fish farming, duck farming with rice cultivation. In duck-cum-fish farming the droppings of ducks serve as feed for the fishes and no other feed or manuring of the pond is necessary for fishes (200-300 ducks per hectare of water area). Under integrated duck farming with rice cultivation, the ducks perform four essential functions viz., intertillage as they search for food, their bills loosen up the soil around the rice plants, insect control and manuring.
11. Ducks are good exterminators of potato beetles, grasshoppers, snails and slugs. In areas plagued liver flukes, ducks can help correct the problem. Ducks can be used to free the waterbodies from mosquito pupae and larvae.
12. Ducks are quite intelligent, can be tamed easily, and trained to go to ponds and come back in the evening of their own.

Duck Breeds

Among the egg laying breeds, 'Khaki Campbell' is the best producer. A duck lays about 300 eggs per year. Khaki Campbell ducks weigh about 2 to 2.2 kg, and drakes 2.2 to 2.4 kg. Egg size varies from 65 to 75 g. 'White Pekin' is the most popular duck for meat purpose. It is fast growing and has low feed consumption with fine quality of meat. It attains about 2.2 to 2.5 kg of body weight in 42 days of age, with a feed conversion ratio of 1:2.3 to 1:2.7.

Brooding (0-4 weeks)

The brooding period of 'Khaki Campbell' ducklings is 3 to 4 weeks. For meat type ducklings such as 'Pekin', brooding for 2 to 3 weeks is sufficient. A hover space of 90 to 100 cm^2 is required per ducklings under the brooder. A temperature of 29 to 32 °C is maintained during the first week. It is reduced by about 3 °C per week till it reaches 24°C during the fourth week. Ducklings may be brooded in wire floor or litter. A wire floor space of 0.046 m^2 per bird or solid floor space of 0.093 m^2 per bird would be sufficient up to 3 weeks of age. Water in the drinkers should be 5 to 7.5 cm deep just sufficient to drink and not dip themselves.

Rearing (5-16 weeks)

Ducklings may be reared in intensive, semi-intensive or range system. Under intensive system, a floor space of 0.279 m^2 is allowed up to 16 weeks of age. Under semi-intensive system, a floor space of 0.186 to 0.279 m^2 per bird is allowed in night shelter and 0.929 to 1.394 m^2 as outside run per bird up to the age of 16 weeks. Usually ducklings are allowed to move to runs at the end of 3 to 4 weeks of age depending upon weather. Water in the drinkers should be 12.5 to 15 cm deep to allow minimum immersion of their heads. Partitions up to the height of 60-90 cm inside the pens and the outside runs are adequate for control. Under range system a flock of 1000 can be reared per 0.4 hectare.

Adult Stock (above 17 weeks of age)

Under intensive system, a floor space of 0.371 to 0.465 m^2 per duck is essential, whereas in semi-intensive system, a floor space of 0.279 m^2 in the night shelter and 0.929 to 1.394 m^2 as outside run bird would be adequate. For wet mash feeding in a 'V' shaped feeder, 10 to 12.5 cm feeding space per duck is allowed but for dry mash or pellet feeding adlib in hoppers, a feeding space of 5 to 7.5 cm per duck would be sufficient. High egg laying strains of ducks come into production at 16 to 18 weeks of age. About 95 to 98% of eggs are laid by 9.00 AM. One nest box of size 30 cm × 30 cm × 45 cm to every three ducks is provided. In case of laying breeds a mating ratio of 1 drake to 6-7 ducks and in table breeds 1 drake to 4-5 ducks is allowed. Photoperiod of 14 to 16 hours per day is essential for optimum production.

While handling ducks, they should be caught by neck and not on the side of the body as this might lead to sudden death.

Duck Housing

Ducks do not require elaborate houses. Usually adult ducks do not require housing. But it would be better if they have given some protection. They will lay eggs better and damage less food. Ducks generally love darkness. So, it is not important to lightening the house. However, the house should be well ventilated, dry and rat proof. The roof may be of shed type, gable or half round. The floor of the duck house may be build with dirt, concrete, wood or bamboo. Straw can be used inside the house as bed. It is very easy to clean and make dry of the floor, made with straw bed. Under semi-intensive system the house should have easy access to outside run as the ducks prefer to be outdoors during the day time and even during winter or rains. The run should gently slope away from the houses to provide drainage.

Duck Feeding and Management

Though duck is a water fowl and very fond of water, water for swimming is not essential at any stage of duck rearing. However, water in drinkers should be sufficiently deep to allow the immersion of their heads and not themselves.

If they cannot do this, their eyes seem to get scaly and crusty and in extreme cases, blindness may follow. In addition, they also like to clean their bills periodically and wash them to clear off the feed.

Ducks may be grown on dry mash, a combination of dry and wet mash or pellets. Ducks prefer wet mash due to difficulties in swallowing dry mash. The pellet feeding, though slightly costly, has distinct advantages such as saving in amount of feed, minimum wastages, saving in labour, convenience and improvement in sanitary conditions. Ducks are good foragers. The use of range, pond or supplementary green feed, reduces the feed cost. Ducks should never have access to feed without water. During the first eight weeks, birds should always have access to feed, but later on they may be fed twice a day, i.e. first in the morning and then late afternoon. A 'Khaki Campbell' duck consumes about 12.5 kg of feed up to 20 weeks of age. Afterwards the consumption varies from 120 g and above per bird per day and depending upon the rate of production and availability of greens.

Diseases of Ducks

Ducks are resistant to common avian diseases. Duck diseases are similar to those of chicken and some are common for both, but the course of disease may vary. Since certain infections of chicken may be transmitted to ducks, it is essential that there is strict segregation of different species.

Duck plague: Adult birds are mostly affected by virus disease. It is characterized by vascular damage with tissue haemorrhages and free blood in body cavities. The lumina of intestine and gizzard are filled with blood. There is no treatment for the disease. The birds can be protected by vaccine, which is given at the age of 8-12 weeks.

Duck viral hepatitis: It mainly affects ducklings of 2 to 3 weeks of age. It is characterized by an acute course and primarily hepatitis. There is no treatment for the disease. The day old ducklings can be protected with attenuated virus vaccine. The disease is not stated to be prevalent in India.

Duck cholera: It is an infectious disease, caused by bacterial organism *Pasteurella multocoda* in ducks over four weeks of age. There is loss of appetite, high body temperature, thirst, diarrhoea and sudden death. Most common lesions are pericarditis, arthritis, petechial and echymotic haemorrhages under the skin, in visceral organs, over the serous surface and intestine. Liver and spleen are enlarged. The diseases can be controlled by sulpha drugs. The disease can be prevented by vaccination of the birds with duck cholera vaccine, first at the age of 4 weeks and again at 18 weeks.

Parasites: Ducks are resistant to internal parasites. The infestation is prevalent only among those ducks which have access to stagnant water, over-crowded ponds and small streams. The parasites include flukes, tape worms and round worms. These causes decrease of nutrient assimilation by the bird and anaemia due to toxic material excreted by them, destroying the red cells. The external parasites are an infliction rather than an ailment. These include lice mites, fleas and ticks. These cause irritation and annoyance leading to loss in egg production. They also transmit many disease producing organisms. However, these are not commonly found on water-fowls as in chicken.

Duck Integrated with Fish Farming

This system is very popular and widely practised in our country particularly in Assam, West Bengal, Bihar, Odisha, Andhra Pradesh, Kerala and in North Eastern States. It is one of the best livestock-fish integration systems. Duck droppings directly fall in water or collected and used for fertilization in pond. Fish gather duck droppings as direct food or consume spilled feed. Ducks consume mosquito larvae, tadpoles, dragon fly larvae and snails which also serve as vector for certain parasites. The dabbling habit of ducks increases the available oxygen in pond water. For commercial farming or for maximum profit high egg producing ducks like 'Khaki Campbell' or 'Indian Runner' is preferred instead of local ducks. About 200 to 240 eggs/ duck/ year is expected for commercial farming and on an average 250 ducks/ ha is recommended for duck cum fish farming.

Duck requires night shelter on the pond dyke or over the pond surface. It should made with the help of locally available material such as bamboo cane, thatches etc. If duck night shelter is made over the pond surface, a small bamboo bridge is constructed from the duck house to dyke for feeding the ducks as well as for collecting eggs and duck from the house. Duck house should be well ventilated and it should be exposed to direct sunlight. Peripheries of the pond are to be fenced for protection of ducks. One male duck should be kept in every 5-6 female ducks to get fertilized eggs. Duckling especially up to 3-4 weeks old are very susceptible to disease, hence, care should be taken during this period.

Rice-Duck Farming

Rice-duck farming is an integrated type of farming technology. It is especially suitable for resource poor farmers to produce organic rice in low cost. The evidence from various countries including Japan, Bangladesh, Philippines, and Vietnam has proved the integration of ducks in rice field as a successful and productive farming technology.

The integration of ducks in rice field creates symbiotic relationship between rice and ducks yielding mutual benefits to both entities. Ducks eat harmful insects and weeds averting the use of chemical pesticides and manual weeding in the rice field. Thus they get nutritious diet from eating insects and weeds in rice field. The droplets of ducks act as natural fertilizer to the rice crop preventing the use of chemical fertilizers. The continuous movement of ducks in the rice field provides natural stimulation and aeration which increases the availability of nutrients like Nitrogen, Phosphorous and Potash to the rice crop. Rice-duck technology causes the reduction of emission of methane gas from rice field contributing to reduce the global warming. Against the traditional rice farming system, integrated rice-duck technology supersedes in terms of minimizing the cost of production, increasing rice productivity, providing environmental benefits and increasing the income of farmers through sale of organic rice and duck meat.

Quail Farming

Quail farming is very profitable like other poultry birds, such as chicken or duck farming. Almost all types of weather conditions are suitable for quail farming. Meat and eggs of quail are very tasty and nutritious. Quail eggs are very nutritious than other poultry eggs. Because quail eggs contain comparatively more protein, phosphorus, iron, vitamin A, B1 and B2. Quail farming can play a vital role to meet up the demand of food and nutrition. It requires small capital and labour. Quails can be raised along with other poultry birds for meat or eggs production.

Quails are very small sized bird. An adult quail weights between 150 to 200 g and an egg weights around 7 to 15 g. Female quails start laying eggs within their 6 to 7 weeks of age and continuously lay one egg daily. They lay about 300 eggs in their first year of life. After that they produce about 150 to 175 eggs in second year. Egg production gradually decreases after their first year of laying period. Quail egg is very suitable for human health. It contains 2.47 % less fat than chicken egg. Many people believe that quail eggs help to prevent blood pressure and diabetic. Fat is very low in their meat. So quail meat is very suitable for blood pressure patients. Eggs are very beautiful with multiple colours. Quails do not incubate their eggs. So an incubator or brooder chickens are required for hatching their eggs. For successful breeding purpose one male quail is reared with every five female quails.

Benefits of Quail Farming

- Quails are smaller sized bird, so they can be raised within small place. 6 to 7 quails can be raised in the same place that is required for one chicken.
- Feeding cost of quails is comparatively lower than chickens or other poultry birds.
- Diseases are less in quails, and they are very hardy.
- Quails grow very fast and gain maturity faster than any other poultry birds.
- They start laying eggs within their 6 to 7 weeks of age.
- It takes about 16 to 18 days to hatch their eggs.

- Meat and eggs of quail are very tasty, delicious and nutritious. So it is a great source of food and nutrition.
- Quail farming needs small capital, and labour cost is very low.
- Quail meat contains less fat. So, it is suitable for high blood pressure patients.
- Their food to meat or eggs converting efficiency is satisfactory. They can produce one kg meat or eggs by consuming three kg food.
- As the quail eggs are smaller in size, so the price is also lower than other poultry egg. So marketing is not a problem.

Quail Breeds

Efforts are being made by Central Avian Research Institute (CARI), Izatnagar, to develop breeds for meet purpose. A number of quail breeds are available, which are very suitable for profitable quail farming business. Some of these breeds are famous for egg production and some are popular for meat production. According to their production, quail breeds are of two types such as broilers and layers. Popular layer quail breeds include Tuxedo, Pharaoh, British Range, English White and Manchurian Golden. Popular broiler quail breeds are Bobwhite and White Breasted. Besides these exotic breeds a few breeds like CARI Uttam, CARI Ujjawal, CARI Sweta and CARI Pearl have been developed by Central Avian Research Institute, Izatnagar which are very popular among the farmers.

Quail Housing

Housing is very important for quail farming. Quail can be raised in both litter and cage systems. But quail farming in cage system is more suitable than raising them in deep litter system. In cage system, management is very easy and diseases or other problems are less. There should be proper ventilation system and proper flow of air and light inside quail shelter. 50 quails can be raised in a cage measuring 120 cm length, 60 cm wide and 25 cm height. Wire net is used for making the cages. Measurement of the net would be 5 mm × 5 mm for adult quails. Plastic cages are most convenient for quail farming business. The house must have to be out of the reach of wild animals.

Quail Feeding and Management

For keeping the quails healthy, proper growing and highly productive, they should be provided with balanced feed regularly. An adult quail consumes about 20 to 25 g of food daily. Chick feed should contain 27% and adult feed 22-24% of protein. A chart of balanced feed for quails is shown below. The feed is comprised with broken wheat, sesame oilcake rice bran broken oyster shell salt and mineral mix.

Presence of adequate light is highly recommended for desired egg production from your quails. You can provide artificial light and heat by using electric bulb or heater. You can use 40 to 100 watt bulb for this purpose. Demand of light and heat varies depending on the season. If you want successful breeding and want to hatch their eggs, then keep one male with every five female quails. For getting better egg production, select highly productive breeds and always keep their house dry and clean. Egg production also depends on temperature, feeding, water, care and management. To get desired egg production from your quails, light play a vital role. Lightening period of laying quails is shown below through a chat.

Raising Quail Chicks

Quails never incubate their eggs. So, chicks are produced by hatching their eggs through chickens or artificially through using incubators. Incubation period for quail egg is about 16 to 18 days. For maximum egg production, 16 hours of lighting period is required daily inside the quail house. Newly born quail chicks are kept in a brooder house. Chicks need artificial heat and temperature management system for 14 to 21 days from their birth.

Diseases of Quail

Diseases are less in quails, compared to other poultry birds. But good care and management is a must for profitable quail farming business. Generally they are not provided any disease preventive vaccines. Quail chicks cannot tolerate weather change, and sudden temperature change. So they get affected by disease, if they experience sudden temperature or weather changes. If the quails get affected by coccidiosis disease, coaxial 20 are served to the birds by mixing with water (two grams 2 g/litter) for three days. For ulcerative enteritis one gram streptomycin is mixed with one litter water and served to the quails for three days. This will stop ulcerative enteritis disease. The cages or shelters of the quails should be kept dry and clean. Different aged quails are kept separately from each other. The disease affected quails are kept separately from the healthy ones. The dead bird are burnt or put under soil. Adequate fresh and clean water should be provided to the birds according to their demand.

Guinea Fowl

Compared to chickens, guinea fowl are low-cost and low-maintenance, and do a standout job as chemical-free pest control. Thus guinea fowl has the potential for landless labourers and marginal and small farmers of arid and semi arid region due to its hardy nature as a tool to lift their socio-economic status. Three available varieties are Kadmbari, Chitambari and Swetambari. Weight of the fowl at 8 weeks becomes 500-550 g and at 12 weeks 900-1000 g. The female fowl lays egg at 230-250 days age. Average egg weight is 38-40 g. Egg production in one laying cycle from March to September is 100-120 eggs. A guinea is never caught by its legs, as in a chicken. The correct way to catch a guinea is to clap both hands against its wings. Once caught, the bird is carried by its strong wings, never by its brittle legs.

Benefits of Guinea Fowl Farming

- Guinea fowl are highly free moving birds and possess excellent foraging capabilities with unique ornamental value.
- They act as bioinsecticides and bioweedicides. Working as a team, guineas will eat any pest they can get their beaks on, but unlike chickens, do so without tearing and scratching the garden plants. Since the birds are free-range, these will hunt ticks (or beetles, fleas, grasshoppers, crickets, snakes) all around. These are a more natural option to control the insect pest population than pesticides.
- Guinea fowl are hardy and resistant to many common diseases of other poultry birds.
- Guinea fowls are used as a watch dog in protecting the farm flock from intruders and predators by its loud, harsh, cry and its pugnacious disposition.
- Guinea fowls are extremely good runners which help them to escape from predators.
- Hard egg shell provides minimum breakage and long keeping quality.
- Tolerate weather extremes fairly well after they are fully feathered and can be suitable to any agro-climatic conditions.
- Input requirements are low. Consumes all non-conventional feed stuffs, usually not used in chicken feeding. Birds are more tolerant to mycotoxin and aflatoxin. No requirement of elaborate and expensive housing
- Guinea fowl meat is rich in vitamin and low in cholesterol. Guinea meat is darker and richer than chicken, with less fat and lower cholesterol.
- The nutrient-rich dropping of the birds can be composted and used in the garden.
- The feathers of guinea fowl are used in arts and crafts such as hat and head gears.

Guinea Fowl Housing

Domestic guinea fowl are not fully domesticated and are still a bit wild. They are not used to staying inside a house. They should be kept on free range during the day and kept inside a house at night to be protected against predators and thieves. Guinea fowl will get sick and die if they are kept in a wet or dirty house. Therefore their house should be spacious and well ventilated. This guinea fowl house of 3 m x 3 m is large enough to keep as many as twelve adult guinea fowl comfortably. The house should have a well maintained grass thatch roof, covered with plastic sheeting to ensure that it does not leak. It should be well ventilated with two opposite windows, each 0.75 m ×

0.25 m. In order to protect the birds from predators, the windows of the house and the play area should be covered with chicken wire mesh or closely spaced bamboos. The birds need perches. At least one bamboo perch should be faced to the walls of the house at about 1 metre from the floor. The floor of both the house and the play area should be covered with a thick layer of sand (15 cm deep). Sand is the best bedding material for guinea fowl as it provides them with a source of grit. Droppings should be swept out once a week using a broom. The sand should be changed once a month.

A baby guinea is called a 'keet'. Keets are less tolerant of crowded and dirty conditions and will die also. Young keets are very vulnerable to wet conditions and will certainly die if they get wet. They need to be kept inside the house if it is raining or if the ground outside is wet. The baby guineas become acquainted with their home ground as they broaden their foraging range, while adult guineas are likely to fly the coop the first chance they get. Because they are so small and delicate, keets can be easily trampled or drowned during their critical first two weeks of life. Thus the keets should be kept uncrowded. When they reach three weeks of age, move them into larger facilities offering at least one square foot of space per bird. By the time keets are one month old, they develop their first set of feathers.

Guinea Fowl Feeding and Management

Adult guinea fowl are one of the most self-reliant poultry birds around. Domestic guinea fowl thrive and breed well when they are allowed on free range during the day. They usually move together in groups and scratch for food such as insects, snails, seeds and berries with their feet or their bill. Although they do pick up food while on free range, they should still be fed each day. Feeding your guinea fowl ensures that they remain healthy and productive. By providing food and water inside the guinea fowl house, the guinea fowl are trained to return to their house each evening. Ideally, food for guinea fowl should be easily available, relatively cheap and nutritionally balanced. Guinea fowl need to be fed a well-balanced diet in order to gain weight and produce more eggs. A balanced diet consists of a mixture of different types of food which contain protein, fats, carbohydrates, minerals, vitamins and water.

As most keets are not safe to graze in the wild it is important that they should be given plenty of feed while they are inside the brooder. Simply scatter the feed atop of the newspaper and they will delightedly peck and feed for hours. As for feeding the keets, a 21 to 23 percent protein ration consisting of either commercial turkey starter or mashed hard-boiled eggs mixed with cottage cheese and a little cornmeal or oatmeal is given. After four weeks,

18 percent grower ration, or a mixture of cracked corn and whole wheat supplemented with young grass clippings, chopped lettuce, and other fresh greens are given. Water is always provided to the birds.

Guinea fowl only lay eggs in the breeding season which is from October to March. Sometimes guinea fowl start laying eggs in September and continue until the end of April. Most eggs are laid between the months of November and January. Guinea fowl are prolific layers and will lay many eggs if they are encouraged to keep on laying eggs by removing their eggs each day. Each female guinea fowl lays on average about 4 eggs a week or 17 eggs each month. As the breeding season normally lasts for six months, the total number of eggs which one female can produce can be as many as 100. She will continue laying that number each year until she is five years old or even older. The eggs are light-brown, sometimes speckled, with shells that are three times tougher than the shells of chicken eggs. Guinea eggs have a sharper point than chicken eggs have, and they are smaller; three guinea eggs roughly equal two chicken eggs. Hens lay in late morning or early afternoon and prefer to steal a nest in some secluded spot. Egg fertility is rarely a serious problem. One cock is sufficient for every four or five hens.

Table 4.4: Some Production Traits of Guinea Fowl

Egg laid per year (number)	100
Egg weight (grams)	40-45
Egg fertility	75-80
Hatchability	75-80
Egg weight/body weight (%)	2.8
Mature weight (kilograms)	1.6-1.7
Sexual maturity age (days)	186
Incubation period (days)	26-28
One-day-old keet weight (grams)	24.6

(**Source:** Fani *et al.*, 2004)

Guinea Fowl Meat

Guinea meat is darker and richer tasting than chicken and it contains less fat and fewer calories. Young adult guinea fowl taste better than older guinea fowl. Guineas are also smaller-boned than chickens, but have heavier breasts, making them meatier than they look. The average bird dresses out to 75 percent of its live weight, five percent more than the 70 percent average for a broiler chicken. Young guinea is the most tender and flavoured of all. The best meat comes from 12-week-old keets weighing about 1.3 kg.

Table 4.5: Summary of Some Pests and Diseases of Guinea Fowl

Symptoms	Pest/disease	Treatment
Birds lose weight and are weak, low egg production, most eggs are infertile, presence of lice or fleas around the head and neck	Fleas or lice	Actellic powder or actellic liquid
Birds have no energy, watery droppings with no blood, low egg production	Roundworms	Ruzine or ascarex
Birds lose weight and are weak, watery and bloody droppings, feathers are rough, birds huddle together in groups	Coccidiosis	Amidiostat
Keets lose weight, keets wattles darken, drool from the mouth and smell bad	Trichomoniasis	Amidiostat

(**Source:** Downes, 1999)

Pigeon Farming

Pigeon (*Columba livia*) farming is very interesting, profitable and pigeons are very popular domestic bird. Pigeon farming require less labour and low investment. The meat of baby pigeon (squab) is very tasty, nutritious and restorative. Squabs also have huge demand and price in the market. On the other hand pigeon farming can be a great source of some extra income and entertainment. Generally pigeons are raised in pair. One pair of male and female pigeon stay together for their whole life. Male and female both collect straw together and build a small nest for them to live. Female pigeon start laying eggs at the age of 5-6 months of age. They lay two eggs every time and their breeding capability stays for about 5 years. Both male and female pigeons hatch the eggs. Usually it takes about 17 to 18 days to hatch the eggs. The stomach of baby pigeon contains crop milk, which they eat for 4 days. Female pigeon feed their baby for ten days by their lips. After that, they start taking supplementary food by their own. At their age of 26 days, they become adult. The males are large, aggressive and make a loud cooling noise.

Benefits of Pigeon Farming

- Pigeons are domestic bird and it is very easy to handle them.
- From their six month of age they start laying eggs and produce two baby pigeon per month on an average.
- Pigeon can be raised easily in the home yard and roof of the house.
- It takes about 18 days to hatch their eggs.
- Baby pigeon (squab) become suitable for consumption within their 3 to 4 weeks of age.
- A pigeon house can be built in a small place with little investment.

- Pigeon feeding costs is very low. In most cases they collect food by themselves.
- Pigeon meat is very tasty, nutritious and has a great demand and value in the market.
- Pigeon farming is also very pleasing and entertaining. One can spend some good times through watching the activities of pigeons.
- Diseases are comparatively less in pigeons.
- Closet of pigeon is a good manure for crop cultivation.
- Different types of toys can be made by the feather of pigeons.
- Pigeons help to keep the environment safe by eating different types of insects.
- The squab has a great demand in the market as a patient's diet.
- Pigeon farming is suitable for landless, marginal and small farmers and can be integrated in any farming system.

Pigeon Feeding and Management

Pigeons generally eat wheat, maize, paddy, rice, enamel, legume, mustard, gram etc. Foods are kept in front of their house and they will take the food by themselves. Balanced feed is required for proper growth, good health and for proper production. Commercial chicken feed can also be fed to the pigeons. Nutrient requirement of pigeon is crude protein 913.5%), carbohydrates (65%), crude fibre (3.5%) and fat (3%). A pigeon consumes 35-50 g of grainy feed daily. For fast growing of baby pigeon and for nutrition of adult, oyster shell, lime stone, bone powder, salt, greet mixture, mineral mixture etc. are also fed to the birds with their regular feed. Along with this, some green vegetables are fed them daily. The daily feed intake of an adult pair is about 120 g.

Baby pigeons (squab) do not need extra feed for 5-7 days. They take crop milk from their parents' stomach which is known as pigeon milk. The pigeon milk looks like thick custard and has a high protein content. Male and female pigeon feed their baby in this way for 10 days. After that, they become able to fly and feed themselves by their own. Keep fresh feed and clean water near their house. Pigeons require water for drinking and for bathing to remove external parasites. A pair of pigeons drink about 500 ml of water per day.

Generally male and female pigeon stay in pairs. During laying period they collect straw and make a small nest. Female pigeon start laying eggs when they reach 5 to 6 months of age. As the eggs are very small in size, squab production is very profitable than consuming the eggs. Both partners build their nest and take turns to sit on the eggs. It takes about 17 to 18 days to hatch the eggs. The female starts laying eggs again when the squabs are two weeks old. The young ones become independent in 35 days. Squabs of 30-35 days age are best suited for meat purpose since recovery is high with body weight of 350 g. In addition to meat, pigeon droppings (25 g per bird per day) can be used as fish feed or enriched manure.

Diseases in pigeons are comparatively less than any other poultry birds. They suffer by TB, paratyphoid, cholera, pox, influenza, etc. To keep the birds healthy the pigeon house should be kept clean and germ free. The disease affected birds should be separated from healthy ones.

TURKEY FARMING

Turkey (*Meleagris gallopavo*) occupies an important position next to chicken, duck, guinea fowl and quail among the poultry birds in India. Turkey farming is in infancy in India and forms almost two percent of the total poultry population. They are reared for meat only and its meat is the leanest among other domestic avian species. Turkeys are mostly concentrated in and around cosmopolitan cities of India in small numbers. Indigenous and non-descriptive turkeys are found in good numbers in Kerala, Tamil Nadu, eastern districts of Uttar Pradesh and some other parts of India. Turkey grows faster like broiler chickens and become suitable for slaughter purpose within a very short time. Turkey farming is similar to other poultry birds farming like chickens, ducks, quails, etc.

Serious efforts are being made at Central Poultry Development Organisation (Southern Region), Bangalore to promote turkey farming. Turkey farming is getting popular fast in southern regions. There are three varieties of turkey commonly available in India. They are Board Breasted Bronze, Broad Breasted White and Beltsville Small White. White turkeys seem to be more suitable for Indian conditions. CARI Virat, a variety of Broad Breasted White type turkey has been developed by Central Avian Research Institute, Izzatnagar.

The basic plumage colour of Board breasted bronze is black and not bronze. The females have black breast feathers with white tips, which help in sex determination as early as 12 weeks of age. Board breasted white is a cross between Board breasted bronze and White Holland with white feathers. White plumage turkeys seems to be suitable Indian agro climatic conditions as they have better heat tolerance and also good and clean in appearance after dressing. Beltsville small white variety closely resembles the Board breasted white in colour and shape but smaller in size. Egg production, fertility and hatchability tend to be higher and broodiness tends to be lower than heavy varieties.

Turkey Housing and Fencing

Housing of turkeys may be of range system, confinement or a combination of both. There is a growing trend towards confinement housing. Good housing with all types of essential facilities available is very necessary for commercial turkey production. A permanent house like chicken house may be made and availability of all necessary facilities should be ensured. Turkeys are large in size and become very strong. So, the fencing should be strong enough to protect the birds. Proper protection for the birds from all types of predators and harmful animals should be ensured. Turkeys require a floor space of 0.4 m^2/bird in confinement and 32.5 m^2/bird in range rearing. Turkeys are not allowed grazing in the pasture until they reach grazing age. There should be sufficient flow of fresh air with proper ventilation system and light inside the house. The house should be cleaned regularly. In case of fencing, it must have to be at least four feet above the ground.

Turkey Feeding and Management

Turkeys have much higher growth rate than other poultry birds. Hence they have relatively higher feed and nutrient requirement. Turkeys can be fed with all types of dry feed comprising pellets, wet mash, grain and green feed in well balanced combination. Good and nutritious feed keeps the bird healthy and productive. Turkey needs more protein in their food for first few weeks than other domestic birds. The protein in poultry feed should be at least 28 percent. Chick starter which contain about 28 percent of protein can be fed for first six weeks and after that period chick grower feed which contains 20% protein can be fed. The amount of protein in turkey feed is higher than chickens or other poultry birds feed. Along with providing nutritious food, sufficient amount of fresh and clean water is provided to the birds.

Mating ratio in natural flock is 14 hens: 1 tom for small and 12:1 for medium sized turkeys. The birds should be carefully segregated when they reach the mating stage. Mating takes place during summer. Particular attention should be given in regulating mating. The males should be kept away from their mates in the morning and selectively mated with other birds by turn. Mating in the evening increases the number of fertile eggs. Generally turkey lays egg on alternate days from six months onwards. In a year one hen lays about 150 eggs. The bird attains a weight of 5-8 kg in a year.

Turkeys of all age group can be easily driven from one place to another with the help of a stick. For catching turkeys a darkened room is best, wherein they can be picked up with both legs without any injury. However, mature turkeys should not be kept hanging for more than 3-4 minutes.

Turkey meat has nutritional and sensorial properties which make it almost ideal raw material for rational and curative nutrition. People prefer turkey meat because of its leanest nature. The protein, fat, energy values of turkey meat are 24%, 6.6%, 162 calories per 100 g of meat. Mineral like potassium, calcium, magnesium, iron, selenium, zinc and sodium are present. It is also rich in essential amino acids and vitamins like niacin, vitamin B6 and B12. It is rich in unsaturated fatty acids and essential fatty acids and low in cholesterol.

EMU FARMING

Emu farming in India is emerging as a popular and lucrative business model. Emu farming is very popular in Andhra Pradesh, Delhi, Karnataka, Maharashtra and Tamil Nadu. These are large sized poultry birds of ratite group and have high economic value. They produce valuable eggs, meat, oil, skin and feathers. They can adopt themselves with almost all types of agro-climatic conditions. They can be raised in both extensive and semi intensive farming systems. Indian climate is very suitable for commercial emu farming.

Benefits of Emu Farming

- Emu meat is very healthy and tasty. It is lower in fat and cholesterol and higher in protein and energy.
- Emu products like eggs, meat, skin, oil and features have a high value in the market.
- Emus take less food and convert them to various types of valuable products. They can even survive by eating cost saving foods.
- Marginal and small farmers can easily raise some emus in their household with other livestock animals and poultry birds.
- Diseases are less in emus and they can survive in almost all types of agro-climatic conditions. Indian climate is also very suitable for commercial emu farming business.
- Emu farming business is very profitable and it can be a great source of income and employment for the unemployed people of India.
- Emu farming does not require high technical and management knowledge.

Care and Management of Emu

A newly born emu chick weights around 370 to 450 g which is about 67% of total egg weight. Although the exact weight of chicks depend on the size of eggs. The chicks are kept inside the incubator for first 2 to 3 days. This will help to proper drying and for quick absorption of the yolk. Then the chicks are kept in deep litter floor house. The litter can be prepared with paddy husk and then the litter is covered with new gunny bags. Four square feet space is required per chick for their first 3 weeks. Under the brooder, sufficient number of feeder and water pots should be kept. To avoid straying and jumping of chicks a chick guard of at least 2.5 feet height is provided. A bulb is provided inside the brooder shed burning all time. A 40 watt bulb is sufficient for covering 100 square feet area. The brooder area of chicks is extended after their 3 weeks of age by widening the chick guard circle. The chick starter mash is fed for about 14 weeks or until they reach about 10 kg body weight. Emu chick requires sufficient run space for proper growth and healthy life. Generally, 30 x 40 square feet floor space is suitable for raising about 40 chicks. The floor must have to be free from dampness and easily drained.

Emus are big sized bird. They need big sized waterers, feeders and large floor space. The birds grower mash is fed to the growing birds for their 34 weeks of age or until they reach 25 kg body weight. Along with grower mash about 10% of greens are added. In grower stage, providing 40 x 100 square feet space for 40 birds will be enough. The chicks or grower are never kept with adult emus.

Generally, emu birds become mature at their 18 to 24 months of age. For proper breeding purpose keep the male and female ratio as 1:1. 2500 square feet floor space is required for every pair during mating. More vitamins and minerals are added in their food and fed to the birds before 3-4 weeks of breeding. This will ensure better fertility and hatch ability in birds. Generally an adult bird eats about 1 kg food daily. But during mating period food taking rate get reduced drastically. A female emu lays about 15 eggs during first year and this number gradually increase from the next year. They lay eggs for the first time at one and half years of age. An egg weighs around 475 to 650 g. The eggs are like tough marble and are of greenish coloured. Normally an emu egg takes about 52 days incubation period for producing a chick. Proper temperature and moisture control management is very important for hatching emu eggs. However, proper care and management ensure good and healthy emu chicks.

Like other birds and animals emus also need nutritious and balanced diet for their proper growth and reproduction. Good and high quality foods also keep the bird healthy and diseases free. So, for profitable emu farming in India the birds are fed with high quality and nutritious food according to their demand. Along with good and nutritious food sufficient amount of clean and fresh water is provided to them regularly.

Emus are very strong and live for long time. Mortality rate and other health problems are less in emus. Chicks and juveniles sometimes suffer by some health problems. They may suffer by coli infections, clostridial infections, intestinal obstruction, leg abnormalities, malnutrition and starvation. The main causes of these types of health problems are genetic disorders, improper handling, improper brooding or nutrition and stress. Emus also get infected by some other health problems and diseases like aspergillosis, ascarid infestations, candidiasis, coccidiosis, lice, rhinitis and salmonella. A veterinarian should always be consulted for any health problem.

Along with emu meat, skin, oil, feather, eggs, day old chicks, growing birds are also marketed. Emu farming is absolutely a very profitable business. Indian weather and climate is also very suitable for commercial emu farming business.

CONCLUSION

Integrated farming system has the advantages of increasing economic yield and profitability per unit area per unit time. A judicious mix of cropping system with associated enterprises like dairy, poultry, fishery, duckery, agroforestry, vermicompost, apiary, sericulture, piggery, etc. suited to the given agroclimatic conditions and socioeconomic status of farmers would bring prosperity to farmers, particularly marginal and small farmers. Much attention is being given for the development of poultry farming in India and with improved scientific management practices; poultry has now become a popular rural enterprise in different states of the country. Apart from eggs and meat, poultry also yields manure, which has high fertilizer value. Utilization of this huge resource as manure in aquaculture will definitely afford better conversion than agriculture. Thus, the marginal and small farmers should be educated to take up poultry business in integrated farming systems.

RFERENCES

Anderson, K. E. and Carter, T. A. (2007): Hot Weather Management of Poultry. Poultry Science and Technology Guide No. 30, *North Carolina State University*, USA.

Annadurai, K., Palaniappan, S.P., Chinnusamy, C. and Jayanthi, C. (1994). Integrated Farming System: Need of the Hour. *Kisan World* 21(9): 39.

Das, A. (2013). Integrated Farming: An Approach to Boost up Family Farming. *LEISA India* 15(4): 1-5.

Downes, Anne. 1999. A Guide to Guinea Fowl Farming in Malawi. Department of National Parks & Wildlife, Malawi.

Fani A. R., Fani, Lotfollan, H. and Ayazi, A. 2004. Evaluation in Economical Traits of Iranian Native Guinea Fowl (*Numida meleagris*). The Joint Agriculture and Natural Resources Symposium, Tabriz-Ganja, Iran.

FAO. (1977). Recycling of Organic wastes in Agriculture. FAO Soil Bulletin 40. Food and Agriculture Organisation, Rome.

Fresco, L. O. and Westphal E. (1988). A Hierarchical Classification of Farm Systems. *Experimental Agriculture* 24: 399-419.

http://poultryliveindia.com/integrated-poultry-fish-farming-system

http://www.agriculturesnetwork.org/magazines/india/family-farming/integrated-farming

https://practicalaction.org/integrated-rice-duck-farming

https://www.thehappychickencoop.com/guinea-hen

Hulzebosch, J. (2006): Effective Heating Systems for Poultry Houses. *World Poultry* 22(2): 18-19.

Jayanthi, C., Rangasamy, A. and Chinnusamy, C. (2000). Water Budgeting for Components in Lowland Integrated Farming Systems. *Agricultural Journal* 87: 411-414.

M Khairunnesa, M., Das, S. C. and Khatun, A. 2016. Hatching and Growth Performances of Guinea Fowl under Intensive Management System. *Progressive Agriculture*, 27: 70-77.

Panda, S.C. (2004). Cropping and Farming Systems. Agrobios (India), Jodhpur. 431 pp.

Panke, S. K., Kadam, R. P. and Nakhate, C. S. (2010). Integrated Farming System for Suatainable Rural Livelihood Security. In: 22nd National Seminar on Role of Extension in Integrated Farming Systems for Sustainable Rural Livelihood, 9th-10th December, 2010, Maharashtra, pp. 33-35.

Soni, R. P., Katoch, M. and Ladohia, R. (2014). Integrated Farming Systems–A Review. *Journal of Agriculture and Veterinary Science* 7(10): 36-42.

Suba Reddy, G. and Ramakrishna, Y.S. (2005). Farming System Modules in Rainfed Agriculture. In: Singh, A. K., Gangwar, B. and Sharma, S. K. (eds.). Proceedings of Symposium on Alternative Farming Systems: Enhanced Income and Employment Generation Options for Small and Marginal Farmers, September 16-18, 2004, Project Directorate for Cropping Systems Research, Modipuram. pp. 65-71.

Farming and Development : *Technological Perspectives* **Pages 84-100**
***Edited by:* Dr. Pawan Kumar 'Bharti' & Dr. Jaswant Ray**
ISBN: 978-93-88854-08-5
***Edition:* 2019**
***Published by:* Discovery Publishing House Pvt. Ltd., New Delhi (India)**

5

Organic Farming
A Sustainable Agriculture Tool

[1]Sikander and [2]Shivani Garg

ABSTRACT

Sustainable agriculture comprise site specific ranching and agricultural practices designed to meet the current and future needs for food, fodder, fibre, energy, timber and ecosystem services. Sustainable agriculture emphasizes the production of food systems that are healthy, profitable, environmentally sound, energy efficient, and will improve the quality of life of both the farmers and consumers. Indian agriculture sector has witnessed a sharp increase in food grain production after the green revolution and helped the country not only to attain the state of self-sufficiency but also enabled us to export significant amount of grains, cereals and fruits despite our huge population. In a time of increasing population, decreasing health of people, climate change and environmental degradation, we need an agricultural system that comes with a more balanced portfolio of sustainability benefits and is more eco-friendly. Organic farming is one of the healthiest and strongest sectors in agriculture today and will continue to grow and play an important part in feeding the world producing adequate yields and better uniting human health, environment and socio-economic objectives than conventional farming. Organic farming systems offer a wide range of conservation benefits, including improved soil and water quality, resilience to climate disruption, lower use of non-renewable energy, increased biodiversity, and wildlife habitat quality. This paper attempts to discuss likely opportunities and challenges for the proper adoption of organic farming in India.

Keywords: Agriculture, Sustainable agriculture, Organic farming, Conservation.

1 Department of Geology, Kurukshetra University, Kurukshetra, Haryana, PIN-136119, India.

2 Institute of Environmental Studies, Kurukshetra University, Kurukshetra, Haryana, PIN-136119, India.

Background of Organic Farming

From 1905 to 1924, Organic Agriculture started simultaneously in India and Central Europe. Sir Albert Howard, a British botanist, referred to as the father of modern organic agriculture, working as an agricultural adviser in Pusa, Bengal, (now in Bihar) documented traditional Indian farming practices and regarded them as superior to his conventional agriculture science. J. I. Rodale in the United States began to popularize the term and methods of organic growing among farmers and particularly among consumers through promotion of organic gardening. Lord Northbourne used the term "organic farming" for the first time in 1939. The term derived from his concept of "the farm as organism", explained in his book, "Look to the Land" (1940). Lady Eve Balfour did first scientific study of organic and conventional farming after being influenced by Sir Albert Howard's work.

Introduction

Agriculture is the back bone for sustenance of life of people since time immortal. This has been and is a dynamic system changing practices with time and new technological inventions. Increasing population demands for more grain production thereby exerting a stress on the natural factors such as land and water without much concern to the concept of sustainability. According to the estimates of UN population projection, world population could reach 9.15 billion by 2050, thus the expected rate of increase in world population will be 2.25 % over the next forty years (Alexandratos and Bruinsma, 2012). In 1972, the International Federation of Organic Agriculture Movement (IFOAM) was founded in France, pressing for government regulation of organic production. This led to legislation and certification standards being enacted beginning in the 1990s. Modern agriculture system is chiefly oriented towards higher production without much concern for conservation of natural resources thereby putting severe pressure on them.Indian farmer is using wide ranges of chemical pesticides to limit the losses from pests and diseases, in which insecticides account for 73%, herbicides 14%, fungicides 11% and other 2% (FAO, 1998). All this is inherently self-depleting and unsustainable and adoption of organic farming practices is referred as a long term solution for this problem which will work as an effective tool for sustainable agriculture and also for sustainable development particularly in India and all across the globe as a whole,its acceptance and popularity are growing due mostly to environmental and health related concerns (Biao et al., 2003; Galantini and Rosell, 2006). According to the latest survey of FiBL-IFOAM, 2012 (Researchinstitute of organic agriculture-International Federation of Organic Agriculture Movements) data,organic agriculture is available from 164 countries and 37.5 million hectare land iscultivated organically worldwide including those in the process of conversion. All the aspects and benefits of organic farming in sustainable agriculture development are discussed in this chapter.

Organic Farming

Organic farming is the agricultural practices that do not cause any harm to the environment and works in harmony with the nature. Organic farming shares the fundamental objectives of agricultural sustainability and is deserves to be assessed as a mainstream part of sustainable agriculture (Edward-Jones and Howells, 2001). It is also referred to as, low input farming and uses natural sources of nutrients such as compost, crop residues and manure, and natural methods of crop and weed control, instead of using synthetic or inorganic agrochemicals. Sir Albert Howard is widely considered to be the "father of organic farming". Organic farming works in a more eco-friendly manner, to make a harmony between biotic and abiotic components of ecosystem, to improve long term soil health, to minimize the use of water in the fields for irrigation purpose, to maintain the quality of water, to ensure the nutrition value and quality of the food grains, fruits or vegetables, to minimize the overall investment of farmers by reducing expenditure for pesticides and fertilizers and it also enables farmers to earn more money by selling their products. The International Federation of Organic Agriculture Movements (IFOAM) carries out the tasks related to setting standards and regulation of organic farming activities worldwide.

Organic Farming and the Concept of Sustainability

Sustainability must be widespread not only globally, but forever in time, and to all living organisms including plants, animals and humans. In simple terms, sustainable agriculture refers to the ability of a farm to produce food indefinitely, without causing permanent damage to the health of ecosystem. Sustainable agriculture means farming system that is capable of maintaining their productivity & usefulness to society indefinitely. Such systems must be resource-conserving, socially supportive, commercially competitive and environmentally sound. Sustainable agriculture is an agricultural system which sustains agriculture without either reduction or any break in future, while ensuring to meet the needs of the present, without compromising the ability of future generations to meet their own needs. The goal of sustainable agriculture is to reduce adverse impacts to the immediate environments while providing a sustained level of production and ensuring profit in terms of money.

Organic Farming for Sustainable Agriculture

Our necessity for nutritional security and environmental sustainability makes it inevitable to resort to the organic or eco-farming system as it appears to be a possible option to meet both these objectives. An organic farming system is that primarily aims at cultivating land and raising crops under ecologically favourable condition. It emphasizes restricting the use of chemical inputs whether it is inorganic fertilizers or pesticides and instead, relies more on an integrated approach of crop management practices making use of cultural, biological and natural inputs. Addition of organic manures, recycling of organic wastes through composting, green manures and biological inputs like vermicomposts and bio-fertilizers etc. constitute important components for plant nutrient management in organic farming. Similarly it also takes utmost advantage of the natural mechanism for pest management with utilization of bioagents such as predators and parasites available in nature in plenty and the botanical pesticides which are effective in controlling crop pests posing no risk to the environment. Agronomic practices such as crop rotation with judicious selection of crops, intercropping and companion cropping, stubble mulching and use of resistant varieties are among the important factors contributing to organic farming.

Principles of Organic Farming

1. **The principle of health** – Organic farming should enhance the health of soil, plant, animal, human and planet as one and indivisible and help in sustainable development of agriculture. The role of organic agriculture (whether in farming, processing, distribution, or consumption) is to sustain and enhance the health of ecosystems and from the smallest organisms present in the soil to human beings. Organic agriculture in particular is proposed to produce high quality, nutritious food that contributes to preventive health care and well-being. In this context it should avoid the use of fertilizers, pesticides, animal drugs and food additives that may have adverse health effects.
2. **The principle of ecology** – Organic farming should be based on living ecological systems and cycles, and eco-friendly and help sustain them. Organic agriculture should attain ecological balance through the design of improved farming systems, establishment of natural habitats and maintenance of genetic and agricultural diversity. Producers, processors, traders, and consumers of organic products should protect and do good to the common environment including habitats, biodiversity, landscapes, climate, air and water masses.
3. **The principle of fairness** – Organic farming should ensure fairness between the common environment and life opportunities. This principle emphasizes that those involved in organic agriculture should conduct human relationships in a manner that ensures fairness at all levels and to all parties related to it professionally. Organic agriculture should endow with good quality of life, and contribute to food autonomy and poverty reduction. It should aim to produce a sufficient supply of good

quality food and other commodities. Natural resources that are being used for production and consumption should be managed in a way that is socially and ecologically just and should be held in trust for future generations also. Fairness requires a system of production, distribution and trade that is open and impartial and account for real environmental and societal costs.

4. **The principle of care** – Organic farming should be managed in such manner to protect the health and wellbeing of current and future generations and the environment. This principle states that precaution and responsibility are the key concerns in technology choices, management and development of organic agriculture sector. Science is necessary to ensure health, safety and ecological soundness of organic agriculture. However, scientific knowledge alone is insufficient. Practical experience, accumulated wisdom and traditional and indigenous knowledge may recommend valid solutions. Organic agriculture should prevent significant risks by adopting appropriate technologies and rejecting unpredictable ones, such as genetic engineering. Values and needs of all who might be affected should be reflected in the decisions through transparent and participatory processes.

Components of Organic Farming

Major components of organic farming include use of organic manure, soil microorganisms, crop residues, bio-pesticide/bio-herbicide, biogas slurry and farm-waste etc. for effectively enhancing the soil fertility and producing qualitatively and quantitatively better crops in a sustainable manner. The various components of organic farming have been discussed in details below:

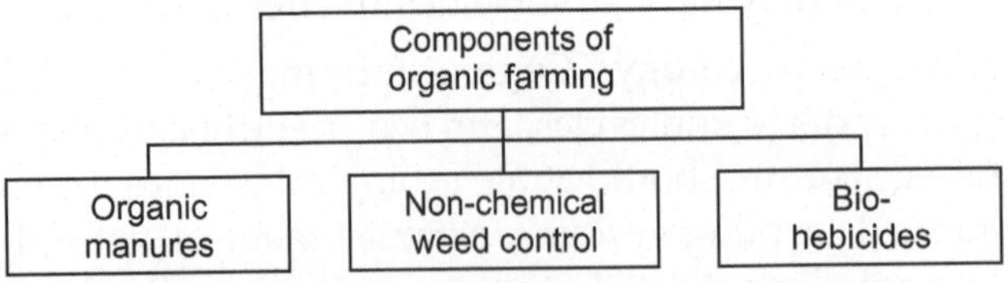

Fig. 5.1: Different components of organic farming

1. Organic Manures

Manure is organic matter used as a fertilizer in agriculture. Manures contribute to the fertility of the soil by adding organic matter and nutrients, such as nitrogen that is trapped by bacteria in the soil. Organic manures commonly in use in organic farming are:

- **Farm Yard Manure (FYM):** Farmyard manure is the semi decomposed to decomposed mixture of leftover material from cattle feed/fodder, urine and dung of farm animals along with some plant residues. Farm Yard Manure is a valuable soil improver which improves and restores a range of natural properties of the soil that is ideal for mulching in the fields. It also adds humus, Improve water and nutrient retention and slow releasing nutrients to the soil.

- **Green manure:** Green manure is a type of cover crop which is grown primarily to add nutrients and organic matter to the soil. The practice includes ploughing of undecomposed green plant tissue (mainly green leaves) for the purpose of improving physico-chemical condition as well as fertility of the soil is known as Green manuring. For example in northern India, some legumes are grown in the field while taking a crop of sugarcane. Later these legumes are left for natural decay and decomposition in order to improve the soil quality and add nitrogenous nutrients to it.
- **Vermicompost:** In this process earthworms are used to convert organic materials into vermicompost (humuslike material). A number of researchers throughout the world have found that the nutrient profile in vermicompost is generally higher than traditional compost. It is suggested by various studies that vermicomposts should be applied at moderate concentrations in order to obtain maximum yield after seeking some ill effects of the higher concentration of soluble salts found in the vermicompost as compared to normal compost.
- **Crop residues:** Management of crop residues is a big problem in some developing countries such as India. On burning crop residues pollutes the air very badly, but residues of common cultivated crops may be an important resource which can add nutrients to the soil and affect physical, chemical, and biological functioning of soil. Data on nitrogen benefits and nitrogen recoveries from residues show that a considerable potential exists from residues, especially leguminous residues, not only in meeting the Nitrogen demands of the next crops, but also in increasing the long-term fertility of the soils. The constraints to more production and environmental conservation should be identified in each cropping system and conceptualized to mark toward the best management of crop residues for a sustainable agriculture system.
- **Bio-fertilizers:** Biofertilizers or microbial inoculants can be defined as preparations containing live or inert cells of suitable strains of nitrogen fixing, phosphate solubilising and cellulolytic microorganisms used for direct application to soil, seeds or composting areas in order to increase the availability of nutrients which later can be easily assimilated by plants. The Bio-fertilizers may include bacteria, algae & fungi and may broadly be classified into two categories:
  - **Nitrogen fixing** like *Rhizobium, Azospirilum, Acetobacter, Azotobactor,Azola,* Blue Green Algae

* **Phosphorus solubilizers/ mobilisers** like Phosphate Solubilizing Microbes (PSM) & Mycorrhizae.

The bio-fertilizers were identified for the first time by a Dutch scientist in 1888. Nobbe & Hiltner (1895) produced biofertilizers commercially for the first time under the trade name "Nitragin" in the USA. After the first study on legume-*Rhizobium* symbiotic association by N.V. Joshi in India, there has been a constant effort made by various academicians, agriculturists, scientists and government agencies. The usage of biofertilizers was observed in Tamilnadu (1956) and among Soybean growers in Madhya Pradesh (1964). However, the commercial organizations practically came forward during 1990's in India. It is a matter of concern that bio-fertilizer could not really become popular amongst farmer community despite many decades have passed.

2. Non-Chemical Weed Control

Direct weed control methods are very common and environment friendly as compared to chemical methods. When preventative measures of weed management do not adequately control weeds in the field, direct weed control may be necessary. Mechanical and biological control practices are commonly used on organic farms and have the potential to also allow conventional farmers to reduce herbicide use and risk. Mechanical weed control involves the physical removal of weeds or placement of barriers to weed growth but after removal proper management should be necessary of weeds. Biological pest control refers to the deliberate application of a living organism to control pests. Biological control of weeds is not a very common practice in annual cropping systems.

3. Bio-Herbicide Approach

In this approach indigenous plant pathogens are isolated from weeds and are cultured to produce large quantity of infective material. These are applied at amounts that will bring about enough infection, leading to partial or complete elimination of the target weed before it causes much of the economic damage in the field. Bio-herbicides can target one weed and leave the rest of the environment unharmed. Bio-herbicides are made up of microorganisms (e.g. bacteria, viruses, fungi) and certain insects (e.g. parasitic wasps, painted lady butterfly) that can target very specific weeds. This selective response makes bio-herbicides very useful because they kill only certain weed plants that interfere with crop productivity without damaging the crop itself. Once the weed problem has been removed, natural constraints ensure that the pathogen population returns to a low level once again. The bio-herbicide approach has been successfully implemented for a number of important agricultural weeds (both invasive and exotic).

Need of Certification in Organic Farming

This is a certification process for producers of organic food and various other organic agricultural products. Any business directly involved in food production can be certified, including farmers, seed suppliers, retailers and food processors. A business cannot label its products organic if it does not comply with the criteria set and regulated by the law in their respective countries.If a producer/seller wants to label their business products as organic, they need to be certified first and for this they must fulfill the requisite standards that apply to organic products in their respective country and comply with consumer law. Businesses that label their products as organic should be able to defend their claims, whenever questioned so by consumers. The certification can be obtained with the completion of applications, audit procedure, and the process of getting approval for organic labeling. After certification, producers can legally label their products with an organic symbol, logo or trademark to indicate their status. For example, in the U.S., when a food or beverage product is labeled as organic, it means that the product has been grown, produced, examined, and certified to be following the organic standards mandated by the National Organic Programme (NOP), a program of the United States Department of Agriculture (USDA). If a company is labelling a product as USDA Organic, it indicates that it has met the standards of USDA (NOP), which indirectly denotes that the product is chemical pesticide-free, fertilizer-free, bioengineering & radiation-free, antibiotics & growth hormone-free and production process involves conservation of soil and water to protect and improve environmental quality and use of renewable resources of energy, thereby keeping the concept of sustainability its focal theme.

World Initiatives to Check the Development of Sustainable Organic Agriculture

In many countries, standards for organic products are formulated and regulated by the government. Putting the word "organic" on a food product is a valuable marketing advantage these days, but there is no guarantee for the genuineness of the product to be legitimately organic. Certification is intended to protect consumers from misuse of the term, and ensure good quality of organic products. There are also international certification bodies, including members of the International Federation of Organic Agriculture Movements (IFOAM) working on harmonization efforts. In 2011 IFOAM introduced a new program - the IFOAM Family of Standards - that attempts to simplify harmonization. The vision was to establish the use of one single global reference (the COROS) to access the quality of standards rather than focusing on bilateral agreements. The Certcost was a research project that conducted research and prepared reports about the certification of organic food. The project was supported by the European Commission and was active from 2008-2011. Some of the countries which have comprehensive organic legislation and their certifying/ regulating bodies are having their specific logo (Fig. 5.2). This logo may be used only by certified producers.

Fig. 5.2: 'ORGANIC' certifying bodies of some countries

Government Policy for Organic Agriculture

As per National Standards for Organic Production (NSOP), Agricultural and Processed Food Products Export Development Authority (APEDA) is the regulating body for the certification of organic products in India. Organic food products produced/manufactured/prepared and exported from India are marked with the 'India Organic' certification mark issued by the APEDA. Ministry of Agriculture, Commodity Boards, Food Processing Industries, Forests and Environment, Science and Technology, Rural Development and Commerce, and Trade and Exports are some organizations or agencies that work for promotion of organic farming and sustainable agriculture in the country. The main objectives of the National Program for Organic Production (NPOP) have centralized around the export market and economic development. The Ministry of Agriculture developed an organic agriculture task force in October, 2000 that was separate from the NSCOP. The objectives of this separate task force were to advise the Ministry of Agriculture on all aspects of organic agriculture, to promote general awareness of organic agriculture, and to developing a map for organic agriculture in the country. State governments have also initiated several projects throughout the 26 states of India. These projects include setting up organic farm models, providing guidance about certification, promoting composting, and other practices relevant to organizing conferences, extending subsidies and providing training related to the organic farming. The main outcome of the global survey based on certified organic farming is that total 32.2 million hectares of agricultural land is being managed organically by more than 1.2 million producers, including small holders (2007). In addition to the agricultural land, there are 0.4 million hectares of certified organic aquaculture. The total organic area in Asia is nearly 2.9 million hectares. This constitutes only 9% of the world's organic agricultural land.

Organic Farming in India

Organic farming in India came in light after launching of National Project on Organic Farming (NPOF) in 2004-05. Organic farming is being promoted under National Project on Organic Farming (NPOF), National Horticulture Mission (NHM) and Rashtriya Krishi Vikas Yojana (RKVY) (Meena and Sharma, 1970). Emerging from 42,000 hectare under certified organic farming during 2003-04, the organic agriculture has grown almost 29 fold during the last 5 years. India has brought more than 4.48 million hectare area under organic certification process by March, 2010. Out of this cultivated area accounts for 1.08 million ha while remaining 3.4 million ha is wild forest harvest collection area (Yadav, 2010). Ion Exchange, Mumbai is a private company engaged for export and domestic marketing of organic products in India. It found to be 2–3 times higher production both in case of maize and wheat and also for higher price were obtained by organic produce wheat because of 25–30% price premium on organic products and lower cost of production and marketing. In Maharashtra, popularization of organic cotton production was due to high cost benefit ratio of organic cotton. Organic production of chickoo, banana and coconut had higher profitability in Gujarat. Groundnut, jowar, cotton, coconut and banana were grown as organically in Karnataka. The major problems faced by organic farmers were found to be initial lower yields, no price incentives, no separate markets for organic produce, besides lack of and high costs of certification.

Organic Farming Mitigates Climate Change

Organic farming reduces greenhouse gases emission, especially nitrous oxide, as no chemical nitrogen fertilizers are used and nutrient losses are minimized. The water quality is also improved as the absence of the harmful agrochemical (Fertilizers and pesticides) residues which otherwise run-off into the underground water when used indiscriminately under organic farming management system. It helps to stores carbon in soil (carbon sequestration) and plant biomass by building organic matter, encouraging agro-forestry and forbidding the clearance of primary ecosystems. It also minimizes energy consumption by 30-70% per unit of land by eliminating the energy required to manufacture synthetic fertilizers, and by using internal farm inputs, thus reducing fuel used for transportation.

Advantages of Organic Farming

1. **Nutritionally valuable food:** The nutritional value of food depends upon its vitamin and mineral content. Organically grown food is dramatically superior in mineral content to that grown by modern conventional methods. A major benefit of consuming organic food is that it is free from health harming chemical contaminants such as pesticides, fungicides and herbicides. There are reasonably consistent findings for higher nitrate and lower vitamin C contents in conventional vegetables

(Woese et al., 1997). Several studies indicate that 10-60 percent more healthy fatty acids (like CLA's) and omega-3 fatty acids occur in organic dairy (Butler et al., 2008). In organic crops, 5-90 percent more vitamin C and 10-50 percent moresecondary metabolites are found. Also, less residues of pesticides and antibiotics are found in organic food stuffs (Huber and van de Vijver, 2009). According to Heaton (2002) organic food contains higher minerals and dry matter and 10-50 percent higher phytonutrients. Decreased cell proliferation of cancer cells was observed on extracts of organic strawberries (Olsson et al., 2006), which may prove to be a milestone in promoting organics. The Parsifal study showed 30 percent less eczema and allergy complaints and less body weight among 14000 children fed with organic and biodynamic food in five EU countries (Alfven et al., 2006). In animals, organic feed leads to increased fertility (Staiger, 1988) and improved immune parameters (Finamore et al., 2004). Other studies indicate that the most systematic differences between organic and conventional crops are the contents of secondary metabolites (Brandt & Mølgaard, 2001). Organically grown food tastes better than that conventionally grown. The tastiness of fruit and vegetables is directly related to its sugar content, which in turn is a function of the quality of nutrition that the plant itself has enjoyed. This quality of fruit and vegetable can be empirically measured by subjecting its juice to brix analysis, which is a measure of its specific gravity (density). The brix score is widely used in testing fruit and vegetables for their quality prior to export. Organically grown plants are nourished naturally, rendering the structural and metabolic integrity of their cellular structure superior to those conventionally grown. As a result, organically grown foods can be stored longer and do not show the latter's susceptibility to rapid rotting and molding.

2. **Minimise growing cost:** The economics of organic farming is characterized by increasing profits via reduced water use, lower expenditure on fertilizer and energy, and increased retention of topsoil. To add to this the increased demand for organic produce makes organic farming a profitable option for farmers.
3. **Enhances soil fertility:** Organic farming effectively addresses soil management. Organic farming performs better than conventional farming with regard to soil organic matter (Stolze et al. 2000). Even damaged soil, subject to erosion and salinity, are able to feed on micro-nutrients via crop rotation, inter-cropping techniques and the extensive use of green manure. The absence of chemicals in organic farming does not kill microbes which increase nourishment of the soil. Biodynamic farms had better soil quality such as greater in organic matter, content and microbial activity, more earthworms, better soil structure, lower

bulk density, easier penetrability, and thicker topsoil (Reganold et al., 1993); according to Dobbs and Smolik (1996); Drinkwater et al. (1998) and Edwards (2007) agricultural productivity doubled with soil fertility techniques like compost application and introduction of leguminous plants into the crop sequence.

4. **More energy efficiency:** Growing organic rice was four times more energy efficient than the conventional method (Mendoza, 2002). Organic agriculture reduces energy requirements for production systems by 25 to 50 percent compared to conventional chemical-based agriculture (Niggli et al., 2009).
5. **Carbon sequestration:** German organic farms annually sequester 402 kg Carbon/ha, while conventional farms had losses of 202 kg (Clark et al., 1999; Küstermann et al., 2008; Niggli et al., 2009). Thus organic farming indirectly reduces global warming by lowering greenhouse gases.
6. **Less water pollution:** According to Drinkwater et al. (1998), 60 percent more nitrates are leached into groundwater over a 5-year period in conventional farms.

Problems and Constraints

There are more than a few obstacles in the way of adopting organic farming, such as: A sound knowledge of organic farming practices is necessary and unfortunately we in India do not have much of the trained or skilful farmers for organic farming. For organic farmers, in many cases it becomes very difficult to control pathogens or pests without using chemical pesticides, in the starting phase organic farming gives poorer production, foods which are derived from organic resources may be harmful because they produces more bacterial infections, small farmers cannot opt organic farming because of lack of crop safety and lesser subsidy from the governments. Availability of traditional varieties of seeds, organic manure, bio-fertilizers and bio-pesticides are also some of the major challenges.

1. Lower productivity: An organic farm cannot produce as much yield as a conventional or industrialized farm. Though there is a debatable point as the productivity and soil quality of an industrialized farm decreases rapidly over the years. A survey and study conducted by the UN Environmental Program (2008) concluded that organic methods of farming result in smaller yields even in developing areas, compared to the conventional farming techniques.

2. Requires skill: An organic farmer requires better understanding along with regular and close watch of his crops as there are no quick fixes involved, like pesticides or chemical fertilizers. Many times it becomes very hard to meet all the strenuous requirements and the experience to practice organic farming at a commercial scale.

3. Time-consuming: Significant amount of time and energy are required to execute the detailed methods and techniques that are required for a farm to be called an organic farm. Failure to comply with any of these requirements could result in loss of certification, which the farmer will not be able to regain in up to three years. Organic farming increases soil fertility by way of compost, and organic fertilizers and mulch. Organic fertilizers tend to be slow-release. As with control by botanicals, horticultural oils, and insecticidal soaps, organic fertilizers may need several applications before the desired results are brought about and if the desired results.

4. Labour intensive: Organic farming can be more labor intensive. For organic farming considers biological, cultural and mechanical responses to production challenges. It focuses on plant and soil health through proper aeration, drainage, fertility, structure and watering. So there's more above and below ground labour work involved.

Future Perspectives of Organic Farming

The relatively high success of organic farming in some countries is because of awareness regarding health problems caused by the consumption of contaminated food products, the ill effects of environment degradation, appropriate support by the government and organizations like the European Union and International Federation of Organic Agriculture Movements (IFOAM). The modern system of farmingis becoming unsustainable as evidenced by declining crop productivities and nutritional value of the food, damage to environment, chemical contaminations much higher than the threshold value etc. The necessity of having an alternative agriculture method which can function in a friendly eco-system while sustaining and increasing the crop productivity is realized now. Organic farming is recognized as the best known alternative to the conventional agriculture. The major hurdles of organic agriculture in the country are absence of linkages between the farmers and markets and absence of financial support from the governments. India has the potential to become a major player in organic production given the international demand for our organic farm products, different agro-climatic regions for the cultivation of a variety of crops, the huge size of the domestic market and above all the long history of environment friendly farming and living. The movement started with developed world is gradually taking pace among the developing countries also. But demand is still concentrated in developed and most prosperous countries. However, local demand for organic food has grown. India is poised for faster growth with growing domestic market. Success of organic agriculture in India depends mainly upon the growth of its own domestic markets. India has traditionally been a country of organic agriculture, but the growth of modern scientific, input intensive agriculture has pushed it to wall. But with the increasing awareness about the food safety and quality, long term sustainability of the system and accumulating evidences of being equally productive, the organic farming has emerged to be an alternative system of farming which not only addresses the food quality and sustainability concerns, but also ensures a debt free and advantageous livelihood option.

Suggestions and Recommendations

In a country like India there is a huge agricultural land and many people working in agriculture or agriculture related sectors. This land comes under arid to semi-arid zones which are known as the best places for organic farming as bacterial activity is higher in such areas to improve the soil health by natural processes like nitrogen fixation etc. Many developed countries have converted their 25-35% land into organic farming while India is still lagging far behind in this case. It is a farming technique that aims to work in harmony with nature. Organic farming is a farming method which is sustainable as it uses only bio-inputs which do not harm the environment, but there are many social, economical and political problems in following the organic farming in India. These problems can be overcome by continuous efforts of the farmers and with the help of the Organic Farmers' co-operative societies, Government as well as the Non-Governmental Organizations. As Organic Farming practices are location specific, decentralized research should be promoted in the farmer's fields. During starting phase, there will be a decline in the yield and for that farmers Co-operative societies should help the farmers. The need for special markets for organic products is also felt. State and Centre Government should provide more subsidies to the farmers for the purchase of organic seeds, bio-fertilizers, organic pesticides and repellents etc. at an affordable price; Government should withdraw the subsidies given to chemical fertilizers and pesticides and ensure a good amount for the organically farmed products, the best performers should be given appropriate awards to enhance and promote the adoption of organic farming amount small and medium farmers. Funding for research and development focussing on organic farming and quality of organic products should also be increased. Farmer should be trained for organic farming practices from time to time. Hence there should be collective efforts from the government, PSUs, NGOs, researchers, academicians, business entrepreneurs and farmers to adopt organic farming for a better future for our next generations.

Discussion and Conclusions

Though agriculture has always remained the backbone of the Indian economy and despite our huge population we still occupy a place of pride by exporting our agricultural products. With the tremendous increase in population our compulsion has shifted not only to stabilize agricultural production but to increase it further in a more sustainable eco friendly and pollution free manner.

In India agriculture has become a yield and profit based profession rather than health benefits. It lowered the average lifespan of people in India and also diminished their health status. Ecology, environment and natural balance are totally being discarded by the excessive use of technology, chemical fertilizers and pesticides in quest to grow more and more grains. Organic farming system in India is not new and is being followed from ancient time. Thus, a natural balance needs to be maintained at any cost for continuity of existence of life on this planet. Taking advantage of the diverse soil types, climatic conditions, diversified geographic, geologic, monsoon and groundwater conditions, organic farming will progress tremendously in India providing better quality food and without adversely affecting ecology and environment and thereby bringing peace, prosperity and ample employment opportunities in the country.

REFERENCES

Alexandratos, N. and Bruinsma, J., 2012. *World Agriculture Towards 2030/2050: The 2012 Revision* (Vol. 12, No. 3). FAO, Rome: ESA Working Paper.

Alfvén, T., BraunFahrländer, C., Brunekreef, B., Von Mutius, E., Riedler, J., Scheynius, A., Van Hage, M., Wickman, M., Benz, M.R., Budde, J. and Michels, K.B., 2006. Allergic Diseases and Atopic Sensitization in Children Related to Farming and Anthroposophic Lifestyle–the PARSIFAL study. *Allergy, 61*(4), pp.414-421.

Berzsenyi, Z., Győrffy, B. and Lap, D., 2000. Effect of Crop Rotation and Fertilisation on Maize and Wheat Yields and Yield Stability in a Long-term Experiment. *European Journal of Agronomy, 13*(2-3), pp.225-244.

Butler, G., Nielsen, J.H., Slots, T., Seal, C., Eyre, M.D., Sanderson, R. and Leifert, C., 2008. Fatty Acid and Fatsoluble Antioxidant Concentrations in Milk from Highand Lowinput Conventional and Organic Systems: Seasonal Variation. *Journal of the Science of Food and Agriculture, 88*(8), pp.1431-1441.

Chandra, S., and Chauhan, S.K., 2004. Prospects of Organic Farming in India. *Indian Farming, 52*(2), pp.11-14.

Chhonkar, P.K., 2002. Organic Farming Myth and Reality. *Fertilizer News*, pp.1-9.

Choudhary, R.S., Das, A. and Patnaik, U.S., 2003. Organic Farming for Vegetable Production using Vermicompost and FYM in Kokriguda Watershed of Orissa. *Indian Journal of Soil Conservation, 31*(2), pp.203-206.

Clark, M.S., Horwath, W.R., Shennan, C., Scow, K.M., Lantni, W.T. and Ferris, H., 1999. Nitrogen, Weeds and Water as Yield-limiting Factors in Conventional, Low-input, and Organic Tomato Systems. *Agriculture, Ecosystems & Environment*, 73(3), pp.257-270.

Dobbs, T.L. and Smolik, J.D., 1996. Productivity and Profitability of Conventional and Alternative Farming Systems: A Long-term on-farm Paired Comparison. *Journal of Sustainable Agriculture*, 9(1), pp.63-79.

Drinkwater, L.E., Wagoner, P. and Sarrantonio, M., 1998. Legume-based Cropping Systems have Reduced Carbon and Nitrogen Losses. *Nature*, 396(6708), p.262.

Edwards, S., Asmelash, A. and Araya, H., 2007, May. The Impact of Compost Use on Crop Yields in Tigray, Ethiopia. In Institute for Sustainable Development (ISD). Proceedings of the International Conference on Organic Agriculture and Food Security. FAO, Rom.

FAO, F., 1998, November. Agriculture Organization, 1998. Evaluating the Potential Contribution of Organic Agriculture to Sustainability Goals. Environment and Natural Resources Service. In *Sustainable Development Department. FAO's Technical Contribution to IFOAM's Scientific Conference, Argentina.*

Finamore A, Britti MS, Roselli M, Bellovino D, Gaetani S and Mengheri E. 2004. Novel Approach for Food Safety Evaluation. Results of a Pilot Experiment to Evaluate Organic and Conventional Foods. *Journal of Agricultural and Food Chemistry*, 52: 7425-7431.

Francis, C.A., 1990. Sustainable Agriculture: Myths and Realities. *Journal of Sustainable Agriculture*, *1*(1), pp.97-106.

Gaur, A.C., 2006. Handbook of Organic Farming & Biofertilizers. Ambica Book Agency.

Heaton S., 2002. Assessing Organic Food Quality: Is it better for you? In: in Powell J. et al., (eds.) Proceedings of the UK Organic Research 2002 Conference, pp 55-60. Organic Centre Wales, Institute of Rural Studies, University of Wales Aberystwyth.

Henning, J., Baker, L. and Thomassin, P., 1991. Economics Issues in Organic Agriculture. *Canadian Journal of Agricultural Economics/Revue canadienne d'agroeconomie*, *39*(4), pp.877-889.

Huber M. and van de Vijver L., 2009. Overview of Research Linking Organic Production Methods and Health Effects in the Lab, in Animals and in Humans. Department of Health Care and Nutrition, Louis Bolk Institute, Netherlands.

Küstermann B., Kainz M., Hülsbergen K.J., 2008. Modeling Carbon Cycles and Estimation of Greenhouse Gas Emissions from Organic and Conventional Farming Systems. *Renewable Agriculture and Food Systems*, 23: 38-52.

Lampkin, N.H., 1994. Organic Farming: Sustainable Agriculture in Practice. *The Economics of Organic Farming: An International Perspective*, p.454.

Meena, V.S. and Sharma, S., 1970. Organic Farming: A Case Study of Uttarakhand Organic Commodity Board. *Journal of Industrial Pollution Control*, 31(2).

Mendoza T.C., 2002. An Evaluation Study of Plan International Sustainable Agriculture Program in Calapan, Oriental Mindoro. Report Submitted to Plan International Philippines, 6th Floor N & M Building Chino Roces Ave. Makati City, Philippines. 123 pp.

Niggli U., Flieβbach A., Hepperly P. and Scialabba N., 2009. Low Greenhouse Gas Agriculture: Mitigation and Adaptation Potential of Sustainable Farming Systems. FAO,

Olsson M.E, Andersson CS, Oredsson S, Berglund RH and Gustavsson KE. 2006. Antioxidant Levels and Inhibition of Cancer Cell Proliferation in Vitro by Extracts from Organically and Conventionally Cultivated Strawberries. *Journal of Agricultural and Food Chemistry*, 54:1248–1255.

Padel, S. and Lampkin, N.H., 1994. Conversion to Organic Farming: An Overview. *The Economics of Organic Farming: An International Perspective*, pp.295-313.

Padel, S., 1994. Adoption of Organic Farming as an Example of the Diffusion of an Innovation–A Literature Review on the Conversion to Organic Farming. *Centre for Organic Husbandry and Agroecology Discussion Paper Series*, *94*(1).

Park, J. and Seaton, R.A.F., 1996. Integrative Research and Sustainable Agriculture. *Agricultural Systems*, *50*(1), pp.81-100.

Reganold J.P., Palmer A.S., Lockhart J.C. and Macgregor A.N., 1993. Soil Quality and Financial Performance on Biodynamic and Conventional Farms in New Zealand. Science, 260: 344-349.

Scofield, A.M., 1986. Organic Farming—the Origin of the Name.

Sharma, A.K., 2001. *A Handbook of Organic Farming*. Agrobios.

Sharma, P.D., 2003. Prospects of Organic Farming in India, in Proceedings of National Seminar on Organic Products and Future Prospects. *Sher-e-Kashmir UAST, Srinagar, Pp: 21, 29.*

Staiger D. 1988. The Nutritional Value of Foods from Conventional and Biodynamic Agriculture. IFOAM Bulletin No. 4, pg 9-12. Stuttgart, pp 1437–6512

Tate, W.B., 1994. The Development of the Organic Industry and Market: An International Perspective. *The Economics of Organic Farming: An International Perspective*, pp.11-25.

Veeresh, G.K., 1999. Organic Farming Ecologically Sound and Economically Sustainable. *Plant Horti Tech, 1*(3), pp.512-520.

Willer H and Youssefi M. 2007. The World of Organic Agriculture – Statistics and Emerging.

Woese K., Lange D., Boess C. and Bogl K.W., 1997. A Comparison of Organically and Conventionally Grown Foods –Results of a Review of the Relevant Literature. *J. Sci. Food Agric.*, 74: 281-293.

Yadav, A.K., 2010. Organic Agriculture (Concept, Scenario, Principals and Practices). Director National Centre of Organic Farming, Ghaziabad National Centre of Organic Farming Department of Agriculture and Cooperation, Ministry of Agriculture, Govt of India, Uttar Pradesh.

Farming and Development : *Technological Perspectives* **Pages 101-110**
Edited by: **Dr. Pawan Kumar 'Bharti' & Dr. Jaswant Ray**
ISBN: 978-93-88854-08-5
Edition: **2019**
Published by: **Discovery Publishing House Pvt. Ltd., New Delhi (India)**

6

Gender Issues in Farm Enterprises in India

[1]Dr. Esakkimuthu M

ABSTRACT

Agriculture development has been a major concern to most developing nations for the last twenty years. It includes a cluster of some related but separate concepts such as agricultural expansion, increased production per acre of cropped land; agricultural growth, rising per capita income and complete agricultural transformation. It is a well known fact that agriculture is the mainstay of Indian economy employing about two third of the population but the contribution to Gross Domestic Product (GDP) is much lower. There might be many reasons; one of them could be women's work not recognized as gainful employment. Men and women are two wheels of a cart that leads to development and yes, agricultural development. There has been a growing recognition of the importance of gender to some specific development sectors in recent times. It has also been a cross cutting issue in agriculture, health and infrastructural development. Women in India play a significant and crucial role in agricultural development and allied fields including crop production, livestock production, horticulture, post harvest operations, agro-social forestry and fishing etc. The last decade of the twentieth century has seen the emergence of gender as a one of the basic issues of human progress. The focus of gender rather than makes it critical to look not only at the category women but at women in relation to men. 'Gender' insists that women cannot be viewed in isolation. In examining the different roles of women and men. 'Gender analysis' provides the principle for separating out and differentiating the work men and women. When compared to men, women encounter additional constraints in their gendered role. This occurs particularly in household enterprises where men recruit their wives to unpaid tasks as sewing, weaving etc. The crucial role of women in agriculture, allied occupations and household activities have been under estimated and undervalued. The multiple role played been under estimated and undervalued. The multiple role played by women in terms of work hours contributed or equivalent. Income generated in the family are neither attended nor recorded.

Keywords: Agriculture, cluster, development, economy and gender.

1 Kerala Agricultural University, Thrissur, Kerala 680656, India

Introduction

Women in India play a significant and crucial role in agricultural development and allied fields including crop production, livestock production, horticulture, post harvest operations, agro-social forestry and fishing etc. The last decade of the twentieth century has seen the emergence of gender as a one of the basic issues of human progress. The focus of gender rather than makes it critical to look not only at the category women but at women in relation to men. 'Gender' insists that women cannot be viewed in isolation. In examining the different roles of women and men. 'Gender analysis' provides the principle for separating out and differentiating the work men and women. When compared to men, women encounter additional constraints in their gendered role. This occurs particularly in household enterprises where men recruit their wives to unpaid tasks as sewing, weaving etc. The crucial role of women in agriculture, allied occupations and household activities have been under estimated and undervalued. The multiple role played been under estimated and undervalued. The multiple role played by women in terms of work hours contributed or equivalent. Income generated in the family are neither attended nor recorded.

Concept of Gender

Gender in general is a system relationship rather than a set of attributes which distinguish males and females. Gender is the relative status of men and women in a given society because of their being "men" and "women". Gender describes roles, identification and power relations of men and women that are defined by society and socially constructed.

Gender Derived Needs

Gender derived needs are those women and men develop by virtue of their social positioning through gender attributes. These gender needs can be either practical or strategic each derived in a different way.

(i) Practical Needs

This refers to satisfying the men and women within their existing roles in society. For examples, reduced work load, increase income through improved success to markets and skill training, improve health etc.

(ii) Strategic Needs

Strategic needs refers to changing the structure and nature of relationships between men and women. For examples, Gender equality aspects like equal success to productive assets like land, education etc.

Gender based Roles

Role

Role means a unique combination of talent and attitudes adopted to discharge of specific assignment.

Gender Role

The gender roles ascribed to men and women in a particular society are largely due to men and women in a particular society are largely due to attitudinal predispositions. The perceived men's role is "provider" and "supporter" and the perceived women's role is "homemaker". In reality this may not true because in a third of poor families in India women are the heads of house hold and other third of the families women's income is a decisive factor in the household.

Role of Women in Agriculture

In India agricultural labour and fare activities are the main areas of economic activities for women. The National Sample Survey Organisation (NSSO, 2012) report has shown that the 65 percentage contribution of women in agriculture is higher than men where most of the key operations at farm are done by women. They work as,

1. Paid labourers
2. Cultivators – doing labour in their own land as unpaid workers
3. Managers of certain aspects of agricultural production by way of labour supervision, participating in post-harvest processing etc.

Table 6.1: Role of Women in Farm and Non-farm Activities

S.No.	Farm			Non-farm	
	Crop	Animal	Ancillary	Household	Non-household
1.	Sowing	Grazing/feeding the animal	Collection of fodder	Cooking	Marketing
2.	Weeding	Chaffing of fodder	Filling of manure pits	Child care	Rope making
3.	Harvesting	Cleaning the animals and Cattle sheds	Kitchen gardening	Making cow dung cakes	Dari making
4.	Irrigation	Milking and Processing of milk	Firewood collection	Fetching of drinking water	Weaving

Gender Issues in Agriculture

Agricultural development has been a major concern to most developing nations for the last 20 years. It includes a cluster of some related but separate concepts such as agricultural expansion, increased production per acre of cropped land; agricultural growth, rising per capita income and complete agricultural transformation. It is a well known fact that agriculture is the mainstay of Indian economy employing about two third of the population but the contribution to GDP is much lower. There might be many reasons; one of them could be women's work not recognized as gainful employment. Men and women are two wheels of a cart that leads to development and yes, agricultural development. There has been a growing recognition of the importance of gender to some specific development sectors in recent times. It has also been a cross cutting issue in agriculture, health and infrastructural development **(Rathore S, 2012).** The major gender issues in agriculture are the followings:

1. Sexual division of labour
2. Impact of male out migration on women
3. Decision-making privileges to women
4. Disparity in wage rate
5. Access to credit and land
6. Impact of farm technology on women
7. Access to extension services
8. Training to women
9. Impact of development schemes on women in agriculture

1. Sexual division of labour

All societies have division of labour based on sex i.e. work that is seen as women's work. Evidences clearly suggest that the sexual division of labour is socially constructed and not based natural sex differences. In general, women are exempted from doing certain operations in the field. For example, ploughing, plant protection operations etc. The involvement of farm women in land preparation and plant protection operations was found to be less. It stated that except ploughing, which in entirely male domain, all other farm operations are done by females. Therefore, none of the farm women participated in ploughing, irrigation management and during operations. Women are allotted more arduous, time consuming and low paid works. Activities in which women participated traditionally are transplanting, weeding, sowing and harvesting. These activities requires more time. Above all, these are more arduous in nature. The task performance of feminine gender it was high in five operations like sowing, weeding, grain storage, land preparation and cleaning seeds for sowing. It was found that transplanting and harvesting of paddy where done exclusively by female workers. In Kuttanad, one of the paddy prominent rice farming tract of Kerala. The operations like weeding, harvesting and processing which requires maximum work force were solely undertaken by women. Women have high level of involvement in threshing, storage, harvesting and packing activities in the farm.

2. Impact of male out migration on women

Migration: It refers to the shifting of an individual from his native place to some other place for employment.

The effect of male out migration on women:

(*i*) **Increase of female headed households:** Male out migration directly leads to increase in households solely by women. World economic profile of women shows that women represents 50% of the population and 40% of the world farms are said to be managed by women. In India 30-35% rural families are said to be managed by women as a result of men's migration to urban areas. In rural eastern India, women do 60-80% of rice farming work with the seasonal migration of men.

(*ii*) **Increase in the work load of women:** As a result of men's migration, women are forced to manage in a households and farms at the same time. These women are caught in an often impossible position having to provide the cash as well as food needs of the family.

(*iii*) **Productivity of women decreases:** Because of the women's lack of access to input, new technologies, extension, training and credit facilities, productivity of women is female household decreases.

(*iv*) **Change in the division of labour:** As a result of male out migration, women are forced to carry out the works that are traditionally done by men in which the women lack training. It revealed that lack of access and control over productive assets by Indian women is leading to lower productivity in the wake of increased male migration to the urban centres. It also stated that as a result of male migration, women have to carry a greater burden of the agricultural labour.

Reasons for male out migration:

(*i*) Migration is motivated by rural residents' desire for cash income.

(*ii*) Insufficient farm size and poor local wage labour opportunities oblige some men to seek migratory work.

(*iii*) It found out that the males from poor and landless households have the highest prosperity to migrate.

(*iv*) Economic reasons were the major factor contributing towards male migration.

3. *Decision-making Privileges to Women*

Decision making: Decision making as the degree to which an individual justifies by selection of most efficient means from among the available alternatives. On the basis of scientific criteria for achieving maximum economic profits.

Need for female decision making: Women's participation in economic decision-making was vital means by which their economic dependency and social inequity could be removed. The female participation in decision making result in development of their entrepreneurial and leadership qualities. In agriculture there are clear cut gender demarcation ion case of making decision about various farm activities. In general female participation in farm decision-making is limited. The decision on farm activities were predominantly husband-oriented. It indicated that women made lesser independent decisions on matters relating to farming when compared to collective decisions. More than 51% of the total decisions with respect to agricultural operations were solely by and only 29% of the decisions were by the women. Participation of women in decision making is more with respect to purchase and sale of land, marketing of produce and livestock. In Kerala more than 90% of farm women took part in decision relating to storage and marketing of produce and management and care of animals. This pattern of decision making between males and females has a detrimental effect on women firstly,

(1) It hinders the acceptance of improved agricultural technology because the real workers i.e. women is different from the real decision maker.

(2) The extension workers approach only the males and thus the communication of message about the improved agricultural practices to the real workers becomes indirect and less effective.

4. Disparity in wage rate

In agricultural sector the remuneration and division of labour is highly sex based. Inequality in the wage disparity between female and male agricultural labourer. Women need to work twice as long to achieve the same level of earnings as men. The wage rate of agricultural labourers is highest in Kerala followed by Punjab and Haryana. In Kerala State the wage rate between men and women is equal in many districts whereas in other States of India discrimination wages are still prevalent which need great attention.

The basic reasons for disparity in wages:

(i) Operations that fetches higher wages are male preserve whereas work of arduous nature bringing in lower wages is done by women.

(ii) Seasonal nature of the demand of labour. Only during peak season women get employment. For example, during sowing, transplanting and harvesting season. Remaining period they remain without any earnings.

(iii) The traditional classification of some jobs as the monopoly of women.

(iv) Poverty, illiteracy and ignorance regarding laws.

(v) Poor bargaining power of women.

5. Access to credit and land

The crux of the problem is the ownership of property and controlling at least a certain amount of assets. In almost all cases ownership of the rights of land is bestowed on the male head of household regardless of traditional inheritance rights of men and women. In Indian the patrilineal allocation of lineage land or inheritance has great implications for women's role in food productions and for women's economic authority. Other detrimental effects are,

Lack of access to bank credit:

(*a*) Since land has been the major source of collateral security, women's lack of ownership has barred them from the access to the formal credit.

(*b*) Banks under estimate the women's potential agricultural productivity and mistrust women's ability to repay loans. But the report of the National Commission of Self-employed Women and Women observed that, women when given institutional support demonstrated high productivity, better record of repayment of loans and assets are sustained.

(*c*) Non-availability of loans and the financial institutions hesitance to extend credit to women farmers.

(*i*) An in-depth study of credit flow by gender in regional rural bank branch and a commercial bank branch in one district of Andhra Pradesh suggest that disbursement to women ranged between 6 and 12 percent overall but dropped to zero for agricultural loans.

(*ii*) The percentage of women members in Indian Co-operative Societies was found to be only 10%. The reason being the domination of rural elites in the management of the Co-operative Societies who are averse to providing credit to weaker sections including women.

(*iii*) Women by and large unaware of the existing credit facilities and bank policies.

(*iv*) Women farmers were apprehensive of banks cumbersome procedures which they find it more difficult to deal with.

(*v*) Lack of women's group/co-operatives which could help women in obtaining the required credit.

(*vi*) As a result of all these the women are accustomed to taking informal credit from pawn brokers, money lenders and relatives who charge high interest.

6. *Impact of Farm Technology on Women*

By technology what we mean is the application of science into the process of production.

Need for technology:

(*i*) To improve the earning capacity and increase output.

(*ii*) Widen employment opportunities especially for women.

(*iii*) Lessen drudgery in daily life.

(*iv*) Encourage participation in activities which promote the development of the community.

(*v*) To offer labour and time saving appliances not only in agriculture but in household tasks.

Whatever the technology developed it should:

(*i*) Be adapted to local cultural and economic conditions.

(*ii*) The tools and processes utilized should be under the maintenance and operational control of the people and whenever possible the technology should use locally available materials.

(*iii*) The technology should match the skill of both male and female farmers.

(*iv*) Cost of technology should not be too high.

(*v*) Finally it should reach the farmers.

Displacing Effect of Technology

To cope up with the increasing demand of food grain production many new scientific innovation in agriculture technology is getting introduced every day. Mechanization and new farming practices resulted in an overall decline in demand for family and hired labour. The displacing effect of technology is more for women than men. It also reported that as a consequence of change in harvesting practices and crop establishment methods and of the introduction of mechanical rice thresher more females than male labourers was displaced. **(Choudhary *et al*, 2012)** reported that the green revolution in Northern India resulted in displacing women from the available work in turn they allotted jobs which pay less and require less skill.

7. Access to Extension Services

Extension activities can strengthen the tie between the introduction and spread of innovative techniques. In recent past an increasing awareness has created to make the agricultural services more accessible and responsive to women farmers. But, the existing extension frame work was found to have been not very successful in bringing such women orientation.

Reasons:

(*i*) Traditional extension approaches have often failed to reach the women farmers in large measure because of cultural and social factors.

(*ii*) It stated that in many Asian countries cultural constraints in the rural areas prevent male extewnsion workers from communicating effectively with women farmers.

(*iii*) The research and extension system in agriculture has been largely male oriented.

(*iv*) More than 20% of the framers worldwide were females but the percentage of extension workers was barely 1%. Therefore, the availability of female extension workers were found to be minimum.

(v) It was observed the extension workers almost exclusively male aim their advise at men and at men's activities and crops and ignore women farmers.

(vi) It was found that even in states like Odisha and Tamil Nadu, which have set targets of at least one female contact farmer per village the women selected were not agriculturalists but simply members of the elite local families often with limited contact with active women farmers.

Importance of Female Extension Workers in Agriculture

It is accepted that female extension personnel will be more successful in reaching female farmers with advisory service. It also reported that female extension personnel are more likely to be influential and effective in reaching female farmers than male extension workers regardless of socio-cultural, agro-climatic and politic and economic conditions.

8. Training to Women

Agriculture is thought in a much different way at the present, than it was formerly. Now the farmer must use good judgement and careful management if he has to make a profit. So training is very much essential to equip women with the improved technology. However, women farmers are mostly trained on home economics than farming aspects. The farmers need training in many aspects of farming to which they devoid off. **(Badiger *et al*, 2009)** observed that intense training was required by the farm women since they were included in farming activities and often joined with their husbands in performing different agricultural operations. They required training on methods of sowing, transplanting, harvesting and knowledge on developed storing techniques to avoid loss.

9. Impact of Development Schemes on Women in Agriculture

Ever since Independence, Government of India started several schemes and development programmes to uplift the rural poor and women. Unfortunately the impact of these programmes on women on women's development is reported to be insignificant.

Conclusion

Much has been written about the past failures of government extension services in reaching women farmers and the cultural bias which has in many countries prevented women from active participation in group training, extension meetings and most importantly, access to inputs such as fertiliser and credit. These services have been predominantly staffed by men and they have tended to direct their services to male farmers or heads of households, excluding female-headed households and women members of male-headed households. However, any consideration of gender in relation to these points must be considered in the context of the changes which are taking place.

REFERENCES

Badiger, C. Gavimath, U. and Nadagoudar, B.S. (2009): Knowledge and Participation of Farm Women, *Maharastra Journal of Extension Education*, 10 (1): 87-91.

Choudhary, H. and Singh, S. (2012): Knowledge of Farm Women about Agricultural Activities. *Rural India*, 4 (1). 13-14.

Rathore, S. (2012): Advances in Extension Methodologies for Agricultural Development, Report on ICAR Sponsored Summer School, Govind Ballabh Pant University of Agriculture and Technology, Pantnagar, Uttarakhnad, pp:106.

Farming and Development : *Technological Perspectives* **Pages 111-125**
Edited by: **Dr. Pawan Kumar 'Bharti' & Dr. Jaswant Ray**
ISBN: 978-93-88854-08-5
Edition: **2019**
Published by: **Discovery Publishing House Pvt. Ltd., New Delhi (India)**

7

Sustainable Farm Enterprise Development in Kerala

A Case on Samagra banana farming

[1]Dr. Esakkimuthu M

Introduction

In India mostly small and marginal holdings constitute 80% of the total holdings in India. Small farmers face several problems like absence of marketing network, lack of value addition technology, non-availability of quality inputs, lack of timely credit, etc. The small scale agriculture can be made profitable through product diversification, value addition and agri-entrepreneurship. Small scale agri-enterprises provide an excellent opportunity for employment generation and improving their socio-economic condition.

India is an agrarian country. Over 58% of India's population is supported by agriculture. Even while India's industrial and service sectors are growing by leaps and bounds, growth rate of agriculture is below 2%. However, in the long run, growth of other sectors is invariably linked to the fortunes of agriculture due to intricate forward and backward linkages. Hence, India's economic status continues to be determined by agriculture sector, and the situation is not likely to change in the foreseeable future.

Status of Land Resources and Farm Economy

The country recorded impressive achievements in agriculture during three decades since the onset of green revolution in late sixties. This enabled the country to overcome widespread hunger and starvation, achieve self-sufficiency in food, reduce poverty and bring economic transformation to millions of rural families. The situation, however, started taking a downturn in the mid-nineties with slowdown in growth rate of output, which then resulted in stagnation or even decline in farmers' income leading to agrarian distress. Over the years, this has been turning more and more serious. Agriculture now supports 58% of the population, as against 75% at the time of independence. During the same period, the contribution of agriculture and allied sectors to the gross domestic product has fallen from 61 to 19%. As of today, India supports 16.8% of World's population on 4.2% of World's water and 2.3% of land resources

[1] TKerala Agricultural University, Thrissur, Kerala-680656, India.

and per capita availability of resources is about 4 to 6 times less as compared to the world average. This will decrease further due to increasing demographic pressure and consequent diversion of the land for non-agricultural uses.

Sustainable Farm Productivity

Around 51% of India's geographical area is already under cultivation as compared to 11% of the world average. The present cropping intensity of 136% has registered an increase of only 25% since independence. Further, rainfed drylands constitute 65% of the total net sown area. There is also an unprecedented degradation of land (107 million ha) and groundwater resources, and also fall in the rate of growth of total factor productivity. Natural resource base of agriculture, which provides for sustainable production, is either shrinking or degrading leading to adverse affects on production capacity. However, demand from the sector is rising rapidly due increase in population and per capita income and growing demand from industry sector. There is, thus, an urgent need to identify the problems confronting agriculture sector, restore its vitality and put it back on high growth trajectory. The deceleration needs to be arrested and agricultural productivity has to be doubled by 2050 to meet the growing demands of the population.

Agriculture System in India

The concept of innovation is opined by (Freeman, 1987) and (Lundwall, 1992) proposed that the origin of innovation systems thinking can be traced to the idea of a national system of innovation. The concept brings together thinking from a broad set of theoretical debates that view development and change in systems terms. More importantly it is based on empirical observations of 'good practices' in different countries and technology sectors. At its heart lies the contention that change or innovation results from and is shaped by the system of organizations and institutions in particular locations and points in time. This system includes organizations involved with research and the application and adaptation of research findings, as well as intermediary organization that promote knowledge transfer. A simple definition of an innovation system would be the system of all the actors and their routines and habits that in a given policy context produce, use, diffuse and adopt knowledge in socio-economically significant ways (Sulaiman, 2008). The concept of innovation system stresses that the flow of information among people, enterprises and institutions is key to an innovative process. It contains the interaction between the actors who are needed in order to turn an idea into a process, product or service in the market.

Kerala's Decentralised Farm Economy

Decentralized planning is strongly entrenched in the Kerala society since late 1990's. With experience spread over a decade and half in this regard, the Kerala state has to its credit many innovative projects in the agricultural sector which have left a lasting impact on the community. When it comes to sustainability and scaling up of such innovative projects, a large number of factors come into play (Surendran, 2000). There has been some model projects such as the 'Samagra (comprehensive) Project' on Banana cultivation initiated in Thiruvananthapuram District Panchayat with active participation of a host of institutional and individual stakeholders. The resounding success of the Project has paved the way for the further extension and expansion of the Project to benefit more 'Activity Groups' to be organised under the Kudumbashree Mission (Kudumbashree, 2010).

Local Self Government Interventions in Farm Development

A preliminary impact assessment of the Project indicated that 1691 ha. of land has been brought under banana cultivation involving 2915 Activity Groups . Production credit to the tune of Rs. 24 crores has been absorbed with repayment exceeding 80 per cent. The productivity of banana has gone up to 12 MT/ha. Most critical and innovative elements in the project have been the successful handholding of the beneficiaries by the Private Partner and the escorting services rendered by the project laboratories justify set up by the three-tier Local Self Governments. The sustainability and innovation system analyses conducted among 150 respondents representing various stakeholder groups have brought to focus a set of dimensions which need to be reckoned in decentralized planning for development particularly in the primary sector. This paper epitomises these interesting findings leading to the prescription of some policy perspectives for effective local self governance.

Strategies for Eradication of Poverty and Hunger

It is an interesting historical fact that the entire Millennium Development Goals could be traced back in the Stockholm Declaration of 1972 and subsequently the Agenda 21 of the Rio Declaration of 1992. Alleviation of poverty and hunger is the major pillar of sustainable development. Again within the frame work of the mechanisms for ending poverty and hunger, the role of women becomes the most important guiding factor. To instrumentalise women for achieving comprehensive socio-economic-ecological sustainable development the skill development and empowerment of women is the exact policy initiative any country in the world has to focus.

Keeping the above policy perceptions in mind the District Panchayat, Thiruvananthapuram (through its Kudumbashree Programme) and a Development Innovation Promotion Agency in Thiruvananthapuram (Prowins Agri System) initiated an entirely pioneering programme to alleviate poverty and hunger through women empowerment and skill formation initiated with specific focus an organic agriculture development (Samagra- Nendran banana cultivation programme).

Development innovation promotion agency, Prowins Agri System, along with this programme also implemented a comprehensive women development model encompassing almost all sectors of the rural economy through entrepreneurial development programme and skill development trainings for women. These entrepreneurship and skill development programmes resulted in a wide variety of multiplier effect resulting into more demonstrative income generation and poverty alleviation.

For the first time in India the Samagra Programme and comprehensive Sustainable Development skill formation designed by Prowins Agri System in association with the District Panchayat Thiruvananthapuram and implemented through women resulted in conspicuous increase in agriculture productivity (banana production) and total socio economic empowerment and development in rural areas. Following table illustrates details showing the area benefitted number of beneficiaries, production, productivity and net profit obtained under the Samagra programme in various blocks where it was implemented.

Table 7.1: Samagra Project-beneficiaries, Area, Production, Productivity in Various Blocks

Sl. No.	Name of Block	No. of Panchayat	Area (Ha)	No. of Beneficiaries	Loan (in Lakhs) Rs.	Production (M.T)	Average Cost of Cultivation	Price/ M.T (in Lakhs) Rs.	Returns generated	Net Profit in Lakhs Rs.
1.	Athiyanoor	2	223	880	170	4460	301.05	0.2	892	590.95
2.	Perumkadavila	7	996.5	7324	1163.27	19930	1345.275	0.2	3986	2640.725
3.	Parassala	3	680	1565	664.35	13600	918	0.2	2720	1802
4.	Nemom	4	518.37	1000	274.7	10367.4	699.7995	0.2	2073.48	1373.681
5.	Vamanapuram	7	201.2	1220	86.6	4024	271.62	0.2	804.8	533.18
6.	Vellanadu	5	281.71	1182	138.75	5634.2	380.3085	0.2	1126.84	746.5315
7.	Nedumangadu	4	113	1020	25.6	2260	152.55	0.2	452	299.45
8.	Kazhakoottam	2	15.5	355	9.75	310	20.925	0.2	62	41.075
	Total		3029.2	14546	2533.02	60585.6	4089.528		12117.12	8027.592

It is most heartening to note that when many scientists and agricultural practitioners argue that organic agricultural initiatives will not be able to increase the productivity, Samagra banana cultivation through women proved that organic agriculture practices can definitely increase productivity, production and increase in per capita income of the women farmers ultimately leading to considerable reduction in poverty and hunger (see Table 2).

Table 7.2: Comparison of Input Cost and Production (Income) of Samagra Project with Conventional Farming System

Sl. No.	Particulars	Conventional chemical oriented cultivation	Cultivation under Samagra project where integrated fertilizer application avoiding pesticides & fungicides is followed
1.	Cost of cultivation per Ha(in lakhs)	2.10	2.55
2.	Production per Ha(in MT)	20.00	27.00
3.	Price per MT	20000.00	20000.00
4.	Total income per Ha (in lakhs)	4.00	5.40
5.	Net profit (in lakhs)	1.90	2.85

It is most interesting and encouraging that the sustainable agricultural development programme undertaken by women through Samagra project shows that the final net profit is 35% more compared to the conventional farming system in which chemical inputs are applied (Ashaletha, 2000). An encouraging result emerging out of the comparison between conventional cultivation with chemical inputs and organic cultivation under Samagra, it can be seen that the total input cost is more in case of Samagra project due to high input cost while it is less in case of conventional cultivation. Even though the input cost analysis happened to be so, it is heartening that the income analysis shows that under organic agricultural practices (Women involved Samagra banana project) 35% more income and profit is recorded compared to conventional agriculture. This is a paradoxical phenomenon.

The input cost in case of Samagra Project happened to be high because of the usage of bio-fertilizers, organic plant growth promoters such as humic acids, nutrich, salvic acid, sea weed extract and bio pesticides such as metarhyzium, Beaveria, Pseudomonas etc. These inputs are comparatively more costlier than the conventional chemical oriented inputs.

When the input cost scenario happened be so the output (income) increased because of the optimum nutritional application to the plant. It is an encouraging experience we came across that when we have avoided the application of toxic carbofuran and replaced the same with Neem Cake and Neem Kernel crush the total health of the plant increased especially the pseudo stem become very sturdy and as a result the plant was able to withstand even moderately high wind velocity. At the same time it is experienced that the nearby farmers who followed the conventional pattern of agricultural practices (including application of carbofuran), not only experienced low weight of bunches but also the strength of pseudo stem was comparatively less and as a result even wind with low velocity caused dislodging of the plant resulting in huge crop loss.

Win-win phenomenal Factors

Committed administrative determination shown by the political leadership and the district level officials of the District Panchayat, Thiruvananthapuram in implementing the project without any hurdles. Efficient field level implementation by the Sustainable Development Innovation Agency (Prowins Agri System) in providing appropriate technology support, supplying quality bio inputs, credit linkage services to women farmers and field level co- ordination by their dynamic field experts. Timely credit support given by leading banks such as Sate Bank of Travancore and State Bank of India. Comprehensive Technical support provided by Prowins Agri System such as soil testing, plot specific inputs recommendation etc. Comprehensive Training on Sustainable organic banana cultivation practices provided by Prowins to all women participants in the project.

Innovative Farm Developmental Model

This innovative development model which we have experimented in Kerala through women empowerment in a multi sectoral and multi dimensional skill formation techniques is most unique. The Prowins Agri System developed an entrepreneurial development and skill development model for women in such a way that women were given multi-sectoral and multi-dimensional Skill formation training. For example a women who was given entrepreneurial development training for food processing (banana chips, Pickle, cereal powder, dairy etc) was also given training on goat rearing and organic agriculture (banana, vegetables, etc). The women who have got such a multi-sectoral skill formation training were able to identify which is the most sustainable entrepreneurship initiative they can adopt comparing the experience they have received from the training programme provided by Prowins Agri System in different sectors. Some of the successful women who later on revealed that they have experimented with two three entrepreneurial ventures and then they realized that their attitude and knowledge is more suitable for a particular venture which ultimately made them successful entrepreneurs.

Sustainable Development through Farm Women Empowerment

The women empowerment programme designed within the frame work of Sustainable Development proved that the women could become instrument in achieving comprehensive sustainable development, resulting in conspicuous increase in family income and reduction in poverty. From a macro perspective of Kerala, a State which experience food and vegetable shortage for a long time the Samagra Sustainable Development Project through women made a humble contribution in increasing the supply of vegetables especially banana. Along with this programme it is most encouraging that the Prowins Agri System provided entrepreneurship and skill formation training programme for a total number of 22715 women and out of these 22715 women who received entrepreneurship training (including technical Skill refined for specific value addition Programme) 19610 women have established their own ventures. A preliminary survey revealed that in more than 60% of the cases the entrepreneur ventures started by women resulted in giving employment to 2-5 people (An exact multiplier effect have to be assessed through a detailed study in future). It can also be observed from the table 2 that the skill formation training was given to women encompassing almost all sectors of the rural economy using locally available materials/ resources.

Table 7.3: Profile of Integrated Training Provided by Prowins Agri-System to Women Entrepreneurs in Various Ventures

Sl. No.	Microenterprises Unit	No. of Beneficiaries	No. of units established by women after getting the training	No. of women involved in the units after getting the trainings
1.	Food Processing	1849	71	718
2.	Fruits & Vegetable Processing	2196	61	605
3.	Crop Cultivation	14320	5420	14308
4.	Animal Husbandry	3966	463	3755
5.	Industrial Units	384	14	224
	Total	22715	6029	19610

It is a heartening fact that the women who were producing the basic raw material (eg. Cultivating banana for preparing banana chips) were also using the same raw material for preparing banana chips themselves. Total training was provided to women encompassing food processing, fruit and vegetable processing, agriculture, animal husbandry and industrial units like soap making , sanitary napkins production etc. An interesting outcome from the training provided to 22715 women is that majority of them adopted banana cultivation. A win-win outcome of the project is that the women who cultivated banana also themselves prepared banana chips using the banana produced by them. This has resulted in avoiding the middle men and ultimately able to compete with the banana chips market successfully. A most interesting information we could gather from the women who established banana chips were that when they used organic banana the weight of the final fried chips was comparatively more than the chips produced from banana procured from market which were raised under chemical cultivation practices. It was gathered from the women entrepreneurs that the chemically produced banana is having more water content compared to organically produced banana and breakage of banana chips is less in case of organically produced chips (This is an area where a serious research investigation is required by the food technologists to identify the nutritional and study characteristics of organically produced and chemically produced banana)

Skill Development for Entrepreneurship

The comprehensive sustainable development programme undertaken in the form of Samagra shows that if scientifically designed entrepreneurship and skill development programme are provided to women they could definitely become the agents for promoting socio-econo-ecologically sustainable development (Chandran, 1989). The Samagra project also revealed that when a systematically integrated development programme is evolved in which the government agency, the beneficiary, the credit providing agency and skill formation training providing agency like, Prowins Agri System, work together in a perfect tandem historically successful results can be achieved. The Samagra project also provides concrete evidence that scientifically designed skill formation, especially multi sectoral and multi dimensional training given to the same target group proved to be an innovative training technique which give a comprehensive skill testing opportunity to the targeted training group (here women) enabling them to choose a particular entrepreneur venture which is more suitable to them. This technique can definitely be identified as a replicable sustainable development skill development training programme especially for women in different countries where similar socio-ecological system exists (Sanjeev, 1987). The Samagra experience shows that there is a need for establishing an institutional entity for providing permanent and continuous training and skill formation program in comprehensive sustainable development to women. Such training programme should encompass training and skill formation relating to all sectors of the economy both in urban and rural systems. The Government (including Panchayats), -Private industry, public sector banks, NABARD and international development agencies may come forward to establish such a comprehensive training institute with special focus on empowerment of women.

Analysis of Socio-economic and Communication Characteristics of Farmers

Age: According to Manjusha (1999) reported that there is non-significant relationship between age and extent of adoption of recommended practices by the farmers in bitter gourd cultivation; Sreedaya (2000) reported a non significant relationship of age with the extent of adoption of recommended practices among vegetable growers of both Intensive Vegetable Development Programme (IVDP) and Vegetable and Fruit Promotion Council, Keralam (VFPCK); Thomas (2000) reported that age had positive and significant relationship with the knowledge of farmers; Geetha (2002) reported that age had negative and significant correlation with the functioning of 'Thozhil Sena'.

Area under cultivation: According to Jha and Shaktawat (1972) found that size of holding was not significantly related to adoption behavior of farmers in their study; Muller (1997) reported non significant relationship between farm size and group relationship of women; According to the study conducted by

Manoj (2000), total area under paddy was found to have positive relationship and significant correlation with adoption behaviour; Surendran (2000) reported that large farm size resulted in more returns from farming which was conductive for higher group participation.

Experience in banana cultivation: According to Manjusha (1999) found a non significant relationship between experience in bitter gourd cultivation and extent of adoption; Sreedaya (2000) reported that experience in vegetable cultivation was positively and significantly correlated with need satisfaction among VFPCK self help groups.

Annual income: According to Vehra (1971) reported that those who had greater economic resources participated more and higher levels of income were conducive for higher participation; Kailasam (1980) found that income had positive and significant association with extent of participation; Rao (1989) said that there are many resources at the farm level that can be used more effectively on group basis. Technologies which are very costly and uneconomic for individual farmers can be used more economically at group level ; NABARD (1995) identified that majority of the farmers of SHGs were possessing low level of annual income; Jayalekshmi (1996) reported that the annual income of majority of rural women in SHGs range from Rs.15, 000/- to Rs. 20,000/-.

Educational status: According to Rathinasabapathi (1987) reported education had positive and non-significant association between education and adoption of improved paddy cultivation practices; Sanjeev (1987) reported that there was no significant relationship between education and adoption of improved paddy cultivation practices; Agarwal and Arora (1989) opined that the educational level was significantly associated with adoption of biogas plant; Quazi and Iqbal (1991) reported that education was an important determinant of innovation adoption.

Cosmopoliteness: According to Murthy and Singh (1974) reported positive and significant correlation between cosmopoliteness and information input and output ideas of farmers; Jayalekshmi (1996) found that women who had started an enterprise usually sold their produce in nearby towns to increase profit. This increase cosmopoliteness ensuring discussion of problems with similar enterprise owners and their trainers and marketing institutions; Surendran (2000) reported that farmers in non-governmental organisation groups had shown high levels of cosmopoliteness behaviour as compared to others.

Social participation: According to Govind (1984) reported that social participation of farm women had significant and negative association with the extent of involvement in farm activities; Hussain (1992) indicated that group management approach had brought in favourable changes in the character of the social participation of rice farmers; Sindhu (2002) reported that the old farmers are likely to loose interest in active participation within and outside the social system; Narayanasamy *et al.* (2010) observed that around 93 per cent of the respondents reported to have participated in the Gram Sabha meeting convened specially to discuss the matters related to MGNREGS.

Training attended: According to Vashistha (1987) reported positive relationship of training with adoption behaviour; Sivaprasad (1997) reported that majority of youth in sericulture and bee keeping had undergone training duration of training and stipend given acted as incentives; According to Ashaletha (2000), training was positively and significantly related to the awareness about the National Agricultural Research Project ; Parthasarathi and Govind (2002) reported that the knowledge level of trained farmers was much higher on biological and physical methods of integrated pest management, identification of pests and predators on economic threshold levels. This shows that the training on integrated pest management had positive effect on farmers.

Information need perception: According to Rao and Sathyanarayanan (1992) reported that the majority of the respondents required much information on banking procedures to secure the loans followed by mode of disbursement of the loan; Ranganathan (2001) reported that beneficiaries of nationalized banks needed maximum information about the mode of repayment at first position followed by banking procedures to be followed to secure loans and interested prevailing in the bank on second and third position.

Credit orientation: According to Nizamudeen (1996) observed that credit orientation behaviour of Kuttymulla growers had prompted them towards the successful adoption of cultivation practices; Jayalekshmi (2001) reported negative and significant relationship brtween credit orientation and empowerment.

Risk orientation: According to Basram (1966) found that farmers, after using old varieties of seeds and traditional implements for years, feel insecure in the outcome of latest techniques and Bhaskaran (1978) found out that there was no relationship between farmers' perception of risk and their extent of adoption and credit utilization; Sivaprasad (1997) reported that by imparting proper training orientation, the risk bearing ability of the individual can be increased.

Economic motivation: According to Chandran (1989) found positive and significant relationship between economic development and attitude of pepper growers in Pepper Development Programme; Sivaprasad (1997) found that economic motivation was an important character that prompted people to adopt improved practices that are proven worthy and Thomas (1998) reported that the more one is motivated by economic ends, the more he/she will try to adopt the practices which are aimed at increasing sustainable returns.

Innovativeness: According to Momi and Sohal (1975) found that cost was least important factor in the adoption of the innovation and Bhaskaran (1978) reported there was no relationship between farmers perception of cost of innovation and their extent of adoption and credit utilization.

Achievement motivation: According to Sivaprasad (1997) reported positive and significant relationship between achievement motivation and extent of adoption of scientific practices in sericulture and in beekeeping and Thomas (1998) found that achievement motivation had significant correlation with extent of adoption of watershed development programmes.

Attitude of respondents: According to Allport (1935) stated that attitude is a mental and neutral state of readiness organized through experience, exerting a directive or dynamic influence upon the individual's response to all objects and situations with which it is related and Thrustone (1946) defined attitude as the degree of positive or negative effect associated with some psychological objects towards which people can differ in varying degrees and Katz and Scotland (1959) stated that attitude is a tendency or disposition to evaluate an object or the symbol of that object in a certain way; Rai (1965) revealed that adopters of new ideas had favourable attitude towards government programmes; Singh *et al.* (1966) found that farmer's attitude towards the package programme had positive and significant influence on the level of adoption of package of practices; Singh (1978) showed that high scores on attitude towards farming and continuous decision making were associated with progressive farm behaviour; Sajeevchandran (1989) found significant difference in the level of attitude among beneficiaries towards pepper development programmes; Shilaja (1990) reported that majority of the farm women possessed favourable attitude towards mixed farming; According to Rajendralal (1997) any development programme aimed at the welfare of the people, calls for maximum participation of people to achieve this participation the beneficiaries should have a positive attitude towards the development programmes he added and the views of the above authors revealed that the attitude of human beings towards an object, programmes etc., varied with situation. It can be calculated from the above studies that favourable attitude towards a development programme, technology or innovation is a prime requirement for the effective implementation and success of the project.

Experienced and Encountered Farm Constraints Farm Development

According to Norman (1982) identified the problem in vegetable cultivation as the high attack of pests and diseases and high input cost. Farmers also stated that they experienced serious transportation problems in marketing their produce; Prasad (1987) classified those factors influencing the development of agricultural sector in India to common basic constraints, technological constraints, organisational and administration constraints, extension constraints and social constraints; Menon and Bhaskaran (1988) found that lack of sufficient land and fragmented land holding were the major constraints to agricultural technology transfer in Kerala; Nelson (1992) reported that lack of clerical support in office work was the most important constraint perceived by Agricultural officers in the effective functioning of *Krishi Bhavan* followed by lack of conveyance facilities, lack of funds to meet traveling expenses and lack of office facilities.

According to Rajendran (1992) while analysing the feasibility and utilisation of selected agricultural enterprises among Schedule Caste farmers observed that lack of technical knowledge, lack of necessary supporting services and unavailability of raw materials as the major constraints in the utilization of agricultural technologies in general; Bhaskaran and Sushama (1994) cited lack of infrastructural facilities, absence of technology evaluations and up gradation efforts, inadequate training for farmers, extension personnel's and researchers, lack of functional linkages among the research, extension, input and farmer sub-systems as some constraints in technology transfer in Kerala agriculture.

Conclusion

The innovations in the implementation of the Samagra project are also excellent examples of good agricultural extension practices which are a sine-quo-non for the sustainability of development projects in the decentralised planning process. The case of the Samagra project provides an insight to the local self governments into the processes of empowering the local community to innovate in the assessment of needs, formulation of action plans, mobilisation of resources and institutions, implementation of development activities and evaluation of the results so as to ensure that the development process is truly a "hand up" rather than a "hand out".

REFERENCES

Ashaletha, S. (2000): Impact of NARP on Agricultural Development in the Southern Agro Climatic Zone of Kerala, *Ph.D. Thesis, Kerala Agricultural University*, Vellanikkara, pp:14.

Chandran, S.A. (1989): Impact of Development Programme of Promoting Pepper Production in Kerala, *M.Sc. (Ag.) Thesis, Kerala Agricultural University*, Vellanikkara, pp:141.

Kudumbashree. (2010): Kudumbashree Documentation on Samagra – Nendran Banana Project, *Kudumbashree Mission*, Thiruvanathapuram, pp: 23.

Sanjeev, K.V. (1987): Training programme of KAU Krishi Vigyan Kendras – An Analysis, *M.Sc (Ag.) Thesis, Kerala Agricultural University*, Vellanikkara, pp:155.

Surendran, G. (2000): Participatory Group Approach for Sustainable Development of Agriculture in Kerala, *Ph.D. thesis, Kerala Agricultural University*, Vellanikkara, pp: 268.

Agarwal, A. and Arora, D.R. (1989): Factors Affecting Adoption of Gober Gas Plants in Ludhiana, *Social Change*, 19: 69-71.

Allport, G. (1935): Attitude, *Handbook of Social Psychology*, Mass Clark Univ. Press, Worcester, pp: 798-844.

Ashaletha, S. (2000): Impact of NARP on Agricultural Development in the Southern agro-climatic Zone of Kerala, *Ph.D. Thesis, Kerala Agricultural University,* Vellanikkara, pp: 14.

Basram, G.S. (1996): Motivational and Resistance Forces Related to the Acceptance of New Ideas in Farming, *Ind. J. Extn. Edn.(* 2): 107-115.

Bhaskaran, C. and Kumari Sushama, N.P. (1994): Problems of Technology Transfer in Kerala Agriculture, *Centre for Research and Studies,* Thiruvananthapuram, pp: 82-83.

Bhaskaran, S. (1978): To Study the Impact of Institutional Credit and Its Influence in the Behaviour of Farmers in Adopting High Yielding Varieties of Paddy Cultivation, *M.Sc. (Ag.) Thesis, Kerala Agricultural University,* Vellanikkara, pp:108.

Chandran, S.A. (1989): Impact of Development Programme of Promoting Pepper Production in Kerala, *M.Sc. (Ag.) Thesis, Kerala Agricultural University,* Vellanikkara, pp: 141.

Freeman, C. (1987): Technology and Economic Performance- Lessons from Japan, *Pinter Publications,* London, pp:342.

Geetha G. Nath. (2002): Role of Labour Force (*Thozhil sena)* in Agricultural Development Implemented through People's Plan in Kerala, *M.Sc. (Ag.) Thesis, Kerala Agricultural University,* Vellanikkara, pp:102.

Govind, S. (1984): Participation of Farm Women in Farm and Home Activities, *M.Sc.(Ag.) Thesis, Tamil Nadu Agricultural University,* Coimbatore, pp:140.

Hussain, M.M. (1992): Group Management in Rice Production: An Action Research, *Ph.D. Thesis, Kerala Agricultural University,* Vellanikkara, pp:283.

Jayalekshmi, G. (1996): Entrepreneurial Behaviour of Rural Women in Thiruvananthapuram District, *M.Sc. (Ag.) Thesis, Kerala Agricultural University,* Vellanikkara, pp:144.

Jayalekshmi, G. (2001): Empowerment of Rural Women Through SHGs – An Action Research, *Ph. D. Thesis, Kerala Agricultural University,* Vellanikkara, pp:144.

Jha, P.N. and Shaktawat, G.S. (1972): Adoption Behaviour of Farmers Towards Hybrid Bajra Cultivation, *Indian J. Ext. Edn (.*8): 24-31.

Kailasam, S. (1980): Credit Seeking, Repayment, Utilization Pattern and Information Need Perception of Borrowers, *M.Sc. (Ag.) Thesis, Tamil Nadu Agricultural University,* Coimbatore, pp: 28.

Katz, D. and Scotland, E. (1959): A Preliminary Statement to a Theory of Attitude Structure and Change, A Study of Science. *Mc Grew Hill Book,* New York, pp: 200 -205.

Lundvall. (1992): National Systems of Innovation: Towards a Theory of Innovation and Interactive Learning, *Pinter Publications,* London, pp: 123.

Manjusha, J. (1999): Techno-economic Assessment of Farmers' Practices in the Cultivation of Bittergourd (*Momordica Charntia L.)* in Thiruvananthapuram District., *M.Sc. (Ag.) Thesis, Kerala Agricultural University,* Vellanikkara, pp: 106.

Manoj, S. (2000): Techno-economic Assessment of Farming Practices in Rice Cultivation in Thiruvananthapuram District, *M.Sc. (Ag.) Thesis, Kerala Agricultural University,* Vellanikkara, pp:102.

Menon, A.G.G. and Bhaskaran, C. (1988): Technology Alters Traditional Attitudes, *Indian Farming, 28 (8): 45-47.*

Momi, G.S. and Sohal, T.S. (1975): Significance of Characteristics of Innovation for Adopters and Non-adopters, *Ind. J. Ext. Edn,(11):74-75.*

Muller, Sherin. (1997): An Analysis of the Characteristics of Women's Groups and their Role in Rural Development, *M.Sc. Thesis, Kerala Agricultural University,* Vellanikkara, pp:14.

Farming and Development : *Technological Perspectives* **Pages 126-142**
Edited by: **Dr. Pawan Kumar 'Bharti' & Dr. Jaswant Ray**
ISBN: 978-93-88854-08-5
Edition: **2019**
Published by: **Discovery Publishing House Pvt. Ltd., New Delhi (India)**

8

Innovations and Sustainability of Farm Technology Commercialization

[1]Dr. Esakkimuthu M. and [2]Dr. Bhaskaran C.

ABSTRACT

Many of the poverty alleviation programmes in India are not showing the expected results. However, the 'Samagra' project on Banana cultivation is one of the successes stories. This project has a multiple stakeholder partnership in Kerala, India. Launched in 2007 by the Thiruvananthapuram District Panchayat and Kudumbashree Mission(one of the world's leading and successful poverty eradication programmes), the aim of the project is to enhance banana productivity through the promotion of innovations in technical backstopping. The study was conducted in three Grama Panchayats of the Thiruvananthapuram district. Three categories of respondents namely beneficiary respondents (60), implementing officials (30) and people's representatives (30) were involved in the study. The dependent variable innovations in technical backstopping were measured in terms of perception about the innovative procedures, processes and institutions. The major findings of the study indicate that majority of the beneficiary respondents, officials and people's representatives-felt that the innovative procedures, innovative processes and innovative institutions adopted in the 'Samagra' were excellent.

Keywords: Innovative institutions, innovative procedures, innovative processes, multi-stakeholder partnerships, production centered and technical backstopping.

Introduction

India is an agricultural country. Over 70 per cent of India's population is supported by agriculture. Even while India's industrial and services sectors are growing by leaps and bounds, growth rate of agriculture is below 2% Pawar (2010). Industrial and services sectors are invariably entangled with the fortunes of agriculture due to various intricate forward and backward linkages. Kerala's agriculture has its own uniqueness and peculiarities. Kerala is a land for the cultivation of variety of crops such as plantation crops, food grains, fruit crops, spices, vegetables, tubers etc. Kerala is considered as the land of spices. Homestead farming systems are mostly common in Kerala. The main problems in Kerala's agriculture are lack of land, labour and capital, high labour and input cost, lack of mechanisation, low productivity of major crops, unstable prices etc. Kerala is a pioneering state in India in the matter of implementation of decentralized planning process. In the agricultural sector, many demands driven initiatives towards technology commercialization have been undertaken as a part of these Local Self Governments. One among them is the promotion of scientific banana cultivation, taken up by the Thiruvananthapuram District Panchayat as the nodal agency. This Project entitled 'Samagra Banana Project' was implemented in the year 2007.

Women are the backbone of agricultural workforce. 'Kudumbashree' is the women oriented programme. 'Kudumbashree' mission is a poverty eradication mission officially launched by the Government of Kerala with the objective of wiping out of poverty from the state Kudumbashree (2010). It plays a vital role in co-coordinating the activities of 'Samagra' Project. 'Samagra' Banana Project is for the establishment of market - oriented banana production and processing network by effectively utilizing organized 'Kudumbashree' units Shilaja and Sobhana (2010) Co-ordinated efforts of the State 'Kudumbashree' mission and the Thiruvananthapuram District Panchayat could effectively build up this kind of an innovative venture to improve banana cultivation utilizing high end technologies and enabling steady market. The 'Samagra' (Comprehensive) Project on banana cultivation stands out in many ways. It is a multi-stakeholder participatory effort in agricultural development emphasising on 5 Ps-Public-Private-Panchayat-People Partnerships.The partners in the Project are the Thiruvananthapuram District Panchayat, 'Kudumbashree' Mission, the Agricultural Department, the Kerala Agricultural University ,the State Horticultural Mission, the Nationalised Banks, and the private partner 'Prowins Agri system'. All the institutions are contributing to the various aspects of the 'Samagra' Project. It includes various innovations in technical backstopping systems. The innovation in technical backstopping stresses that, the flow of information among people, enterprises and institutions are key to an innovative process. It contains the interaction between the actors who are needed in order to turn an idea into a process, product or service in the market. 'Samagra' Project was aimed at enhancing the net income of the 'Kudumbashree' activity groups through improved productivity and reduced cost of cultivation. It promoted of Good Agricultural Practices and Good Extension Practices such as NHGs formation, women empowerment, Public-Private-Panchayat-People-Partnerships, forward and backward linkages, value addition, marketing process and strengthening the linkage between various service providers. A comprehensive study of the innovations in technical backstopping perceived as part of the Samagra Banana Project is very much desirable to take stock of the situation. The study will also useful for scaling up of the Project in future in more areas covering more crops. Therefore, the present study has been designed with the following specific objectives.

To study the technical backstopping for the 'Samagra' project on banana cultivation of the Thiruvananthapuram District Panchayat and to identify the innovative procedures, processes and Institutions involved in the implementation of the 'Samagra' project. Besides, it is also proposed to analyse the perception of the people's representatives and officials at various levels and Beneficiaries about the innovations in the implementation of the 'Samagra' project.

Perspective of Samagra Projects

'Samagra' means comprehensive development of either an agricultural produce or an industrial product or a traditional job. This is an all inclusive programme encompassing all the components from production to marketing, helping the people involved to derive maximum possible income and thereby improving the general living standards of the people in that area (Kudumbashree, 2010).

Samagra is a novel initiative independently developed by Kudumbashree and being implemented in the state in collaboration with the three – tier Local Self Governments (LSGs) and other agencies. It is an attempt to address the entire production – supply chain holistically, by scaling up productivity both qualitatively and quantitatively and seeking viable marketing opportunities.

(Kudumbashree, 2010) Details of Samagra projects that are implemented in various Districts in Kerala as follow:

1. Nendran Banana (Thiruvananthapuram)
2. Nivedyam (Thrissur) Pooja Kadali Banana
3. Harithashree (Thiruvananthapuram) Vegetables
4. Haritham (Ernakulam) Vegetables
5. Ksheerashree (Thiruvananthapuram) Milk
6. Ksheerasagaram (Idukki) Milk
7. Nedumpana Mini Apparel Park (Kollam) Readymade Garments
8. Madhuram (Pathanamthitta) Honey
9. Ornamental fish project (Kottayam)
10. Thirumadhuram (Ernakulam) Pineapple
11. Kondattom (Palakkad) Crispy Fries
12. Manufacturing of footwear uppers (Kozhikode)
13. Goat Village (Kannur)
14. Saphalam (Kasargod) Cashew

Samagra-Nendran banana is a community based income generating/ livelihood project which involves farming, application of technology, marketing and value addition. The Nendran banana project implemented in Thiruvananthapuram District aimed to bring 2,400 ha land under Nendran banana cultivation by generating employment opportunities to 30,000 women beneficiaries.

With unique partnership between public institutions, Non-Govenmental Organizations (NGOs), farmers, private sectors and innovative approach, a momentum has been developed to increase profitability, income generation and employment in agriculture (Ayyappan, 2010). A host of institutions at various levels – National, State, District and Grass root levels including the Rural Business Hub, Kerala Horticultural Mission, Kudumbashree, Kerala Agricultural University, technical and marketing agencies, Banks and Self Help Groups (SHGs) are involved in the project.

The Government, in association with the Confederation of Indian Industries (CII) has undertaken an initiative to promote Rural Business Hubs (RBH), first of its kind, based on Public-Private-Partnership (PPP) model to facilitate direct business linkage between industry and the rural community (Ministry of Panchayati Raj, 2008). The 'samagra' project - formulated in the model of Rural Business Hub (RBH) programme is for establishment of market oriented banana production and processing network by effectively utilizing organized Kudumbashree units (Shilaja, and Sobhana, 2009).

Importance of Samagra Project

'Samagra' Banana Project is for establishment of market - oriented banana production and processing network by effectively utilizing organized 'Kudumbashree' units. Co-ordinated efforts of the State 'Kudumbashree' mission, and the Thiruvananthapuram District Panchayat can effectively build up this kind of an innovative venture to improve banana farming.

Even though Thiruvananthapuram farmers are cultivating Nendran banana for years, the efforts on brand building, value addition and streamlining production process with international quality standards to get larger market access are very meager. Utilisation of advanced technologies in production is also at low rate. The emerging expectations of global market access in present scenario calls for higher productivity per unit of land, water and other inputs in an equitable and sustainable manner. Critical areas that would require pinpointed attention are quality and productivity of the farm product.

Adequate marketing support is important for successful implementation of 'Samagra'. The private agency associating with this project will take over the responsibility of marketing. For effective market strategy planning and marketing intervention private sector participation was hoped to be more effective in Samagra project, it was felt.

Kerala Agricultural Scenario

Kerala's agriculture has its own uniqueness and peculiarities. Kerala is a land for the cultivation of variety of crops such as plantation crops, food grains, fruit crops, spices, vegetables, tubers etc. Kerala is considered as the land of spices. Homestead farming systems are mostly common in Kerala. The main problems in Kerala's agriculture are lack of land, labour and capital, high labour and input cost, lack of mechanisation, low productivity of major crops, unstable prices etc.

Decentralization in Kerala

Kerala is a pioneering state in India in the matter of implementation of decentralized planning process. In the agricultural sector, many demand driven initiatives towards technology commercialization have been undertaking as a part of these Local Self Governments. One among them is the promotion of scientific banana cultivation.

Samagra Project

Innovations play an important role in food production as well as in optimizing resource utilization by farmers (Venkatasubramanian, 2010). In general, Samagra means comprehensive development of either an agricultural produce or an industrial product or a traditional job. This is an all - inclusive programme encompassing all the components from production to marketing, helping the people involved to derive maximum possible income and thereby improving the general living standards of the people in that area. 'Samagra' is a novel initiative independently developed by Kudumbashree and the three – tier Local Self Governments (LSGs) and other agencies. It is an attempt to address the entire production – supply chain holistically, by scaling up productivity both quantitatively and qualitatively and seeking viable marketing opportunities (Kudumbashree Mission.2009).

Multistakeholder Partnership

The 'Samagra' (Comprehensive) Project on banana cultivation stands out in many ways. It is a multi-stakeholder participatory effort in agricultural development emphasising on 5 Ps-Public-Private-Panchayat-People Partnerships. The partners in the Project are the Thiruvananthapuram District Panchayat, 'Kudumbashree' Mission, the Agricultural Department, the Kerala Agricultural University, the State Horticultural Mission, the Nationalised Banks, and the private partner 'Prowins Agri system'. All the institutions are contributing to the various aspects of the 'Samagra' Project. It includes various innovations in technical backstopping systems.

Samagra Project Activities

The activities delineated in the" Samagra Project" are:

1. Scale up of enterprise activities: Increased number of units in economically feasible activity, subject to carrying capacity, attempting to bring economies of scale and greater focus for facilitation and handholding support.
2. Convergence of different activities: While preparing projects on agricultural crops, animal husbandry, fish farming etc. there should be an integrated approach involving different sectors like training, crop development, production of planting materials, improvement in quality, marketing etc.
3. Convergence of different projects/ programmes: "Samagra" brings together different projects and programmes implemented through different departments and LSGs by uniting them under a common agenda and goal.
4. Convergence of different departments: Under the present set up, different departments are carrying out poverty reduction, marketing, crop development etc. This has led to duplication of efforts, wastage of time and money. "Samagra" envisages convergence of activities of different departments in these sectors.
5. Effective utilization of other stakeholders in production and marketing: There are areas where the knowledge and skills within government are limited (e.g. marketing). "Samagra Project" arranges mutually beneficial tie ups so that efficiency gaps are made up – "Samagra" visualizes this especially in production, marketing, quality control etc.
6. Ensuring product diversification and quality enhancement in the production process.
7. Employing modern technologies in marketing: Modern technologies available in research institutions for product diversification, quality enhancement and marketing should be made use of to improve the level of intervention in the market. "Samagra" looks at newer marketing strategies for packaging, branding, networking etc.

Sustainability vis-a vis Innovation Systems of the Project

Research evidences indicate that the linkage between innovations and growth appears fairly straight forward (Joseph, 2010; Sunilmani, 2009). Innovation and sustainability are also reported to be positively related (Hall, 2010). A field study conducted among 150 stakeholders of the Project revealed the evaluative perception of these respondents regarding the relative importance of the dimensions of sustainability as follows.

Various dimension of sustainability of the Samagra project:

Sl. No.	Dimension of sustainability	Relative Weightage to a maximum of 5
1.	Clearly stated objectives	3.7
2.	Effective Leadership	3.3
3.	High level of participation	3.2
4.	Strong strategic plan	3.1
5.	Good financial management	3.0
6.	Capacity to mobilise funds	2.8
7.	Good information flow	2.7
8.	Good documentation	2.5

Innovation Systems

A simple definition of an innovation system would be the system of all the actors and their routines and habits that in a given policy context produce, use, diffuse and adopt knowledge in socio-economically significant ways (Sulaiman, 2008). The concept of innovation system stresses that the flow of information among people, enterprises and institutions is key to an innovative process. It contains the interaction between the actors who are needed in order to turn an idea into a process, product or service in the market.

Innovative procedures, processes and institutions identified under the Samagra project:

Sl.No.	Items
I.	**Innovative procedures**
1	Credit linkage.
2	Full technical support given by exclusive staff of private agency.
3	Public – Private – Panchayat – People – Partnership.
4	Holistic support given by private agency.
II.	**Innovative processes**
1	Assured supply of quality inputs.
2	Capacity building activities.
3	Kudumbashree giving fund for technology support.
4	Socio – economic – ecologically sustainable development.
III.	**Innovative Institutions**
1	One product – one village concept.
2	Private agency linkage with governmental agencies.
3	Ensures people's participation.
4	Kudumbashree linked with LSGIs.

Need for the Hour

'Samagra' is the first multistakeholder partnership effectively implemented in the Kerala state. It is the flagship project of the public and private Institutions. It aims at enhancing economic empowerment, women empowerment, social empowerment, livelihood security of rural poor by the promotion of scientific banana cultivation. poverty and hunger is a major problem in rural areas. This study was undertaken to assess the effective utilization of 'Samagra' Banana Project with respect to innovative procedures, processes and Institutions involved in the implementation of the 'Samagra' project.

Materials and Methods

The study was conducted in Thiruvananthapuram district which was purposively selected. Respondents in this study were the beneficiaries of 'Samagra' Banana Project in the three selected gram panchayats, namely Kottukal, Kunnathukal and Kalliyoor. From each grama panchayat, twenty beneficiaries were selected at random. In addition, 30 implemeting officials and 30 people's representatives from the State Poverty Eradication Mission, District Kudumbashree Mission, Thiruvananthapuram District Panchayat, Kerala Agricultural University, Kerala State Department of Agriculture, Prowins Agri System were selected by simple random sampling method. Accordingly, the total number of respondents for the study was 120 comprising of 60 beneficiaries, 30 implementing officials and 30 people's representatives. Ex-post facto design was adopted in the study (Table 1). 'Innovations in technical backstopping of 'Samagra' project' were measured in terms of innovative procedures, innovative processes and innovative institutions. The term innovation is defined as a process through which the nation creates and transforms new knowledge and technologies into useful products, services and processes for national and global markets leading to both value creation for stakeholders and higher standards of living. Perception about innovative procedures, processes and institutions involved in the 'Samagra' project was evaluated on the basis of their effective utilization in "Samagra' project. The innovative procedure is defined as the fixed step-by-step sequence of activities or course of action that must be followed in the same order to correctly perform a task envisaged in the "Samagra" project. The innovative procedures are; credit linkage, full technical support given by private agency, Public – Private – Panchayat – People – Partnership, Holistic support given by private agency. Based on the response of the respondents they were grouped into three categories of perception, i.e. bad, good, or excellent. The innovative processes are defined as the sequence of interdependent and linked procedures which constitute a process. The innovative processes are; Assured supply of quality inputs, Capacity building activities, Kudumbashree giving fund for technology support and Socio – economic – ecologically sustainable development. Based on the response of the respondents they were grouped into three categories of perception - bad, good, or excellent. The innovative Institution is defined as the newly established organisations, ways and means in the implementation of "Samagra" project. The innovative Institutions are; one product – one village concept, private agency linkage with governmental agencies, ensures people's participation and Kudumbashree linked with Local Self Government Institutions (LSGIs). Based on the response of the respondents they were grouped into three categories of perception as bad, good, excellent. The responses of respondents were collected on three point continuum viz., excellent, good, bad with scoring of 3,2 and 1 respectively. In order to study the relationship between the independent and dependent variables, correlation analysis was done.

Results and Discussion

Perception about beneficiaries about innovations in technical backstopping

Based on the response of the respondents three categories of perception as Bad, Good, Excellent were formed and the results are presented in Table 8.1.

Table 8.1: Distribution of the 'Samagra' Beneficiaries on Their Perceptions about Innovations in Technical Backstopping)

Perception category	Score	Perception about					
		Innovative procedures		Innovative processes		Innovative institutions	
		f	%	F	%	F	%
Bad	Upto 3	0	0	0	0	0	0
Good	4 – 8	18	30	21	35	23	38.33
Excellent	9 and above	42	70	39	65	37	61.67
Total		60	100	60	100	60	100

From the data in Table 1, it could be inferred that the majority (70 %) of the beneficiaries had the opinion that innovative procedures in the 'Samagra' project were excellent. Thirty per cent of the beneficiaries opined that innovative procedures in the 'Samagra' project were good and none of them had bad remark about innovative procedures in the 'Samagra' project. Sixty five per cent of the beneficiaries opined that innovative processes in the 'Samagra' project were excellent. Thirty five per cent of the beneficiaries opined that innovative processes in the 'Samagra' project were good and none of them had bad remark about innovative processes in the 'Samagra' project. Majority (61.67 %) of the beneficiaries opined that innovative institutions of the 'Samagra' project were excellent. Over 38 per cent (38.33 %) of the beneficiaries opined that innovative institutions formed in the 'Samagra' project were good. None of the respondents perceived the innovative institutions in 'Samagra' project as bad. This may be due to fact that 'Samagra' is the only project providing assured market to the banana produced by the beneficiaries. This could also be attributed to the good technical backstopping provided in the project by the private agency 'Prowins'.

Profile Characteristics of the Respondents

Profile characteristics of selected sixty respondents with reference to age, area under cultivation, experience in banana cultivation, annual income, educational status, cosmopoliteness, social participation, trainings attended, information need perception, credit orientation, risk orientation, economic motivation, innovativeness, achievement motivation and attitude towards 'Samagra'are as follows in the table 8.2. Kudumbashree activity groups are respondents in this study were the beneficiaries of 'Samagra' Banana Project in the three selected gram panchayats, namely Kottukal (20), Kunnathukal (20) and Kalliyoor (20).

Table 8.2: Distribution of Respondents based on their Profile Characteristics

Variables	Category	Frequency	Percentage
Age	Young (upto 35)	15	25
	Middle (36-50)	30	50
	Old (51 and above)	15	25
Area under cultivation in cents	Low (upto 60)	42	70
	Medium (61-70)	7	11.66
	High (71 and above)	11	18.33
Experience in banana cultivation in years	Low (upto 3)	29	48.33
	High (4 and above)	31	51.67
Annual income	Low (upto 50,000)	13	21.67
	Medium (50,001-1,00,000)	46	76.67
	High (1,00,001 and above)	1	1.66
Educational status	Illiterate	1	1.67
	Can read and write only	1	1.67
	Primary school level	17	28.33
	Middle school level	16	26.67
	High school level	18	30
	College level	7	11.66
	Professional college status	0	0
Cosmopoliteness	Low (upto 12)	14	23.33
	Medium (13-24)	38	63.33
	High (25 and above)	8	13.34

Social participation	Low (1)	16	26.6
	Medium (2-3)	38	63.3
	High (4 and above)	6	10.1
Trainings attended	Low (upto 1)	1	1.67
	Medium (2)	19	31.7
	High (3 and above)	40	66.63
Information need perception	Low (upto 19)	36	60
	High (20 and above)	24	40
Credit orientation	Low (upto 11)	20	33.33
	Medium (12-15)	25	41.67
	High (16 and above)	15	25
Risk orientation	Low (upto 18)	1	1.66
	Medium (19-25)	37	61.67
	High (26 and above)	22	36.67
Economic motivation	Low (upto 20)	30	50
	Medium (21-23)	27	45
	High (24 and above)	3	5
Innovativenes	Low (upto 2)	4	6.67
	High (3 and above)	56	93.33
Achievement motivation	Low (upto 7)	46	76.67
	High (8 and above)	14	23.33
Attitude	Unfavourable (upto 12)	0	0
	Neutral (13-18)	24	40
	Favourable (19 and above)	36	60

Perception of Officials about Innovations in Technical Backstopping

The results presented Table 3 indicate that all the officials opined that innovative procedures adopted in the 'Samagra' project were excellent and that none of them had bad remark about innovative procedures adopted in the 'Samagra' project. Over 73 per cent (73.3%) of officials had opined that the innovative processes adopted in the 'Samagra' project were excellent. More than a quarter of the respondents - officials (26.7%) opined that innovative processes in the 'Samagra' project were good. Nobody expressed bad remark about innovative processes in the 'Samagra' project. All the officials opined that innovative institutions observed in the 'Samagra' project were excellent. None had a bad remark about innovative institutions in the 'Samagra' project. The officials are responsible to implement the programme at field level. For the first time, these officials were exposed to the innovations in technical backstopping for the 'Samagra' Banana Project and they were possibly impressed by these innovations. This could be the probable reason for the present finding.

Table 8.3: Distribution of the 'Samagra' Officials on their Perception about Innovations in Technical Backstopping

Perception category	Score	Perception about					
		Innovative procedures		Innovative processes		Innovative institutions	
		F	%	F	%	F	%
Bad	Upto 3	0	0	0	0	0	0
Good	4 – 8	0	0	8	26.7	0	0
Excellent	9 and above	30	100	22	73.3	30	100
Total		30	100	30	100	30	100

Perception of the People's Representatives about Innovations in Technical Backstopping

The results presented in Table 4 indicate that all the people's representatives included in the study had the opinion that the innovative procedures in the 'Samagra' project were excellent. None of them had bad opinion about these innovative procedures. Ninety per cent of the people's representatives opined that the innovative processes in the 'Samagra' project were excellent. Ten per cent of the people's representatives felt that innovative processes in the 'Samagra' project were good. None of them had bad opinion about innovative processes adopted in the 'Samagra' project. A similar trend was observed in the case of perception about innovative institutions too.

Table 8.4: Distribution of the People's Representatives on Their Perception about Innovations in Technical Backstopping for the 'Samagra' Project

Perception category	Score	Perception about					
		Innovative procedures		Innovative processes		Innovative institutions	
		F	%	F	%	F	%
Bad	Upto 3	0	0	0	0	0	0
Good	4 – 8	0	0	3	10	3	10
Excellent	9 and above	30	100	27	90	27	90
Total		30	100	30	100	30	100

Relationship between Independent and Dependent Variables of Beneficiaries

The results presented in Table 5 revealed that among the selected fifteen independent variables, experience in banana cultivation, educational status, credit orientation, achievement motivation had a positive and significant relationship with innovative procedures, innovative processes and innovative institutions. Economic motivation had a positive and significant relationship with innovative procedures and innovative institutions whereas it had no significant relationship with innovative processes. Innovativeness had negative significant relationship with innovative processes whereas it had no significant relationship with innovative procedures and innovative institutions. The majority of the respondents were literate and high educational status. This may be the reason for positive significant relationship of education with perception about innovative procedures, processes and institutions. This is because of the farmers are adopting the scientific banana cultivation farming practices and also the literate farmers familiar with innovations in 'Samagra' project. The majority of the respondents in the study was literate. The relatively better literacy status as a result of the availability of educational facilities even in rural Kerala predisposes increased awareness which may be the reason for the positive and significant relationship of education with perception about innovative procedures, processes and institutions as observed in the study. The majority of the beneficiaries were traditionally banana growers with more experience in the indicates of banana cultivation. This could be attributed as the reason for positive and significant relationship of experience in banana cultivation with perception about innovative procedures, processes and institutions. Most of the farmers are having a medium level of credit orientation. Their positive mindset about increased use of capital through credit borrowing for banana cultivation in the 'Samagra' Project would have led to the positive and significant relationship of credit orientation with perception about innovative procedures, processes and institutions. Economic motivation is important in promoting a person to perform more effectively to improve his/her economic status. This is a favourable psycho physical disposition which could cultivate in the positive significant relationship of economic motivation with perception about innovative procedures, processes and institutions. A person with a high need for achievement would be viewing innovations in any sphere of activity with a positive frame of mind. This could be cited as a reason for the positive and significant relationship of achievement motivation in banana cultivation with perception about innovative procedures, processes and institutions as evidenced in the present study.

Table 8.5: Relationship between Independent and Dependent Variables of Beneficiaries of 'Samagra' Project

Sl. No.	Name of the independent variable	Correlation coefficient (Y1-Perception about innovative procedures)	Correlation coefficient (Y2-Perception about innovative processes)	Correlation coefficient (Y3- Perception about innovative institutions)
1.	Age	–0.1006	–0.0962	–0.0736
2.	Area under cultivation	0.0661	0.2166	0.1320

3.	Experience in banana cultivation	0.4778**	0.5846**	0.5390**
4.	Annual Income	0.1580	0.1775	0.1703
5.	Educational status	0.3708**	0.4110 **	0.3370**
6.	Cosmopoliteness	0.2309	0.0574	0.1580
7.	Social participation	0.0165	0.1572	0.1215
8.	Training attended	0.0433	0.0532	0.1335
9.	Information need perception	0.1300	0.1263	0.1987
10.	Credit orientation	0.6524**	0.7443 **	0.5983 **
11.	Risk orientation	0.0379	0.1763	0.0019
12.	Economic motivation	0.4617**	0.2402	0.4165 **
13.	Innovativeness	0.1309	- 0.2507*	– 0.1592
14.	Achievement motivation	0.3451**	0.4074**	0.3423 **
15.	Attitude	- 0.1320	0.2285	0.0873

** Significant at 0.01 level
*Significant at 0.05 level

Constraints Perceived by the 'Samagra' Beneficiaries

Table 8.6: Constraints Perceived by the 'Samagra' Beneficiaries

S. No.	Item	Score	Rank
1.	Lack of land for cultivation	3.65	I
2.	Lack of Village Knowledge Centers	3.55	II
3.	Lack of Video conferencing facilities	3.3	III
4.	Lack of technical know how	3.27	IV
5.	Lack of transportation facilities	3.2	V
6.	Lack of processing facilities	3.17	VI
7.	Lack of assured quality planting materials	2.93	VII
8.	Lack of diagnostic services	2.88	VIII
9.	Lack of timely credit supply	2.62	IX
10.	Lack of assured quality manures / fertilizers	2.58	X
11.	Lack of marketing facilities	2.57	XI
12.	Lack of assured quality Bio pesticides	2.57	XII
13.	Lack of technical trainings	2.53	XIII
14.	Lack of proper guidance from the Regional consultant	2.5	XIV

Lack of land for cultivation, Lack of Village Knowledge Centers and Lack of Video conferencing facilities were the major constraints perceived by the beneficiaries. Eventhough beneficiaries are more interested in banana cultivation, there is great dearth in Kerala for cultivativable land. In leased land farming also heavy land rent for cultivable land is a serious constraint. Sometimes, beneficiaries are not getting the leased land also to a sufficient extent. In each Grama Panchayat it was proposed in the Project document that Village Knowledge Centres will become functional so that farmers easily clarify their doubts regarding banana cultivation aspects. But this promise could not be kept by the implementing agencies and therefore the respondents had indicated this as an important felt constraints of the 'Samagra' Project. Similarly, in the 'Samagra' Project proposal Video conferencing facilities were contemplated. But it could not be implemented at field level resulting in the disappointment among the beneficiaries.

Achievement of the 'Samagra' Project

The Project has covered 1691 ha. under banana spread over 34 Grama Panchayats involving 2915 Activity Groups so far. The Nationalised Banks have disbursed Rs.24 crores with a reported repayment of over 80 per cent. Enhanced productivity of 12 MT coupled with a return of Rs. 2.28 lakhs per ha. through an attractive buyback system have made the Project a commercial success. Encouraged by the positive turn of events, the TDP has proposed scaling up of the Project to cover 2400ha. under Banana spread over 45 Grama Panchayats in the district.

Samagra project becomes a win-win phenomenon because of the following factors:

1. Commited administrative determination shown by the leadership and the district level officials of the Thiruvananthapuram District Panchayat in implementing the project without any hurdles.
2. Efficient field level implementation by the innovative sustainable development agency (Prowins Agri System) in providing appropriate technology support, supplying quality bio inputs, credit linkage services to women farmers and field level co-ordination by their dynamic field experts.
3. Timely credit support given by leading banks such as State Bank of Trivancore and State Bank of India.
4. Comprehensive technical support provided by Prowins Agri Syatem such as soil testing, plot specific input recommendation etc.
5. Comprehensive training on sustainable organic banana cultivation practices provided by Prowins Agri System to all women participants in this project.

The innovations in technical backstopping of 'Samagra' Banana Project studied have been rated well by the respondents but the sustainability of these innovations must be studied further. Studies are required to explore the role of Public-Private partnerships and rules and regulations must be formed on the basis of such studies. Increasing the efficiency of the group leadership through action researches must be another priority in the land - locked Kerala State.

Conclusion

The Samagra project revealed that when a systematically integrated development programme is evolved involving the government agency, the beneficiary, the credit providing agency and skill formation training providing agency like, Prowins Agri System, historically successful results can be achieved. The innovations in the implementation of the Samagra Project are also excellent examples of Good Extension Practices which are a sine-quo-non for the sustainability of development projects in the decentralised planning process. The case of the Samagra Project provides an insight to the LSG's into the processes of empowering the local community to innovate in the assessment of needs, formulation of action plans, mobilisation of resources and institutions, implementation of development activities and evaluation of the results so as to ensure that the development process is truly a "hand up" rather than a "hand out. 'Samagra' is a project achieved at the comprehensive development — improving crop productivity, introducing new technology, building new capacities, product diversification, quality enhancement, new marketing capabilities and initiating innovative procedures, processes and institutions with a view to ensure the livelihood security of the stakeholders.

REFERENCES

Joseph, K.J. (2010): Towards Replanting Plantation Development in India-An Analysis of the Innovation and Production System from Inclusive Growth Perspective, Centre for Development Studies, Thiruvananthapuram, pp: 124.

Sunilmani, M. (2009): Has India Becomes more Innovative Since1991, Centre for Development Studies, Thiruvananthapuram, pp: 06.

Hall, A.J., Dijthman, J. and Sulaiman, R.V. (2010): Research into Use: Investigating the Relationship between Agricultural Research and Innovation, UNU MERIT Working Paper, pp: 62.

Sulaiman, R.V. (2008): Extension from an Innovation System Perspective, IFPRI Conference on Advancing Agriculture in Developing Countries through Knowledge and Innovation, 7-9 April, Addis Ababa, pp: 82.

Ganessamurthy, V.S. (2007): Economic Empowerment of Women, New Century Publications, New Delhi, pp: 32.

Kudumbashree Mission. (2009): Revised Samagra Nendran Project (Joint Venture of State Kudumbashree Mission and District Panchayat, Thiruvananthapuram, pp: 239.

Kudumbashree, (2010): Kudumbashree Report on Samagra-nendran Banana Project, *District Kudumbashree Mission Publication*, pp: 162.

Nair, P.R. (2005): Micro-credit and Women's Empowerment. Rainbow Publishers, Uttar Pradesh, pp: 233.

Pawar, S. (2010): Agriculture Minister Calls for Leveraging Private Sector Resources for Commercialization of Technology, *ICAR Publication,* New Delhi, pp: 3-4.

Shilaja, S and Sobhana, G. (2010): Rural Business Hub-an Innovative Approach for Rural Upliftment, *Maharashtra Society of Extension Education,* Pune, pp. 121-122.

Venkatasubramanian, V. (2010). Farmers' Innovations for Prosperous Agriculture (Farm Innovators- 2010), Indian Council of Agricultural Research, New Delhi, pp: 2.

Farming and Development : *Technological Perspectives* **Pages 143-155**
Edited by: **Dr. Pawan Kumar 'Bharti' & Dr. Jaswant Ray**
ISBN: 978-93-88854-08-5
Edition: **2019**
Published by: **Discovery Publishing House Pvt. Ltd., New Delhi (India)**

9

Needs, Nature and Principles of Farm Credit

[1]R.K. Rai, [2]Prem Chand and [3]Ajay Tripathi

ABSTRACT

Farmers required credit for production activities thus, the financing activities and marketing activities comprises the decisions like what product to be produced and method of production and how much of each product to be produced. The financial activities relate to the decisions of obtaining and use of credit. Marketing activities involved marginal decisions related to procurements of inputs and distribution and sale of output. The famers need to various types of credit for smooth conducting farm activities. For example, nature of enterprises and the quantum of product determine the amount of capital and provide the farm business. The source of credit institution formally comprises informal and formal sector, the informal sector provides the credit to borrowers at higher rate of interest while the informal sector provides the credit at cheaper rate of interest with pledged of some movable and immovable security as well as their principles.

Introduction

Agricultural credit is one of the most crucial inputs for all agricultural development programmers for marginal and smallholder farmers as well agricultural development in country. The credit enables to undertake new investment or adopt new technologies and improve the risk bearing ability to support the framers with higher potential returns. The agriculture sector very few farmers have their own capital to invest in agriculture. From the binging there was major source of informal sector i.e. private money lenders, big merchants and relatives provide agricultural credit to the farmers in the rural areas. Although this source of credit was scant, very expensive and

1 Assistant Professor, Department of Agricultural Economics, College of Agriculture, Banda University of Agriculture & Technology, Banda-210001 (UP), India

2 Senior Scientist ICAR-National Institute of Agricultural Economics and Policy Research (NIAP) D.P.S. Marg, Pusa New Delhi-110012, India

3 Assistant Professor, Department of Agricultural Economics, College of Agriculture, G.B. Pant University of Agricultural & Technology, Pantnagar-263145 (UK), India

exploitative. The multi-agency (formal) approach of co-operative commercial banks, an and regional rural banks would be adopted and to provide cheaper, timely and adequate credit to farmers. The need of credit for agriculture can emphasized where its productivity is still very low due to financial constraints, the credit generally may be required for the purposes of the production and consumption. In other words, credit needs of the farmers can be classified into two parts i.e. productive purpose and un-productive purposes credit. The loans which are used in productive operation of agriculture are known as productive credit, However, productive requirements of the farmers for purchase of cattle, implements, fertilizers, inputs, better seeds and for consumption purpose are called unproductive credit. Between the period of marketing of agricultural produce and harvesting of next crop, there is along interval of time. Most of the farmers do not have sufficient income to sustain them through this period. Hence, they have required loan for meeting their consumption needs. The unproductive loans are also taken for social purpose viz. birth of a male child, marriage or death of person in the family and the time of drought and flood farmers to borrow the credit. According to farm needs the credit are classified in various types.

Classification of Credit

The classification of credit is based on the time span agricultural credit are divided into three types are as follows:

Short Term Loans

This types of loans are given to the farmers for the period of 6 moths to 18 months. It is also known as short term loans, but the length of repayment period varies according to one crop to other crops and duration of crops. The farmer need to this type credit to meet out the ongoing expenses of agricultural operations on the farm i.e. sowing fertilizer and manure application, plant protection measure, payment wage and salary of hired labours etc.

Medium Term Loans

The loans are given for the period of 18 months to 5 years. This type loans are required by the farmers for improvement of their farm, purchasing of machinery and equipment, electronic motor, mulch cattle, sheep and goat etc. The loans have relatively longer repayment period and these loans are due to their partial–liquidating in nature.

Long Term Loans

These loans are given for a long period it is ranging from 5 years to more than 20 years or even more. These loans also include with medium term loans are called investment loans or terms loans. The loans are required for the permanents improvements land such as levelling and reclamation, purchasing of land, construction of form buildings, purchase of tractors, raising of orchards, etc. This type loan are required to activate the large capital, a longer period is required to repay these loans due to their non- liquidating nature.

Based on Purpose

On the basis of purpose, the credit is divided into four types are as follows.

Production Loans

This type of loans given to the farmers for the purpose to increase the production of crops, they also called seasonal agricultural operation (SAO) loans or short term loans or crop loans. The repayment period of these loans are ranging from 6 to 18 months lumpsum.

Investment Loans

The loans are given to framers for the purchase of highly specialized machinery and equipment like tractors, pump sets and tube-well and etc. The farm productivity distributed over more than one time.

Investment Loans

The loans directly help to the farmers during the distress sales and to market the market produce in batter way. The regulated markets and commercial banks given the credit to farmers based on the warehouse receipt provide the marketing debt in advance 75% of the value of produce. These loans help the farmers to payment their old loans and sale the produce to fetch the higher prices.

Consumption Loans

The loans are given in higher in advance for consumption purpose like personal medical, education loans, purchase for refrigerator, air conditioner, computer etc. These loans are looking unproductive loans for agriculture, but indirectly assist more productive use of crop loans i.e. without diverting them to other purpose. Consumption loans not very advanced and resected to the areas which that are affected by natural calamities. These loans are granted on the based on the group of the guarantee with maximum of three members. The loans are to be repaid within five crops sessions or 2.5 years, whichever are earlier. The branch manager has discretionary power to sanctioning these loans up to Rs. 5000 in each individual case with 11% rate of interest.

Based on Security

The loan transactions between lender and borrower governed by confidence and term and conditions is confined by the formal and informal money lenders and agencies, but the formal financial agencies do have their own very long procedure and formalities to passing the loans. Therefore, the secured loans are classified into two categories viz. secured and unsecured loans.

Secured Loans

The secured loans are given to borrower in advanced against some security, termed as secured loans. The various forms of security are offered to obtaining the loans are as follows:

Personal Security

Under this security borrower himself stand as the guarantor, the loans are given to farmers on the basis of promissory note. The third party guarantee may be or may not be insisted upon them, it is based on the understanding between the lender and borrower.

Collateral Security

These loans are called secured loans here the borrower pledged his properties for the loans which include the movable properties i.e. LIC Receipt, Bands, Warehouse Receipts, Machinery and Livestock etc.

Chattel Loans

This type loans are obtained from pawn-brokers by pledging movable properties i.e. jewelry, utensils and various metals.

Mortgage

As against the collateral security, immovable properties are pledged for security purpose i.e. land farm buildings etc. The person who are creation the charge of mortgage is called as mortgagor (borrower) and the person whose favour it is created is known as the mortgagee (bankers). There are two types of mortgage are as follows:

Simple Mortgage

When the mortgaged property is patrimonial or hereditary property of borrower is termed as simple mortgage. Here, the farmers pledged their property keep with banking institution for the loan on the basis of registration and the charges of registration are borne by borrower.

Equitable Mortgage

The mortgage property refers to the self-acquired property of the borrower is called as equitable mortgage property. There is no such type of registration are required because the ownership rights clearly depicted in the title deeds in the name of formers/borrowers.

Hypothecated Loan

The borrower has ownership right on his movable and the banker legal right to take the possession of property to sale the default (or) right to use the owner to bring the property to sale and realization of the amount due. The person who owner the charge of hypothecation is called hypothecator (borrower) and the person whose favor it known as hypothecate (bank) and the property. This happen in the case of tractor loans, machinery loans etc. Under such loans the borrower will not have any right to sell the equipment until the loan are cleared off. The borrower is allowed to use the purchased machinery or equipment so as to enable him pay the loan instalment regularly. Hypothecated loans are two types i.e. key loans or open loans.

Key Loans

The agricultural produce of the farmers /borrower will be kept under kept under control of lending institutions and the loan are given to farmers in advance to farmers. It is helps to the farmers from not restoring the distress sales.

Open Loans

The physical possession of the purchased machinery rest with the borrower, but the legal ownership remains with the lending institutions till the loan is repaid.

Unsecured Loans

These loans given on the basis of confidence, trust and goodwill of the borrower and lender. There is no security kept against the loan amount. These are three types loans are as follows.

Based on the Liquidity

The credit can be classified into two types i.e. self-liquidating loans and partially-liquidating loans.

Self-liquidating Loans

This type loan generate income immediately and are to be paid with one year after the completion of one crop season, it is also known as ex crop loans.

Partially–Liquidating Loans

They will take some time to generate income and can be repaid in 2-5 years or more, based on the economic activity for which the loan was taken dairy loans, tractor loan and orchard loan.

Based on Approach

On the basis of approach, the loans are classified into three types are as follows:

Individual Approach

It is refer to the ordinary loans given by the lending agencies to any potential borrower for the purpose of his needs.

Area Based Approach

These loans given to the persons comes under the given area for the specific purposes will be categorized under this service area approach followed by banks interest rate varies with one area to other areas.

Differential Interest Rate (DIR) Approach

Under this approach loans will be given to the weaker sections at @ 4 % interest rate per annum.

Based on Contact

On the basis of contact loans are classified into two types are as follows.

Direct Loans

The loans given by farmers directly by institutional agencies are called direct loans i.e. crops loans.

Indirect Loans

This loans directly given to the ago-based firm such as fertilizers and pesticide companies are directly beneficial to the farmers are called indirect loans. Indirectly given to organization for activates which contribute to the productivity of agricultural operations are categorized as indirect loans. For examples financing for the establishment of fertilizer and machinery companies, constriction of warehouse, sugar factories and agro chemical.

Credit Delivery Mechanism in India

The Indian farmers borrow the short term, medium term and long term loans form the money lenders, land lord, cooperative credit societies and government organization. The long term credit requirements of the farmers are met by land development banks etc. Consequently, the source of agricultural credit can be divided into two categories i. e. informal and formal source of credit. The details discuss through the table and flow chart.

S. No.	Major source	Sub-source
1.	Institutional (formal sector)	✓ *Government* ✓ *Cooperative banks* ✓ *Commercial banks*
2.	Non-institutional (informal sector)	✓ *Money lenders* ✓ *Employer* ✓ *Shopkeepers/traders* ✓ *Relatives/friends*

Source: WDI 2015 (World Bank)

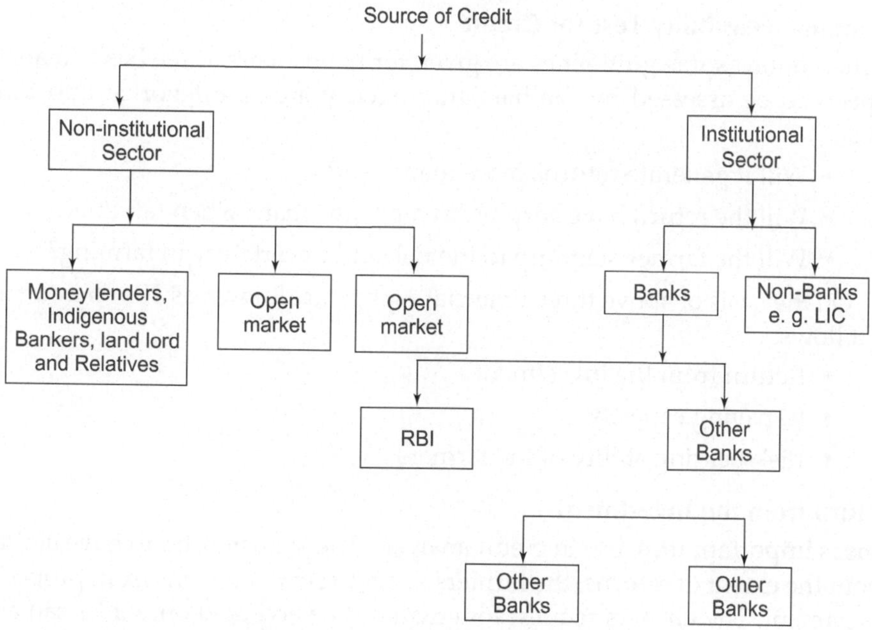

Distribution of Credit by Source in Percentage:

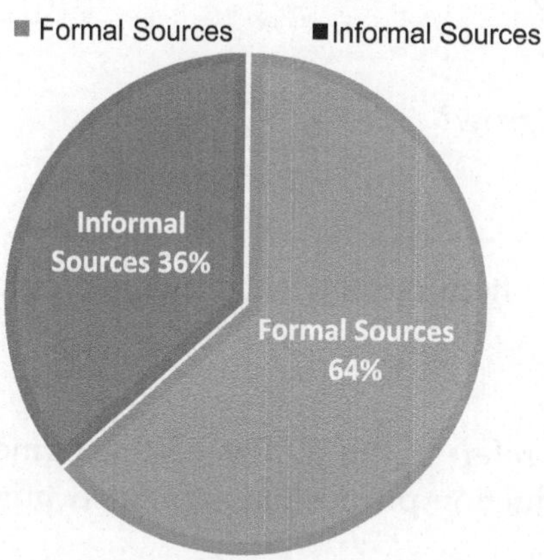

Principles of 3Rs, 5Cs and 7Ps Credit Analysis

Principles 3Rs of Credit Analysis

The technological break-through in Indian agriculture make the agriculture capital intensive. India most of the farmers are capital starve. The farmers need credit at right time, through right agencies and the adequate quantity to realized maximum productivity This is from farmer point of view. When the farmers approach an institutional financial agency (IFA) for the loan, the agency should be convinced about the economic viability proposed investment.

Economic Feasibility Test for Credit

In this context some guidelines are given for the bankers, three basic financial aspects to be assessed by the bankers / agency are as categorize into three parts:

- Will it generate returns more than costs?
- Will the return have surplus, to repay the loans when fall due?
- Will the farmer stand up to the risk and uncertainty in farming?

On the basis of above three financial aspects are known as 3Rs of credit are as follows:

- Return from the investment
- Repaying capacity
- Risk-bearing ability of the farmers

Return from the Investment

This is important measure in credit analysis. The agency need to have an idea about the extent of returns, the farmers likely to get the returns from proposed investment. The farmers request for credit can be accepted only if he can able to generate returns enable meet the costs. Returns depends on the following decision:

- What to grow?
- How to grow?
- How much to grow?
- When to sell?
- Where to sell?

The main concern here is that the farmers should be able to generate incremental income.

Repayment Capacity

Repayment capacity refer to the ability of the farmers to repay the loan obtained for the production purpose in stipulated time period, fixed by the lending agency/banks.

At the time loan may be productive enough to generate additional income but may not be productive enough to repay the loan amount. Hence necessary condition here is that the loan should not only profitable but also have potential for the repayment for the loan amount. Under such conditions only farmer will get the loan amount. The repayment capacity not only depends on returns, but also on several other factors as given below:

$$Y = f(X_1, X_2, X_3, X_4, X_5, X_6, X_7 \ldots\ldots)$$

Where Y is the dependent variable i.e. repayment capacity.

The independent variable viz. X_1 to X_4 are consider as quantitative factor, while x_5 to x_7 consider as qualitative factors.

X_1 (+) = Gross return from the enterprise for which the loan was taken during season/year (in Rs.). X_2 (–) Working expenses in Rs.

X_3 (–) Family consumption expenditure in Rs. X_4 (–)

Others loans due in Rs.

X_5 (+) Literacy

X_5 (+) = Managerial skill

X_7 (+) Moral character like honesty, integrity etc.

Hence, even though the returns are high the repayment capacity is less because of other factors. The estimation of repayment capacity varies from crop loans (i.e. self-liquidating loans) to term loans (partially liquidating loans)

Repayment Capacity for Crop Loans

Gross income – (working expenses excluding the proposed crop loans+ family leaving expenses + other loans due + miscellaneous expenditure).

Repayment Capacity for Term Loans

Gross income – (working expenses = family living expenses + other loans due + miscellaneous expenditure + annual installment due for term loan).

Causes for the Poor Repayment Capacity of Indian farmers

- Small size of farm holdings due to fragmentation of land.
- Low production and productivity.
- Household consumption expenditure are very higher.
- Low prices of agricultural commodities and high fluctuation of repay.
- The credit/or loans are using unproductive purpose.
- Farmers have low equity/ net worth.
- Poor management of limited farm resources.

Measures for Strengthening the Repayment Capacity

- Increasing the net income of farm business by proper organization and operation by proper organization and operation of enterprise i.e. dairy, fisheries, poultry, gotery, etc.
- Improved technology would be increased the production and reduce the cost.
- Removing the imbalances in the resource availability.
- Prepared the loan schedule for the repayment as per flow of income.
- Improving the net worth of the farm households.
- Diversification through high returns enterprises.

- Adoption of risk management strategies like insurance of crops, animal and machinery and hedging to control price.

Risk Bearing Ability

For the estimating the risk bearing ability banks need to find out what has been variation in the yields or returns for the given enterprise over the past 5 – 10 years. This variation can be computed by using of coefficient of variation technique and standard deviation etc. there are various types risk are as follows:

- Production risk
- Technological risk
- Personal risk (risk concerned by illiteracy and ignorance)
- Institutional risk
- Weather uncertainty
- Price uncertainty

Repayment Capacity under Risk

Deflated gross income – (working expenses excluding the proposed crop loan + family leaving expenses + other loans due + miscellaneous expenses).

Measures to Strengthen Risk Bearing Ability

- Increasing the owner's equity/net worth
- Reducing the farm and family expenditure.
- Developing the moral character i.e. honesty, integrity, dependability and feeling the responsibility etc. All these qualities put together *credit rating.*
- Undertaking the reliable and stable enterprises (enterprise given the guaranteed and steady income).
- Improving the ability to borrow funds during good and bad time crop production.
- Improving the ability to earn the save money. A part of the farm earnings should be saved by the farmer so as to meet uncertainty in future.
- Taking up of crop, livestock and machinery insurance.

Principles 5Cs of Credit Analysis

The another important tests are applied to analysis the economic feasibility of the proposed investment activities are called as 5Cs of credit i.e. Character, Capacity, Capital, Condition and Commonsense, transection is trust, even though the bank insists.

Character

The transaction of credit is based on the trust. Even though the bank insists upon the security while the landing a loans, an element of trust by the bankers will also play the major role. The confidence of an institutional financial agency on it borrowers is influenced by the moral character of borrower such as honesty, integrity, commitment, hard work, and efficient etc. Therefore, both mental and moral character of the borrowers will be examined while advancing a loan. Generally, people have good mental and moral character will have good credit as well.

Capacity

These refer to the capacity of an individuals to repayment the loans amount when they fall due. It is depending upon the income obtained from the farm.

C = f (y)

C = Capacity and Y = Income

Capital

Capital indicates the availability of money with the farmer - borrower. When his capacity and character are proved to be inadequate the capital will be considered. It represents net worth of the farmer. It is related to the repayment capacity and risk bearing ability of the farmer-borrower. The small and marginal farmers required the term loan, while the large farmer do not need.

Condition

It refersto the condition needed for obtaining loans from financial institutions i.e. procedure to be followed while advancing loan.

Commonsense

It refers to full understanding lenders and borrowers in credit transection. This is in fact prima-facie requirements in obtaining credit by the borrower.

Principles of 7Ps of Credit Analysis

The increased role of the financial institutions these due to technological changes on agricultural front necessitated the evolving of principles of farm fiancé are expected to not bring only commercial gains to the bankers but also social benefits. The principles so evolved by the institutional financial agencies are expected to have universal validity. These principles popularly called as 7Ps of farm credit as are follows:

- Principles of productive purpose (purpose)
- Principles of personality (Person)
- Principles of productivity (production)
- Principles of phased disbursement

- Principal of proper utilization
- Principal of payment
- Principles of protection

Principles of Productive Purpose (Purpose)

This principle refers that the loan amount given to farmer should be capable of generating additional income. Based on the level of the owned capital available with farmer, the credit needs vary. The requirement of capital is visible on all farms but more pronounced on marginal and small farms. The famers any tiny holdings do need another type of credit i.e. consumption credit, so as to use crops loans and productively (without diverting them from un productive purpose). Inspite of knowing the consumption credit are not given due importance by the institutional agencies. This principle explains that the crop loan of the small and marginal farmers is to be supported with the income generating assets acquired through the term loans. The additional incomes generated from these productive assets add to the income obtained from the farming. The example relevant here are loans for dairy animals, sheep and goats, poultry bird's installation of pump sets on groups action, etc.

Principles of Personality (Person)

The 3Rs credit are sound indicators of credit worthiness of the farmers. Over the years of expenses in lending the bankers have identified an important factor in credit transection i.e. trustworthiness of the borrower. It has relevance with the personality of the individuals. When farmer's borrower fails to repay the loan due to the crop failures caused by natural calamities, he will not consider the willful- defaulter, whereas the large farmers using the who is using the loan amount profitably but fails to repay the loans is considered as willful defaulter. This character of the big farmers is considering as dishonesty. Therefore, that is the safety of the loans is not totally depends on the security offered but also on the personality (credit characters) of the borrower, Moreover, the growth and progress of the lending institutions have depended upon the major influencing factors i.e. personality. Thus, the personality of the borrower and the growth of the financial institutions are positively correlated.

Principles of Productivity (Production)

This principle explains underline that credit increase not only which is not just for increasing production from that enterprise but also it should able to increase the productivity from that enterprise. For example, the use of high yielding verities (HYVs) in crops and superior breeds of animals will increase the productivity of the enterprise. Hence, this principle emphasized on making resource as productive as possible by the selection of most appropriate enterprise.

Principle of Phased Disbursement

This principle explains that the loan amount is to be distributed in phases, so as make to productive and at the same time banker can also be sure about be proper used of the borrowed fund for examples loan for digging wells. The phased disbursement of loan fit for taking up cultivation perennial crops and investment activities to overcome the diversion of fund for unproductive purpose. But the one disadvantage here is that will make the cost of credit higher. That's why the interest rates higher for the term loans as compared to crop loans.

Principle of Proper Utilization

It is explain about the proper utilization of loan amount for the purpose of which are advanced which depends upon the upon the situation of rural area viz. the resources like seeds, fertilizers, pesticides etc., for free from the adulteration, weather infrastructural facilities like storage, transportation, marketing etc. are available. Therefore, proper utilization of fund is possible. If there exist suitable condition for the investment.

Principle of Payment

This principle deals with the fixing of repayment schedule of the loan provided by the financial agencies. For examples as investment credit to irrigation structure, tractor etc. The annual repayments are fixed over a number of years depending upon the incremental returns. With reference to crop loans, the loan is to be repaid in lumpsum because the farmer will have realized the output only once. A grace period of 2-3 months are allowed after the harvest crop to enable the farmer to get the reasonable price for his produce. Otherwise farmer restarts the distress sales. When the crop failed due to unfavorable weather conditions, the repayment is not insisted upon immediately. Under such conditions the repayment period is extended besides assisting the farmers with anther fresh loan to enable him to carry on the farm business.

REFERENCES

Ghosal, S.N. Agricultural Financing in India, Asia Publishing House, 1966.

Kennet, Duft D. Principles of Management in Agribusiness, Reston Publishing Company, Reston, 1979.

Muniraj, R. Farm Finance for Development, Oxford and IBH Publishing Co. Pvt. Ltd., New Delhi, 1987.

Murray, W.G. Agricultural Finance, 1953.

Nelson A.G. Lee, W.F. and Murray, W. G. Agricultural Finance, Iowa State University Press Ames, 1973.

Tandon R.K. and Dhondyal S.P. Principles and Method of Farm Management.

J.P. Bhattacharjee, Studies in Indian Agricultural Economics. WDI 2015 (World Bank).

William G. Murray and Nelson Aron G. Agricultural Finance, The Iowa State University Press, Ames Iowa, 1960.

Farming and Development : *Technological Perspectives* **Pages 156-164**
Edited by: Dr. Pawan Kumar 'Bharti' & Dr. Jaswant Ray
ISBN: 978-93-88854-08-5
Edition: 2019
Published by: Discovery Publishing House Pvt. Ltd., New Delhi (India)

10 Biorational Approaches in Insect Pest Management

Sustainable Agriculture

[1]Manish Kumar, [2]Neelam Yadav and [3]Renu Yadav

Introduction

The utilization of chemicals that affect insect behavior, growth or reproduction, for suppression of insect population is often referred to as biorational control (Dhaliwal and Koul, 2006). These chemicals are based on naturally occurring chemical (e.g. Pheromone, hormones) of microbial agents, and are considered safe to human or the environment (Capinera, 2007). These chemicals affect specific system such as moulting processes, metamorphosis and the insect endocrinology safety.

The term biorational derived from two words, biological and rational, referring to pesticides of natural origin that have limited or no adverse effect on the environment or beneficial organism. They are considered third generation pesticides that are environmentally sound and closely resemble or are identical to chemical produced by insects and plants.

Biorational products are quite different from conventional, broad-spectrum products. They do not control pest in the same way as most broad spectrum products. They are typically target specific. Biorational insecticide includes growth regulators, semio0chemicals and microbially derived products.

Insect Growth Regulators

The chemical that affect the growth and development of insect are called insect growth regulators (IGRs).

The growth regulators that are of interest for pest control include chitin synthesis inhibitors, sclerotization inhibitors, moulting hormone and juvenile hormone (Beckage, 2000; Thacker, 2002; Horowitz and Ishaya, 2004).

1 Department of Chemistry, CCSPG College, Heonra (Saifai), Etawah, (U.P.), India
2 Department of Entomology, Chandra Shekhar Azad University of Agriculture and Technology, Kanpur (U.P.), India
3 Department of Zoology, CCSPG College, Heonra (Saifai), Etawah, (U.P.), India

Chitin Synthesis Inhibitors

Chitin synthesis inhibitors (CSIs) interfere with production of chitin, the structural polysaccharides found in insect cuticle and thus affect the integrity of insect exoskeleton.

Scientists investigating the new derivatives of herbicide, diclobenil, discovered CSIs accidentally. It was found that 1-(2, 6-dichloro benzoyl)-3-(3, 4-dichlorophenyl) Urea (DU 19.111) possessed interesting insecticidal properties against several species of insects. Thereafter, a large number of structural analogues were prepared and screened against a variety of insect pests.

Diflubenzuron [1-(4-chlorophenyl)-3-(2, 6-difluorobenzoyl) urea] was the most successful analogue of the series and is effective against insect pest belonging of Coleoptera, Diptera and Lepidoptera.

A new BPU (Benzoyl Phenyl Urea) insecticide, novaluron, has more contact and translaminar activity as compared with other BPUs, affecting white flies and leaf minor, in addition to lepidopteran and coleopteran larvae (Ishaya *et al.*, 2002).

The benzoyl phenyl urea (BPU) analogues area compound with selective properties, affecting the larval stage, they mainly act as stomach toxicants and kill insects at the time of moulting.

Another compound, buprofezin, is a thiadizine like compound with long residual activity and acts on nymphal stages of sucking insects such as leaf hopper, plant hopper and white flies (De cock and Degheele, 1998).

Plumbagin is a naturally occurring CSI present in the roots of a tropical medicinal shrub, *Plumbago capensis.* Plumbagin possesses high ovicidal activity against eggs of *Dysdercus koenigii* (Fab.), *Spodoptera litura* (Fab.), *Corcyra cephalonica* (stainton) and *Plutella xylostella* (Linn.).

Table 10.1: Important Chitin Synthesis Inhibitors

Chitin synthesis inhibitor	Trade name	Target pests
Buprofezin	Applaud	Brown plant hoppers, white files and scales
Teflubenzuron	Nomolt	Coleoptera, Lepidoptera, white flies
Flufenoxuron	Cascade	Psyllidae and mites
Triflumuron	Alsystin	Lepidoptera, Coleopteran, Diptera, Psyllidae
Chlorfluazuron	Alabron	Thysanoptera, Aleurodidae
Hexaflumuron	Consult	Homoptera, Diptera, Coleoptera
Lufenuron	Match	Thrips, Siphonaptera
Flucyclouron	Andalin	Mites

Sclerotization Inhibitors

Sclerotization is the process of hardening the cuticle due to the tanning of proteins which follows eclosion (emergence of an immature stage from the egg) or ecdysis (shedding of the cuticle and subsequent expansion of an insect under hormonal control) (Ambrose, 2004).

The only commercially available sclerotization inhibitor is MON0585 developed by Monsonto. It is highly toxic to mosquitoes and other dipteran insects. It causes mortality at the time of pupation and dead pupae are white instead of tan colour because of failure of the organism to harden the pupal cuticle via arylation.

Brain Hormone or Prothoracicotropic Hormones (PTTH)

Chemical messengers produced by the central nervous system to regulate various events in the body are known as brain hormones or neurohormones. The first neuropeptide, proctolin, was isolated from *Periplaneta Americana* (Linn.) in 1975 and since thus 50 such structures have been isolated from different insects.

The major problem in commercial exploitation of neuropeptides are their costly synthesis, inability to penetrate the insect cuticle and photo instability. These problems may be overcome by a variety of ways to utilize these regulatory chemicals to the detriment of the insect of the insects (Sukumar, 1994):

- The design of peptide mimics that can penetrate the insect cuticle or gut and block the peptide-medicated response at the target cell.
- Development of control agents that interfere with the secretion of a neuropeptide.
- Incorporation of neuropeptide producing genes into micro organisms will make large scale production economical and also help in overcoming stability and penetration problems.

Juvenile Hormones (JHs)

Juvenile hormones secreted by carpora allata which regulate a variety of function including metamorphosis, vitellogenesis, diapauses and polymorphism (Sparks, 1990).

Williams (1967) first suggested the possibility of utilizing insect hormones as insects' specific environmentally benign pesticides.

The search for JHAs among plants was stimulated by the accidental finding of a paper factor American paper products having JH activity against *Pyrrhocoris apterus*. It was named as Juvabione and was chemically identified as the methyl ester of todomatuic acid.

The natural JHs have limited scope in pest control because these are unstable in UV light and are rapidly metabolized by insect. Therefore, the juvenile hormone analogue (JHA) synthesis was directed towards the stabilization of the molecule by protection or substitution like methoprene, hydroprene, kinoprene, fenoxycard, pyriproxyfen and diofenolan.

- Methoprene are available commercially for the control of mosquitoes, cigarette beetle and flies.
- Kinoprene is a strong highly selective JHA effective against aphids, white files, scales and mealy bugs.
- Pyriproxyfen has proved effective against a number of sucking pest white fly, thrips and scales.
- Diofenolon is highly effective for the control of scale insects and lepidopteran pests.

The exogenous application of JHAs is effective only when the endogenous JH titer in insect is low. This leaves the larval/nymphal stages of most insects unaffected. This limitation could be overcome by blocking the biosynthesis of natural JHs. The chemicals exhibiting this property are known as antijuvanile hormone agents (AJHAs) or JH antagonists. AJHAs were initially isolated from a plant, *Ageratum houstonianum* Mill designated as precocene I, II and III. Additionally, a number of inhibitors of later steps in JH biosynthesis like pipronyl butoxide, imidazoles, acetylenic compounds and cyclopropyl amines also shos AJH activity.

Moulting Hormones (MHs)

Moulting hormone by ecdysone, ecdysterone and other ecdysteroids secreted by prothoracic glands and are responsible for normal moulding, growth and maturation of insects. Ecdysone acts as a hormone or as a precursor for the more active 20-hydroxy ecdysone.

The MHs are hydrophilic because of a number of hydroxyl groups present on the molecule. So analogues of these hormones cannot penetrate the insect cuticle and hence cannot serve as effective pest control agents. However, blocking the biosynthesis of MHs can be used to disrupt the moulting process.

Ecdysone agonist i.e. tebefenozide, halofenozide and methoxyfenozide have been demonstreated to be active against many ledidopterous including *Pieris brassicae* (L.), *Plodia interpunctella* (Hub.) and *Spodoptera Iitura* (Fab.), (Dhadialla *et al.*, 2007).

- Tebufenozide has been found to be effective against codling moth, *Cydia pomonella.*

- Halofenozide is highly effective against the soil dwelling larval stages of scarabaeid beetles such as *Papillio japonica.*
- Mthoxyfenozide has exhibited high filed efficacy against ledpidopteran pests.

Semiochemicals

Substances which are employed in converying messages between organism are termed as semiochemicals. Semiochemicals are divided into intraspecific and interspecific communication chemicals.

Pheromones

A substances that is secreted by an organism to the outside and causes a specific reaction in a receiving organism of the same species.

Types of Pheromones

Sex Pheromones

Sex Pheromones are often produced by the females to attract males for mating, but they may also be produced by males to attract females. They seem to be highly developed in lepidiptera and are frequently produced by eversible glands at the tip of the abdomen. Female sex pheromones are usually received by sensory sensory sensillae on male antennal, and males search up wind, following the odour corridor of the female.

Aggregation Pheromones

These pheromones cause insects to aggregate or congregate at food sites, reproductive habits, hibernation sites etc. They are attractive to both sexes and tend to operate over a long range and have the potential of attracting thousands of individuals.

Alarm Pheromones

Alarm pheromones are common in social insects such as ants and bees, which are usually found to occur in aggregation. The function of this type of pheromone is to raise in conspecifics, to raise a defence response and to initiate avoidance.

Trail Pheromones

Trail pheromones are produced by foraging ants, termites and larvae of some lepidopteran insects. They are essentially used to indicate source of requisites to other number of the colony. While trail pheromones are frequently associated with walking insects such as ants, they are also known from other insects. Bees use trail pheromones during foraging for making attractive foraging sites as well as for scent marking of unproductive food source (Free, 1987).

Pheromones of Insect Pests

Important Insect Pests	Pheromone
American boll worm, *Helicoverpa armigera*	(Z)-11-hexadecenol and (Z)-9- hexadecenal
Pink boll worm, *Pectinophora gossypiella*	(Z, Z) and (Z, E) 7, 11- Hexadecadienyl acetate (1:1)
Tobacco cut worm, *Spodoptera litura*	(Z, E)-9, 11- Hexadecadienyl acetate and (Z, E)-9, 12-Hexadecadienyl acetate 10:1
Diamond back moth, *Plutella xylostella*	(Z)-11-hexadecenol, 11- Hexadecadienyl acetate and (Z) 11- hexadecenal (5:5:1)
Oriental fruit fly, *Dacus dorsalis*	4-allyl-1, 2-dimethoxybenzone
Melon fly, *Dacus cucurbitae*	4-(p-hydroxy phenyl) 2-butanone acetate

Pheromones Use in Insect Control

- **Gossyplure** is commonly used for monitoring the Pink bollworm *Pectinophra gossypiella* (Saunders) throughout the cotton belt.
- **Disparlure** is used for mating disruption of Gypsy moth, *Lymantria dispar* (Linn).
- **Codlemone,** the major sex pheromone component of codling math, *Cydia pomonella* (Linn.), has been used extensively for monitoring and timing of pesticide application.
- Helilure is used for monitoring of *Helicoverpa armigera.*
- (E)-β-farmesene (EBF) has been identified as alarm pheromone and commercially available for use against a number of aphid species including *Aphis gossypii* and *Lipaphis erysimi.*

POTENTIAL USES OF PHEROMONES IN PEST SUPPRESSION

Monitoring:

- Detect the presence of species
- Estimate density of population of a species
- Measure the seasonal abundance of the pest
- Evaluate the effectiveness of mating disruption.

Direct Control:

- Mass deployment of pheromone – baited traps.
- Pheromone – mediated mating disruption.
- Alarm pheromones to move pests away from feeding sites.
- Host-marking pheromones to disrupt landing, feeding or oviposition by pests on their host plant.

Allelochemicals

Allelochemicals are non nutritional chemicals produced by an organism of one species and affect the growth, development and behavior of individual of another species (Whittaker, 1970).

Allomone

Tending to confer an adaptive advantage to the producing organism i.e. the host plant. Allomones are considered to be a major factor of insect resistance in plant.

Kairomones

Tending to give an adaptive advantage to the receiving organism i.e. the phytophagous insect.

One of the most classical example of exploitation of allelochemical is an economic crop is that of resistance in maize to first generation of the Europeann corn borer, *Ostrinia nubilalis.* The chemical compound resistance factor identificed as MBOA (6-methoxy bezoxazolinone), appear to functions as a repellent or feeding deterrent. MBOA does not exist in uninjured corn tissues, but DIMBOA, (2, 4-Dihydroxy 7 methoxy-1, 4 benzoxazin 3-one) in its glucoside form is present in injured corn levels. The yield of MBOA for the decomposition of DIMBOA increases with increases in pH of the midgut of most lepidopteron larvae (Panda and Khush, 1995).

- The major allelochemical imparting resistance to insect pest in cotton has been found to be gossypal which occur in much higher quantities in glanded than in glandless varieties.
- **Cucurbitacins** are a group of about 20 tetracyclic tritepenoids isolated from the family cucurbitaceae. Cucurbitacins are feeding deterrents for a number of arthropods including cucumber leaf beetles, *Phyllotreta spp.*
- Pentadecanal in rice exhibits allomonal properties against *Nilaparvata lugents, Sogatella-furcifera, chilo suppressalis.*
- 2-tridercanone in the leaves of tomato plants is toxic to the larvae of *Manduca sexta and H. zea* and adult of *Aphis gossypii.*
- The aphid parasitoid, *diaeretiella rapae* is attracted by the allylisothiocyanate released cruciferous plants harbouring various aphid species.
- *Chrysoperla carnea* are attracted to caryophyllene, a terpenoid released by damaged cotton leaves.

Miscellaneous

Avermectins

Avermectins are a group of macro cyclic lactones isolated from fermentation of the soil actinomycete microorganism *Streptomyses avermitilis.* These compound exhibited a broad spectrum of activity against agricultural pests such as aphids, mites, caterpillars and other pests that feed on crops (Walia, 2005).

Spinosyns

The spinosyns, a new class of insecticidal macrocyclic lactones, derived by fermentation of the soil actinomycetes, *Saccharopolysopra spinosa.* It has shown contact and stomach activity against Coleoptera, Diptera, Hymenoptera and Lepidoptera (Dowd, 2002).

Polynectins

Polynectins are secondary metabolites from the actinomycete *Streptomyces aureus.* They are very effective in controlling spider mites under wet conditions.

Pyrrole Insecticide

Pyrrol insecticides have been derived from a natural product, dioxopyrrolomycin, isolated from a strain of streptomyces. Chlorfenapyr has been commercially developed because of its broad spectrum of activity against many species of Coleoptera, Lepidoptera and Acarnia.

REFERENCES

Ambrose, D.P. (2004). The Insects: Structure, Function and Biodiversity. Kalyani Publishers, New Delhi.

Beckage, N.E. (2000). Insect Growth Regulators. In: J.E. Rechcigl and N.A.

Capinera, J.I. (ed.) (2007). Encyclopedia of Entomology. Vol 1, A-E. Kluwer Academic Publishers, Dordrecht, The Netherlands.

De cock, A. and Degheele, D. (1998). Buprofezin: A Novel Chitin Synthesis Inhibitor Affecting Specifically Plant Hoppers, White Flies and Scale Insects. In: I. Ishaya and D. Degheele (eds.) Insecticides with Novel Modes of Action: Mechanism and Application. Springer Verlag, Berlin, pp.74-91.

Dhadialla, T.S., Carlson, G.R. and Le, D.P. (2007). New Insecticides with Ecdysterodial and Juvenile Harmone Activity. *Ann. Rev. Entomol.* 52: 545-569.

Dhaliwal, G.S. and Koul, O. (2006). Biopesticides Conference – Biopesticides: Emerging Trends (BET 2005). Highlights and Recommendations. *Biopestic. News* 10(1): 3-5.

Dowd, P.F. (2002). Antiinsectan Compounds Derived from Microorganisms. In: O. Koul and G.S. Dhaliwal (eds) Micribial Biopesticides. Taylor & Francis, Landon, pp. 13-115.

Free, J.B. (1987). Pheromones of Social Bees. Comstock Publ., Ithaca, New York.

Horowitz, A.R. and Ishaya, I. (2004). Biocontrol Insecticides-Mechanisms. Selectivity and Importance in Pest Management. In: A.R. Horowitz and I. Ishaya (eds) Insect Pest Management: Field and Protected Crops. Springer Verlag, Berlin, Germany, pp.1-28.

Ishaya, I., Horowitz, A.R., Tirry, L. and Barazani, A. (2002). Navaluron (Rimon), a Novel IGR-Mechanism, Selectivity and Importance in IPM Programmes. *Med. Landbouww Rijksuniv. Gent.* 67: 617-626.

Panda, N. and Khush, G.S. (1995). Host Plant Resistance to Insects: CAB International, Wlling Ford, U.K.

Rechcigi (eds) Biological and Biotechnological Control of Insect Pests. Lewis Publishers, New York, pp. 123-137.

Sparks, T.C. (1990). Endocrine Based Insecticides. In: E. Hodgson and R.J. Kuhr (eds) Safer Insecticides: Development and Use: Marcel Dekker, New York, pp.103-154.

Sukumar, K. (1994). Neuropeptide Technology in Selected Insect Control. *Phytophaga,* 6: 133-139.

Thacker, J.R.M. (2002). An Introduction to Arthropod Pest Control. Cambridge University Press, Cambridge.

Walia, S. (2005). Allelochemicals as Biopesticides. In: O. Kaul, G.S. Bhaliwal, A. Shankar, D. Raj and V.K. Kaul (eds) Souvenir Conference on Biopesticides: Emerging Trends. November 11-13, 2005, Society of Biopesticides Sciences India, Jalandhar, pp. 19-32.

Whittakar, R.H. (1970). The Biochemical Ecology of Higher Plants. In: E. Sondheimer and J.B. Simecone (eds). Chemical Ecology. Acudemic Press, New York, pp. 43-70.

Farming and Development : ***Technological Perspectives***
Edited by: **Dr. Pawan Kumar 'Bharti' & Dr. Jaswant Ray**
ISBN: 978-93-88854-08-5
Edition: **2019**
Published by: **Discovery Publishing House Pvt. Ltd., New Delhi (India)**

Pages 165-187

11

Drought

Status, Losses and Management in Sugarcane Crop

[1]Ashutosh Kumar Mall, Varucha Misra,
Ashwani Kumar and [2]A.D. Pathak

ABSTRACT

Sugarcane is an important sugar crop. It is one of crops for producing bio-energy. Water is being a scarce commodity in the world and with changing climate, this scarcity will be enhance further due to less rainfall and high temperatures. Sugarcane is a crop which loves water and gives high yield on attaining proper irrigation. Less water availability in its life cycle leads to rapid loss in production and productivity. As per the last four drought occurred, in Brazil (the highest producer of sugarcane in world), drought causes yield losses in sugarcane crop from as low as 6.3% to 40 %. In this chapter, status of frequency of drought in India highlighting state of Uttar Pradesh (highest sugarcane producer of sub-tropical zone of India) has been illustrated along with impact of drought on sugarcane. Furthermore, response of this crop in drought conditions has been described and how could this crop be managed under such a situation has been shown. Besides, in respect to breeding point of view, efforts in developing tolerant variety for drought condition have also been described.

Keywords: Drought, Sugarcane, Sugar, Uttar Pradesh, Yield.

Introduction

Sugarcane (*Saccharum officinarum* L.) is an important crop for sugar and bio-energy worldwide. It is one of the world's major C_4 crops that mainly grow in the tropic and sub-tropic regions. Weather and climate related events are the key factors for sugarcane production worldwide, especially, in many developing countries (Zhao and Li, 2015). Water is already a scarce commodity in many parts of the world, and as the climate is changing unpredictably, this will enhance such conditions in mere future. As the global temperatures are rapidly going down along with the frequency and precipitation level, the problem of water losses are predicted to enhance further through evapo-

1 ICAR-Indian Institute of Sugarcane Research, Lucknow-226 002 (U.P.), India
2 U.P. Council of Agricultural Research (UPCAR), Lucknow, (U.P.), India

transpiration (Lopes *et al.*, 2011). Variation in climate is severely affecting the water sources and as per the present scenario the frequencies of occurrence of drought and floods will be increasing in mere future (Pandey and Shukla, 2015). For a crop to grow properly, it requires water which is not fulfilled just by the uptake from its roots but also additional irrigation is required for it, but if such conditions of water scarcity prevails then this would also lead to groundwater depletion (Oki and Shinjiro, 2006). Water is essentiality not only for humans and animals but also for the plants for their proper growth and development (Larcher, 2006). Reports showed that in 2008, 6.3 per cent of losses in Sao Paulo state (Castro, 2008), in 2010, 40 per cent in Zone da Mata state (Cavalcanti, 2010), in 2012, 20% in Alagaos state (Agencia Globo, 2012; Sindacucar, 2012), in 2013, 30 per cent in Paraiba state (Silva, 2013), in 2014, 15 per cent in Ribeiro preto (Palhares, 2014). Several studies have revealed that deficiency of water causes changes in many physiological activities such as leaf water potential, relative water content, *etc.* (Nogueira *et al.*, 2000; Graça *et al.*, 2010; Silva *et al.*, 2010). Also, as a result of water deficiency, metabolic processes were also altered like osmo-regulators were increased under such conditions (Nogueira *et al.*, 2001; Guimarães *et al.*, 2008; Silva *et al.*, 2009; Medeiros *et al.*, 2012).

Sugarcane crop is known to be a water lover (Table 1), *i.e.*, the requirement of water for its successful growth is high and varies from maximum of 0.24 inches per day in January to a minimum of 0.09 inches per day in June. The amount of water required for this crop depends on the amount required to meet up the needs of evapo-transpiration process as well as metabolic activities. Also, water is required for land preparation as pre-planting irrigation (Shrivastava *et al.*, 2011). Water stress may occur at any time of the year and it plays a rigorous role in suppressing the crop yields, particularly, the short periods of drought occurring in summer (Thompson *et al.*, 1963). Soil looses water through processes like surface evaporation, transpiration by plants and water percolation through root zone. For proper growth of crop, water requirement is fulfilled either by annual rainfall or from ground water and irrigation supplied. This water requirement differs from one place to other depending on the climatic conditions, soil texture and process of growth and development of the pertaining crop (Shrivastava *et al.*, 2011).

The decline in the water table across the country is a matter of serious concern. In India, sugarcane is an irrigated crop and from 1980 to 2006 irrigation coverage has increased from 80 to 93 per cent of the total sugarcane-cultivated area. Sugar producing regions have more than 80 per cent groundwater irrigation through deep-well pumping. As per the estimates showed by Central Ground Water Board, Government of India (2005), just 162 billion cubic metres (BCM)/yr of groundwater is left for future agricultural purposes. Of this around

40 BCM/yr is accessible in the states producing sugars (Srivastava *et al.*, 2011). Following table shows ground water potential of Uttar Pradesh (Table 11.2).

Table 11.1: Production of Different Crops in Lakh Tons in India and Uttar Pradesh

Crops	India	Uttar Pradesh
Rice	2086	111.3
Wheat	917.9	240.7
Sorghum	693.5	2.4
Pearl millet	76.3	12.5
Maize	76.8	10.5
Total pulses	147.1	22.3
Chick pea	133.8	6.6
Pigeon pea	56	3.8
Lentil	27.4	5
Total oilseed	9.9	9.4
Groundnut	252.9	0.9
Rapeseed	81.3	9.1
Sunflower	14.4	0.2
Sugarcane	2811.7	1254.7
Potato	239.1	99.9

Table 11.2: Ground Water Potential of U.P.

(Cu lm yr^{-1})

Total replenishable ground water resource	83.82
Provision for domestic, industrial and other uses	12.57
Available ground water resource for irrigation	71.25
Net draft	26.84
Balance ground water potential available for exploitation	44.41
Level of ground water developed (%)	33.67

(**Source**: Central water commission, 2000)

Drought or water stress is a most important and crucial problem of global sugarcane agriculture. In general, drought conditions are met due to less annual precipitation, late onset of monsoon, early departure of monsoon season, long prevailing dry period at time of monsoon season and the decreasing level of ground water (which is commonly being observed now-a-days). Sugarcane crop may experience any type of drought, *viz.*, occasional drought, frequent drought (now being observed in Maharashtra and Telangana in Andhra Pradesh in India due to deficiency of water), rain fed conditions and last one is experienced when the available water is not sufficient enough for its proper growth and development, generally in months of April–June in sub-tropical zone of India (Shrivastava and Srivastava, 2011). This causes low cane yield and productivity.

Status of Frequency of Drought in India

Sugarcane is the most important cash crop in India, which is widely cultivated in sub-tropical region that comprises of Uttar Pradesh, Uttarakhand, Haryana, Punjab, Bihar, West Bengal and North Eastern States. These account for about 55 per cent of area and about 45 per cent of the total sugarcane production with an average productivity of about 56 tones hectare^{-1}. The severity of disaster correlated with drought is a feature which is frequently being observed in India. About 28 % (on average) of the area of India is considered to be susceptible to drought.

In agro-meteorologist view, there are certain parameters to consider whether the rainfall is normal or not which determines the drought condition of an area. When there is ± 19% deviation in annual rainfall, it is measured as normal but when there is a deficiency of 20–59% and > 60% then it is measured as moderate and severe, respectively. It has been reported that in the past 10 years, Indian districts have faced excess to scanty or deficient rainfall and year 2009 has been declared as drought year due to majority of districts received less rainfall (Fig. 11.1). According to Agarwal (2003), till now 22 droughts have been faced by our country, of which 5 were considered to be severe. The irregular rainfall patterns arising from South West Monsoon or from El Nino phase of the Southern Oscillation are majorly responsible for occurrence of drought in India. Although the drought prone areas are Peninsular and Western regions of our country but in Central, Eastern, Northern and Southern regions, there

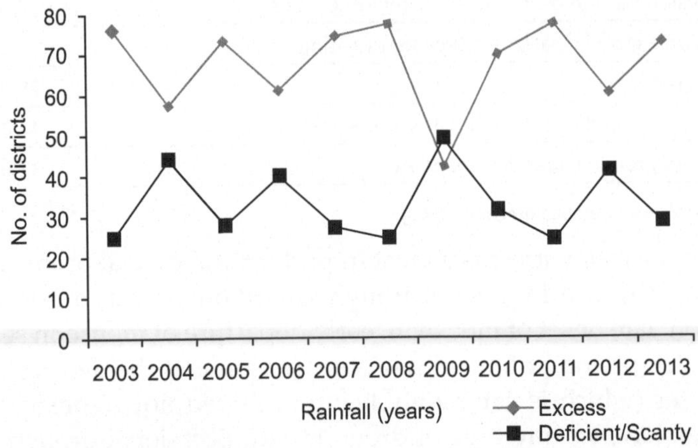

Fig. 11.1: Number of Indian districts facing Excess/ Normal and Deficient/Scanty rainfall

(**Source:** Modified from http://www.tropmet.res.in/~kolli/MOL/Monsoon/year2013/Monsoon-2013-NEW.pdf, 13.02.2017)

are few patches which faces drought due to the increasing effect of changing rainfall pattern, excessive use of water and application of inappropriate agricultural practices (Nagarajan, 2003). As per the data of rainfall from past

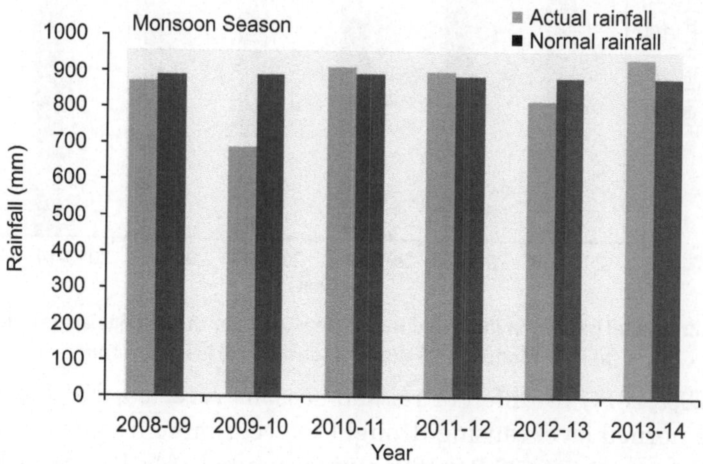

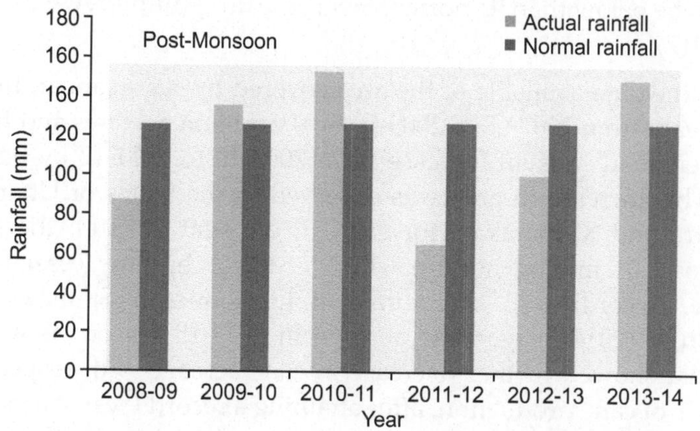

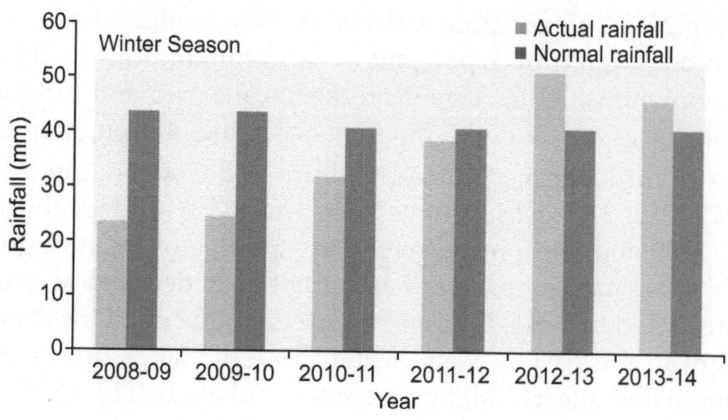

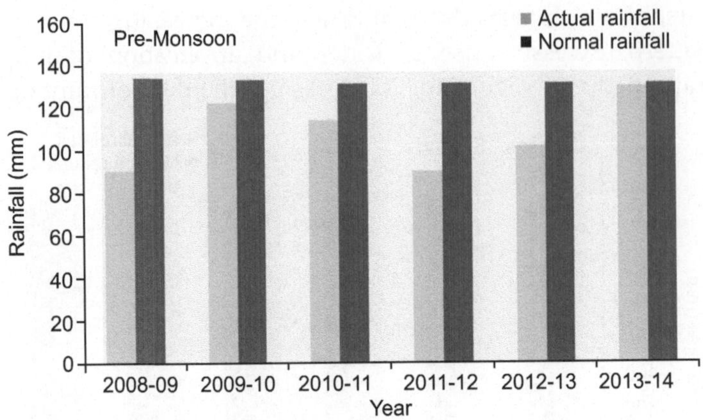

Fig. 11.2: Rainfall pattern in India in different seasons over the last 6 years (a) Monsoon (b) Post-Monsoon (c) Winter monsoon (d) Pre-monsoon

6 years (2008-2014) of different rainfall seasons revealed that the rainfall is below the normal level causing drought to occur more frequently (Fig. 11.2). Even in the recent year (2016), the annual rainfall (846.4 mm) in India was recorded to be below than its normal level (870 mm) (http://www.tropmet.res.in, 14.02.2017).

As per the data available of the area covered by sugarcane in India, there was a decrease from 2007-08 to 2009-10 by 0.9 million hectares and from 2007-08, however, there was an increase from 2009-10 to 2011-12 by 0.87 million hectares. This increase in area was observed in the States of Uttar Pradesh, Maharashtra and Karnataka. However, in the year 2013-14, the sugarcane acreage was 5.01 million hectare which is 13,000 hectare lesser than 2012-13 acreage. According to Directorate of Economics & Statistics, Ministry of Agriculture (2014), sugarcane acreage in 2014-15 seasons is 4.87 million hectares that showed further decrease in cane acreage with respect to 2013-2014. In case of cane production, after attaining a record level of 355.52 million tons during 2006-07, declined in cane production was seen in the subsequent years. During 2013-14, cane production was 350.02 million tones which were projected to be lowered by 2 per cent at 342.8 million tons in 2014-15 sugar seasons (Anonymous, 2016). This decrease in cane area and production over the years may be associated with frequent occurring of drought in India.

Reports from department of Agriculture and Cooperation also showed that 262, 172, 225, 210 districts have been affected with drought in the year 2002, 2004, 2009 and 2015, respectively, irrespective of the drought severity. However, the last mentioned year has yet not been declared as drought year but it is considered to be so. It has been observed that of all the states affected with drought in the past 14 years, Uttar Pradesh stands first in position in which drought had affected highest number of districts (Fig. 11.3).

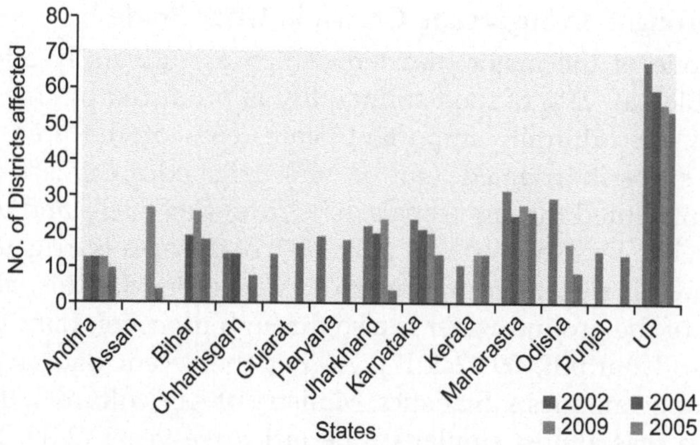

Fig. 11.3: Districts Affected with Drought over the Years

(**Source:** Modified from department of Agriculture and Cooperation http://www.downtoearth.org.in/news/about-100-districts-have-suffered-drought-conditions-for-15-years-50993, 09.02.2017)

Water requirement of sugarcane crop: As stated earlier, sugarcane is water requiring crop. These water requirements under field conditions are met effectively by three sources, *i.e.*, rainfall, groundwater and irrigation. In sugarcane, the requirement of water varies at different stages of its growth (Fig. 11.4) as well as with the type of the soil (Table 11.3) where it is being cultivated.

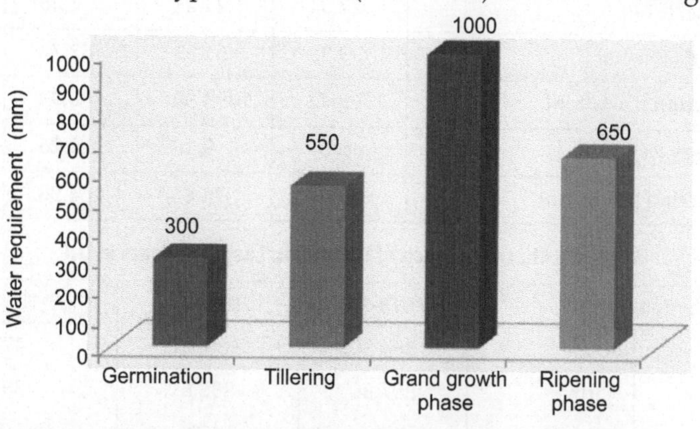

Fig. 11.4: Water requirement for different stages of sugarcane crop

Table 11.3: Irrigation Interval in different Season and Soil Type

Growth phase	Irrigation interval in textured soil (in days)		
	Coarse	Medium	Fine
Germination	5-6	6-7	8-10
Tillering	6-7	7-10	12-15
Grand growth phase	7	10	12-15
Ripening phase	10	12-15	15-20

(**Source:** Marimuthu C. A. (2015). Indian sugar, LXVI (7): 32-36)

Impact of Drought on Sugarcane Grown in Uttar Pradesh

Drought is one of the major disasters which are adversely affecting Uttar Pradesh (Table 4a). 21% of food commodity is produced by this State which makes it an agriculturally important State. 66% of the area utilized for agricultural crops is irrigated. Out of 66% irrigated area, 25% of irrigation supply is contributed through canals, 67% from tube wells and the rest from ponds, lakes, *etc*. This showed that only 1/3rd of the area is irrigated while the rest of the area is dependent on monsoon rains. Besides this, about 80% of total revival of the ground water is also through monsoon rains (http://nidm.gov.in/pdf/dp/Uttar.pdf, 09.02.2017). As per the recent data available from Directorate of Economics & Statistics, Ministry of Agriculture (2014), although the cane area was almost similar in the last three years (2011-2015) yet the cane and sugar production was revealed to be decline. This may be due to the less amount of rainfall occurring due to the climate change. Table 5 clearly demonstrated the sugarcane area in all cities of Uttar Pradesh in years 2013-14 and 2014-15.

Table 11.4a: Sugarcane Area, Average Yield, Production and Sugar Recovery and Sugar Production in U.P. in 2011, 2012, 2013 and 2014

	2011-12	2012-13	2013-14	2014-15
Cane area (Lakh/ha)	22.51	24.24	23.6	21.32
Average yield (Ton/ha)	59.35	61.63	62.74	66.15
Cane production (Lakh/ton)	1335.72	1493.98	1480.93	1389.02
Sugar recovery (%)	9.07	9.18	9.26	9.55
Sugar production (Lakh/ton)	69.74	74.85	64.95	70.9

Table 11.4b: Occurrence of Rainfall in Last Five Years in U.P.

Rainfall (mm)		2013-14[c]	2014-15[a]	2015-16[b](June – Oct)
East U.P.	Actual	864.50	508.90	472.10
	Normal	897.60	865.6	897.60
	Diff	-4%	-41%	-47%
West U.P.	Actual	758.6	240.20	439.9
	Normal	769.4	746.10	769.4
	Diff	-1%	-54%	-43%

(**Source:** [a]http://www.dnaindia.com/analysis/standpoint-india-s-monsoon-report-card-2014-2022685, 13.02.2017

[b]Indian Meteorological Department (2015). https://sandrp.files.wordpress.com/2015/10/1.jpg, 13.02.2017

[c]http://www.tropmet.res.in/~kolli/MOL/Monsoon/year2013/Monsoon-2013-NEW.pdf, 13.02.2017)

Table 11.5: Sugarcane Area in Uttar Pradesh in 2013-14 and 2014-15

Zone	2014-15			2013-14			Per cent increase (+) or decrease (–)		
	Plant	Ratoon	Total	Plant	Ratoon	Total	Plant	Ratoon	Total
Saharanpur	1.17	1.46	2.63	1.33	1.59	2.92	-12.20	-7.80	-9.80
Meerut	1.15	1.53	2.67	1.28	1.69	2.96	-10.40	-9.50	-9.90
Moradabad	1.76	2.02	3.78	1.93	2.12	4.05	-8.70	-4.50	-6.50
Bareilly	1.24	1.34	2.57	1.46	1.65	3.11	-15.60	-18.70	-17.2
Luck now	2.08	2.28	4.36	2.20	2.48	4.68	-5.50	-8.00	-6.80
Faizabad	0.35	0.42	0.77	0.38	0.47	0.85	-8.20	-10.90	-9.70
Devipatan	0.97	1.40	2.37	1.18	1.45	2.63	-17.60	-3.50	-9.80
Gorakhpur	0.31	0.65	0.96	0.46	0.64	1.11	-33.40	-1.20	-13.3
Deoria	0.43	0.79	1.22	0.56	0.76	1.32	-23.70	4.20	-7.70
Total	9.43	11.88	21.32	10.77	12.83	23.60	-12.40	-7.40	-9.70
Western U.P.	2.31	2.98	5.29	2.60	3.27	5.87	-11.30	-8.70	-9.80
Central U.P.	4.44	4.90	9.37	4.96	5.54	10.51	-10.50	-11.10	-10.8
Eastern U.P.	2.69	3.97	6.66	3.21	4.02	7.23	-16.20	-1.10	-7.80

Response of Growth, Productivity, Yield and Recovery on Drought

As moisture content is less in soil in drought conditions, the cane yield was highly affected. This phenomenon rigorously reduces the cane yield (Jangpromma *et al.*, 2010a). After 75-90 days of drought affected soils, the cane yield from such soil had an actual loss in cane yield was of 0.39 mt/day while after 90-105 days this loss increases and amounts to a loss of 0.256 mt/day (Shrivastava *et al.*, 2016). At times when drought condition is preceded by normal weather conditions then there is higher reduction in cane yield than the ones in which there was normal precession of normal weather. In productivity aspect of both plant crop and ratoon crop, the former are affected more than the latter one under drought conditions (Shrivastava *et al.*, 1992). Robertson *et al.* (1999) had showed that there was reduction in cane yield up to 60 % due to drought.

1. Morphological Changes Occurring in Sugarcane under Drought Conditions

Several studies have been conducted on drought that showed reduction in cane yield and growth under such conditions (Inman-Bamber and Smith, 2005; Silva *et al.*, 2008; Smith *et al.*, 2005). The effect on growth, productivity, yield and recovery of sugarcane depends on the severity as well as the tenure of drought faced by the crop. Besides, there are other factors that also depicts the amount of effect showed on the crop like plant genotype, the stage at which the crop faced drought, nature of the stress occurred, *etc.* (Kramer and Boyer, 1995; Gao *et al.*, 2013). Sugarcane grown under drought conditions showed direct effect on the stalk thickness. This is particularly more prominently observed under low moisture content in sugarcane. Higher rate of tillering, leaf number and ratio of weight of tiller/root were also other growth parameters that were related with drought conditions (Lal *et al.*, 1968). Leaf area index was decreased in canes that were imposed to drought conditions but no change in leaf area and leaf weight in canes grown under drought conditions with the ones provided with proper irrigation (Singh and Reddy, 1980). Canes showing early growth favored tiller production when exposed to drought conditions. This has been evident in most of the parts of sub-tropical India where cane is cultivated (Lal *et al.*, 1968). Lal *et al.* (1968) had revealed that under drought conditions, canes having thinner stalks could grow better than the ones having thicker stalks. Roots of canes facing drought conditions are the first one to respond to this phenomenon and are able to notice the changes/ alterations occurring due to it (Wang *et al.*, 2003). These changes are then signaled to other cells, tissues and organs of the plant by roots. Under drought, root system was hampered when water potential is of 0.07 MP which causes a reduction of 50-80% in root system (Saliendra and Meinzer, 1992). The length of roots were also small as they were not able to extend much in dry soil and this was even the reason behind the low uptake of nutrients under such scenario. The low uptake of nutrients is directly responsible for poor growth of canes. Reductions in growth hormones (gibberellins, auxins, cytokinins, *etc.*) were also observed leading to effect on many metabolic processes. Leather (1985) had showed that at times when cane does not show any visible symptoms of drought due to less exposure even at that time cells have lost their turgidity due to which the growth of the cane gets retarded later.

2. Biochemical Changes Occurring in Sugarcane under Drought Conditions

Rise in maliondaldehyde (MDA) level and permeability of plasma membrane was observed when canes were exposed to drought conditions (Abbas et al., 2014). Several studies had revealed that at the initial stage of water stress, occurrence in increase in soluble carbohydrate content may be observed (Pimentel, 1999; Sircelj *et al.*, 2005; Medeiros *et al.*, 2012). In sugarcane grown under drought conditions free amino acids synthesis was increased and this increase was not related to proteolysis as there was no declination in soluble proteins levels in such canes rather it was result of drought imposed on them (Medeiros *et al.*, 2013). Increase in proline level in leaves and roots were also observed in canes grown under drought conditions (Queiroz *et al.*, 2008; Cha-um and Kirdmanee, 2009). The increase in proline level is an initial response of plants to tolerate such conditions (Ashraf and Foolad, 2007). Proline plays an important role in assisting in the osmotic alteration, thus providing tolerance to canes suffered with drought (Kavi Kishor *et al.*, 2005). This also stabilizes the membrane by elimination of oxygen free radicals and prevents damage of cell (Ashraf and Foolad, 2007; Silva *et al.*, 2013). In general, as plants are not able to maintain their turgidity under drought conditions due to which the plant growth ceases along with leaf dehydration, yet there is an increase in osmoregulators content. In order to maintain the cell turgidity, there is an accretion of organic solvents, especially in roots (Medeiros *et al.*, 2013).

3. Physiological Changes Occurring in Sugarcane under Drought Conditions

Physiological processes like leaf temperature, photochemical electron transport, stomatal conductance, rate of transpiration, photosynthesis, respiration and photo-assimilate partitioning were also altered under drought conditions (Negi *et al.*, 1971). It is obvious that canes grown under such conditions had reduced water potential as well as relative water content (Uprety *et al.*, 1999). Ru-Kai *et al.* (1995) had showed that in rigorous drought conditions, the water status in the cane leaves progressively deteriorates in comparison to mild drought conditions. This is basically due to the decline in free water as well as relative water content; however, bound water level was increased under such conditions. Opening of stomata is also inhibited in canes facing drought leading to reduction in photosynthesis. Nitrate reductase activities of such canes are also reduced (Sairam, 1994). During formative phase of cane growth, rise in stomatal diffusive resistance (Ks) on both sides (abaxial and adaxial) of sugarcane leaf will be seen when the period of water stress lies between 60-150 days (Shrivastava and Srivastava, 2006). Other physiological indexes such as PS II photochemical efficiency (F_v / F_m), PS II potential efficiency (F_v /F_o), variable fluorescence quenching rate (δFv/Fo) and efficiency of potential quantum conversion (δFv/Ft) were observed to have negative effect of drought (Gao *et al.*, 2006). The photochemical efficiency of photosystem II was also altered under drought conditions (Gonçalves *et al.*, 2010). Medeiros *et al.* (2013) had showed that plants facing drought had decrease in gas exchange capacity occurring between leaf and the atmosphere leading to less water vapour (because of closure of stomata).This in turn causes reduction in atmospheric CO_2 fixation by the plant.

Certain studies have revealed that water stress causes effect on the sugarcane photosynthetic pigments (Cha-um and Kirdmanee, 2009; Jangpromma *et al.*, 2010; Cha-um *et al.*, 2012). Generally drought conditions causes reduction in chlorophyll content and induces alterations in carotenoids as well as ratio of chl a and chl b. This damage to the photosynthetic pigments is mainly responsible due to oxidative damage occurring in plants facing drought conditions. However, to protect themselves from much damage anti-oxidants, like carotenoids, ascorbate, α-tocopherol, glutathione and flavonoids were synthesized in such plants (Ejert and Tevini, 2002) along with increase in its enzymes such as peroxidases, superoxide dismutase and catalases.

4. Juice Quality of Sugarcane under Drought Conditions

Sugarcane production as well as juice quality is directly related to climatic conditions along with the stage of cane at which it strikes. There are certain critical stages in sugarcane growth cycle at which if drought strikes, cane will not be able to cope up with the water loss attained at that period, even if adequate water supply was given in later stages of its growth. The favorable conditions for high sugar recovery and good juice quality (*i.e.*, high sucrose) are when there is dry weather with low humidity. This is followed by high intense sunlight, lower night temperatures having broad diurnal differences with a scarce rainfall at the time of ripening (Solomon, 2009). Shrivastava and Srivastava (2012) had indicated that when the drought is faced by the canes at the stage of ripening, the juice quality decreases resulting in declination of cane yield. This happens so even in case of over stand canes particularly in sub- tropics. Misra *et al.* (2016) had showed that the canes grown under drought conditions have poor juice quality having low sucrose content, high dextran and acid invertase.

Management of Drought

Several measures have been adopted for managing the crop under drought conditions. The areas where frequent drought conditions occur, following measures are need to be adopted for better growth of sugarcane crop under such condition-

1. Before planting of canes, sugarcane setts may be soaked in saturated lime solution (80 kg lime/1000 l) for 2 hours a day. This method not only improves the cane yield under such condition but also helpful in areas having limited irrigation supply (Anonymous, 2008-09). Another method for inducing hardiness in sugarcane crop is withholding irrigation supply in sugarcane fields for 30 days at 90 days after planting. This causes less damage to the crop when natural drought conditions appear (Rajkumar and Kambar, 1999).
2. In such areas sugarcane are need to be planted a little earlier than its normal time as this will help the plant to face the drought conditions in a better way as the plant in this way is relatively at a higher age (Prasada Rao, 1989).
3. To face the condition of drought for sugarcane crop, the roots need to penetrate deeper in the soil rather than spreading superficially or laterally. For this purpose, deep trench method of planting is preferred. Such type of trenches helps in retaining the soil moisture by application of high dose of bulky manure, earlier to planting. Besides application of trash will also further prevent the moisture loss from evaporation (Naidu *et al.*, 1983). Delayment of first irrigation after planting at reasonable restrictions makes the root to penetrate deeper in the soil which to some extent provide tolerance to canes facing drought conditions (Shrivatsava and Srivastava, 2012).

4. Additional supply of 60 Kg K_2O/ha at 150-180 DAP should be given to the crop. At places where the soil texture ranges from light and medium, pit method of sugarcane planting should be adopted for overcoming such condition. Perez *et al.*, (1996) had showed that application of N at the rate of 100 kg/ha had less loss in cane yield than the fields which lack the application of N under drought condition. In tropical zone of India, application of mixture of urea and KCl at rate of 2.5% each at 60, 90 and 120 days after planting of sugarcane under such condition showed to improve cane yield (Naidu *et al.*, 1983). Application of 2.5 % K_2SO_4 as sprayer revealed as a measure for less loss in cane yield for canes under drought conditions. This improved the cane yield by 10.7% (Jayabal and Chockalingam, 1990). Annadurai *et al.* (2002) had showed that in Coimbatore at places where frequent drought occurs during early stage of cane growth, use of K either solely in soil or as both soil application and foliar one (112 kg K_2O/ha; 2.5% KCl spray at 45, 75 and 105 d.a.p., respectively) helped in improving the juice quality along with its sugar yield. Tandon (1987) had revealed that under drought conditions even the application of P showed improvement in cane productivity.
5. Another method of improving drought tolerance in cane is the application of foliar spray of ethrel at a low concentration of 100 ppm at times when the drought conditions is about to occur. Even soaking cane setts in this solution helps in reducing the loss of cane and sugar yield under such condition (Li and Solomon, 2003).
6. Application of trash mulching in canes facing drought or likely to face drought helps in improving the yield especially in tropical zone of India (Durai, 1997; Jayabal and Chockalingam, 1990; Kathiresan and Balasubramanian, 1991; Manoharan *et al.*, 1990; Parameswaran and Ramakrishnan, 1987; Ramakrishna Rao *et al.*, 1988).
7. Use of FYM, press mud, coir waste, *etc.*, in soil might help in improving cane yield under drought conditions (Manoharan *et al.*, 1990). These soil amendments will not only help in improving cane yield to some extent but also improves the physical condition of soil. Even the application of some moisture absorbents such as *Jalshakti, Stocksorb* and *Alcosorb* were also helpful under such condition (Bendigeri and Pawar, 1997; Durai, 1997).

In respect to managing the effect of drought in sugarcane, IISR had also developed certain technologies like two row plating, skip irrigation, drip irrigation, *etc.*

Breeding Efforts in Developing Drought Tolerant Varieties

Cultivating drought tolerant sugarcane cultivars can lessen the problem of drought and this can also lessen the yield losses occurring due to it. In order to ignore the effects of drought on cane and to enhance tolerance for such conditions, different mechanisms and processes are being concerned for it. Of all, phenology is the crucial factor (Witcombe *et al.*, 2008). For improving cane productivity under such conditions, one inexpensive method is to improve the drought tolerant varieties. To develop a tolerant variety, certain physiological parameters like relative water content, stomatal conductance, photochemical efficiency (PS II) are important for characterizing drought tolerant genotypes (Buckley 2005; Vinocur and Altman, 2005; Shao *et al.*, 2008). Hotta *et al.* (2010) had showed that these parameters along with the genes identified for this purpose can play an important role as a foundation for the development of new tolerant varieties. Also, there are certain physiological and biochemical parameters that gave positive results in identifying the sensitive and tolerant cultivars towards drought (Azevedo *et al.*, 2011; Silva *et al.*, 2007). Nevertheless, it will not be possible in this crop until the mechanism of tolerance is completely understood (Xiong *et al.*, 2006). Selection for physiological traits correlated with tolerance towards drought might augment the achievement of sugarcane breeding for this purpose. To avoid drought, one of the important mechanism that the crop adopt is the modification of its roots so as to capture the water for the process of transpiration (Fukai and Cooper, 1995; Songsri *et al.*, 2009). Drought tolerant canes should maintain its yield under drought conditions (Serraj *et al.*, 2004). As an aid to the breeders for improving the cane varieties for drought conditions molecular markers play an important and strong tool (D'Hont *et al.*, 1995; Bundock *et al.*, 2009; Parida *et al.*, 2009). Detection of novel genotypes having the property of tolerance towards drought condition is necessary for agriculture as well as economics all around the globe. Genes associated with drought tolerance may enhance the knowledge of the evolutionary adaptation to such type of stress. These genes may be used in developing new tolerant varieties by the process of transformation (Nepomuceno *et al.*, 2001; Lenka *et al.*, 2011; Kido *et al.*, 2012). A detailed knowledge of how the plants will response under such condition at molecular level is a pre-condition for managing such conditions (Deshmukh *et al.*, 2014). The genes in response to drought generally belong to two categories, *i.e.*, genes encoding functional proteins and genes encoding regulatory proteins. The former consists of proteins like chaperones or proteases, detoxification enzymes, transporters, water channels, *etc.* The latter consists of those proteins whose functioning is either related to signaling the response or to the factors associated for transcription process (Shinozaki and Yamaguchi-Shinozaki, 2007). As signal transduction encourages response to plants under such conditions, one can easily predict whether these signals are for the adjustment of plant for such conditions or not. Fujita *et al.*, (2005) had showed that to prevail over the injuries occurred due to drought conditions, plants also develop complex pathways for transduction. About 44% of the genes belonging to Hsp70 family along with its co-chaperone have been detected in sugarcane for biotic and abiotic conditions (Borges *et al.*, 2001). As a response to tolerance to stress, gene coding for disulfide isomerase protein (DEF 1) have been expressed in tolerant cane cultivars.

Efforts are being made on sugarcane in order to tolerate drought condition. For breeding a good variety for drought condition breeders emphasize on the variety having deep rooting system, good ratooning ability as well as tolerance to disease particularly, smut mosaic and rust (Flores, 2003). Sreenivasan and Bhagyalakshmi (2001) imparted drought tolerance to a variety Co 87263 wherein Co 312 worked as a parent. *S spontaneum, Narenga* and *Erianthus* used as a parent in breeding a cane variety may impart tolerance to a drought tolerant variety (Krishnamurthi, 1989; Sreenivasan *et al.*, 2001; Roach and Daniels, 1987). Besides, one of the important characters often used to assess whether variety is tolerant or not is the increase in proline content as well as photosynthetic activity in sugarcane (Cha-um *et al.*, 2008). The former plays an effective role in stress phenomenon along with their functioning in cell osmotic adjustment acting as an osmo-protectant but Molinari *et al.* (2007) had showed its association with reactive oxygen species (ROS) scavengers. Certain varieties have already been developed for facing drought conditions in a better way (Table 11.6).

Table 11.6: Cane Varieties Developed and Adopted Well under Drought Conditions with Their Important Characteristics

S. No.	Zone	Varieties	Heavy tillering	Good germinator	Heavy yielder	High sucrose and purity	Resistant to red rot	Resistant to borers	Good ratooner
1.	**Sub-tropical India**	*Hemja*	Yes	No	Yes	Yes	Yes	Yes	No
2.		*Khari*	No	Yes	Yes	No	No	No	Yes
3.		*Ikhri*	No	Yes	Yes	No	No	No	Yes
4.		*Khagri*	No	Yes	Yes	No	No	No	Yes
5.	**Tropical India**	*Kalkya*	Yes	No	No	No	No	No	Yes
6.		*Khadiya*	Yes	No	No	No	No	No	Yes
7.		*Bansi*	Yes	No	No	No	No	No	Yes
8.		*Sunnabile*	Yes	No	No	No	No	No	Yes
9.		*Nannal*	Yes	No	No	No	No	No	Yes

(**Source:** Modified from Sreenivasan, 2004)

In India, the All India Coordinated Research Project on Sugarcane (AICRP), recently have released some of the sugarcane drought tolerant varieties, like Co 94008, (*Shyama*), CoC 01061, *etc.*, for commercial cultivation in Indian areas where drought is prevalent. Following are the newly released varieties especially for areas of Uttar Pradesh (Table 11.7).

Table 11.7: Sugarcane Varieties (Tolerant to Drought) Released by the AICRP (Sugarcane) for Eastern and Central Uttar Pradesh

S. No.	Region	Variety	Year of release	Cane yield (tha^{-1})	Sucrose %	Maturity group	Reaction to disease		Additional tolerance to abiotic stress
							Smut	Red Rot	
1.	For Eastern Uttar Pradesh	Co 87268 (Moti)	2000	78.9	17.5	Early	Resistance	Resistance	Water logging, High soil pH
2.		CoLk 94184 (Birendra)	2008	76.0	18.0	Early	*	Multi-resistance	Water logging
3.	For Central Uttar Pradesh	CoPant 90223 (Pant 90223)	2000	77.3	18.5	Mid late	*	Multi-resistance	Water logging, Low temperature
4.		Co 98014 (Karan-1)	2007	76.3	17.6	Early	*	Multi-resistance	Water logging
5.		CoPant 97222	2007	88.2	18.2	Mid late	*	Multi-resistance	Water logging, Salinity

(**Source:** Shrivastava *et al.*, 2016)

Conclusion

Drought is a naturally frequently occurring phenomenon due to sudden changing climatic conditions. Water is already a scarce commodity in many parts of the world. With the increasing occurrence of drought the problem has increased. Rise in malionaldehyde, proline and permeability membrane are some of the physiological changes observed in sugarcane grown under drought conditions. Also, poor quality of juice at the time of harvest and faster rate of deterioration is also seen in drought affected canes. This chapter gives a clear picture of drought induced changes (morphological, biochemical, molecular and physiological) on the sugarcane crop (Fig. 5) and the efforts towards breeding a tolerant variety as well as steps towards managing such conditions have been discussed. Use of water in a proper way is the need of hour and for sustainable production under water deficit conditions should be followed.

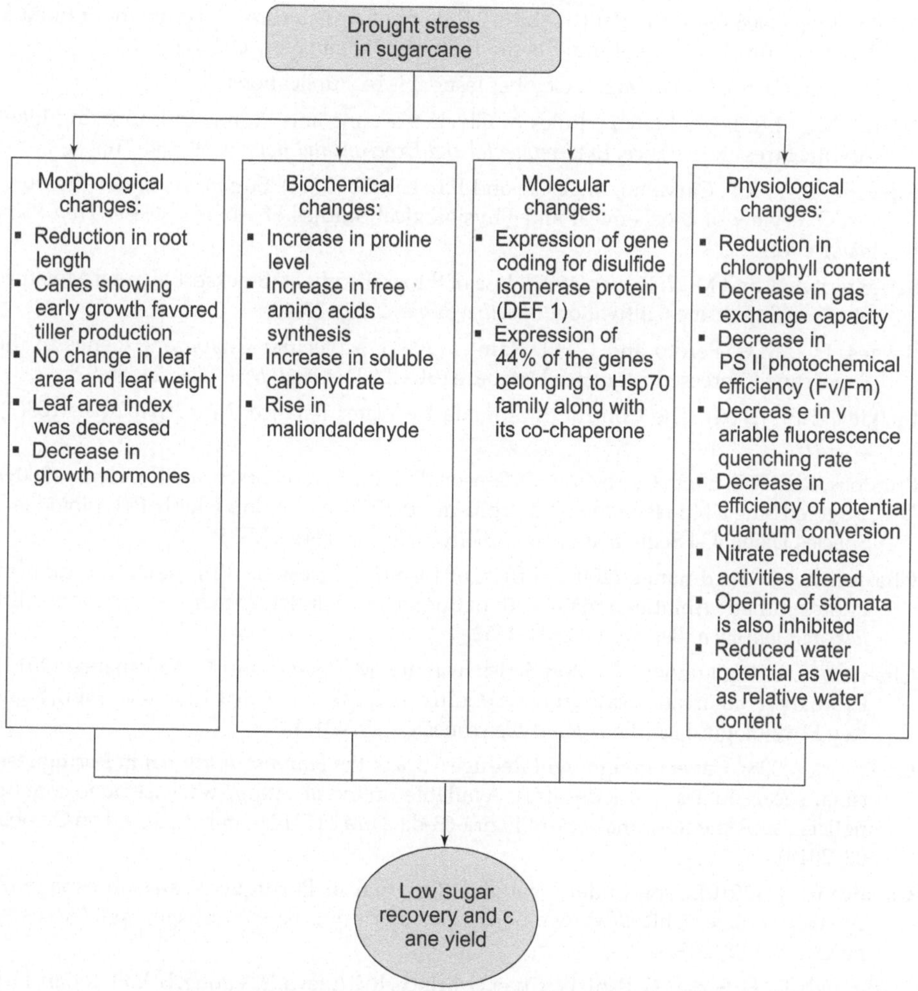

Fig. 11.5: Drought induced response in sugarcane crop causing low sugar recovery and cane yield

REFERENCES

Agencia Globo. (2012). Drought Affects the Development of Sugarcane in Alagoas. (Original in Portuguese: secaafetadesenvolvimentodas lavourasdecana em AL.). Available online at:http://g1.globo.com/economia/agronegocios/noticia/2012/11/seca-afeta-desenvolvimento-das-lavouras-de-cana-em-al. html (Accessed on October 08, 2013).

Abbas, S.R., S.D. Ahmad, S.M. Sabir, A.H. Shah (2014). Detection of Drought Tolerant Sugarcane Genotypes (*Saccharum officinarum*) Using Lipid Peroxidation, Antioxidant Activity, Glycine-betaine and Proline Contents. *J. Soil Sci. Plant Nutr.*, 14(1): 233-243.

Agrawal, P.K. (2003). Impact of Climate Change on Indian Agriculture. *J. Plant Biol.*, 30: 189-198.

Annadurai G., R. Shin Juang and D. Jong Lee (2002). Use of Cellulose-based Wastes for Adsorption of Dyes from Aqueous Solutions. *J. Hazard. Mater.*, 92: 263-274.

Anonymous (2008-09) Annl. Rept., DARE, Ministry of Agriculture, Government of India & Indian Council of Agricultural Research, Krishi Bhavan New Delhi, pp. 47.

Anonymous (2016). Indian Sugar. October Issue. ISMA Publications.

Ashraf, M., M.R. Foolad (2007). Roles of Glycine Betaine and Proline in Improving Plant Abiotic Stress Resistance. *Environmental and Experimental Botany*, 59: 206-216.

Azevedo, R.A., R.F. Carvalho, M.C. Cia and P.L. Gratão (2011). Sugarcane under Pressure: An Overview of Biochemical and Physiological Studies of Abiotic Stress. *Trop Plant Biol.*, 4: 42–51.

Bendigeri, A.V. and M.W. Pawar (1997). Use of Superabsorbent (Stocksorb) Under Moisture Stress in Sugarcane Cultivation. *Bhartiya Sugar*, 22(5): 23-40.

Borges, J.C., M.C. Peroto and C.H.I. Ramos (2001). Molecular Chaperone Genes in the Sugarcane Expressed Sequence Database (SUCEST). *Genet. Mol. Biol.*, 24: 85-92.

Buckley, T.N. (2005). The Control of Stomata by Water Balance. *New Phytologist*, 168(2): 275-292.

Bundock, P.C., F.G. Eliott, G. Ablett, A.D. Benson, R.E. Casu, K.S. Aitken and R.J. Henry (2009). Targeted Single Nu-cleotide Polymorphism (SNP) Discovery in a Highly Polyploid Plant Species Using 454 Sequencing. *Plant Biotechnology J.*, 7(4): 347-354.

Cha-um, S., C. Kirdmanee (2009). Effect of Osmotic Stress on Proline Accumulation, Photosynthetic Abilities and Growth of Sugarcane Plantlets (*Saccharum officinarum* L.). *Pakistan Journal of Botany*, 40: 2541-2552.

Cha-um, S., S. Wangmoon, C. Mongkolsiriwatana, M. Ashraf and C. Kirdmanee (2012). Evaluating Sugarcane (*Saccharum* sp.) Cultivars for Water Deficit Tolerance using Some Key Physiological Markers. *Plant Biotechnology*, 29: 431-439.

Castro, M. (2008). Cane: Drought will Reduce 6.3% of the Harvest. (Original in Portuguese: cana: secareduzirá 6, 3% dasafra). Available online at: http:// www.estadao.com.br/noticias/suplementos,cana-seca-reduzira-63-da-safra,117410,0.htm (Accessed on October 08, 2013).

Cavalcanti, J. (2010).Cane under Drought. (Original in Portuguese:canasob estiagem). Available online at: http://www.modclima.com.br/pdf/cana-sob- estiagem.pdf (Accessed on October 08, 2013).

Deshmukh, R., H. Sonah, G. Patil, W. Chen, S. Prince, R. Mutava, T. Vuong, B. Valliyodan, H.T. Nguyen (2014). Integrating Omic Approaches for Abiotic Stress Tolerance in Soybean. *Frontiers Plant Sci.*, 5: 244.

D'Hont A., P.S. Rao, P. Feldmann, L. Grivet, F.N. Islam, P. Taylor and J.C. Glaszmann (1995). Identification and Char-acterisation of Sugarcane Intergeneric Hybrids, *Saccharum officinarum* × *Erianthus arundinaceus*, with Mo-lecular Markers and DNA *in Situ* Hybridisation. *Theoretical and Applied Genetics*, 91(2): 320-326.

Durai, R. (1997). Stress Management in Sugarcane. *Co-op. Sugar*, 29(2): 102-104.

Egert, M. and M. Tevini (2002). Influence of Drought on Some Physiological Parameters Symptomatic for Oxidative Stress in Leaves of Chives (*Allium schoenoprasum*). *Environmental and Experimental Botany*, 48: 43-49.

Flores, S. (2003). Fifty Years of Breeding Sugarcane in Mexico. *Sugar J.*, 66(5), 23, 25.

Fujita, Y., M. Fujita, R. Satoh, K. Maruyama, M. M. Parvez and M. Seki (2005). AREB1 is a Transcription Activator of Novel ABRE Dependent ABA Signaling that Enhances Drought Stress Tolerance in *Arabidopsis*. *Plant Cell*, 17: 3470-3488.

Fukai, S. and M. Cooper (1995). Development of Drought-resistant Cultivars Using Physiomorphological Traits in Rice. *Field Crop Res.*, 40: 67-86.

Gao, Sanji, Luo Jun, Zhang Hua, Chen Rukai and Lin Yanquan (2006). Physiological and Biochemical Indexes of Drought Resistance of Sugarcane (Saccharum spp.). *Chinese Journal of Applied Ecology*, 17(6): 1051-1054.

Gao, R., K. Duan, G. Guo, Z. Du, Z. Chen, L. Li, T. He, R. Lu and J. Huang (2013). Comparative Transcriptional Profiling of two Contrasting Barley Genotypes under Salinity Stress during the Seedling Stage. *Int. J. Genomics*, 1-19.

Gonçalves, E.R., V.M. Ferreira, J.V. Silva, L. Endres, T.P. Barbosa, W.G. Duarte (2010). Gas Exchange and Chlorophyll *a* Fluorescence of Sugarcane Varieties Submitted to Water Stress. *Revista Brasileira de Engenharia Agrícola e Ambiental*, 14: 378-386.

Graça, J.P., F.A. Godrigues, J.R.B. Farias, M.C.N. Oliveira, C.B. Hoffmann-Campo, S.M. Zingaretti (2010). Physiological Parameters in Sugarcane Cultivars Submitted to Water Deficit. *Brazilian J. Plant Physiol.*, 22: 189-197.

Guimarães, E.R., M.A. Mutton, M.J.R. Mutton, M.I.T. Ferro, G.C. Ravaneli, J.A. Silva (2008). Free Proline Accumulation in Sugarcane under Water Restriction and Spittlebug Infestation. *Scientia Agricola*, 65: 628-633.

Hotta, C.T., C.G. Lembke, D.S. Domingues, E.A. Ochoa, G.M.Q. Cruz, D.M. Mellotta-Passarin, TG Marconi, M.O. Santos, M. Mollinari, G.R.A. Margarido, A.C. Crivellari, W.D. dos Santos, A.P. de Souza, A.A. Hoshino, H. Carrer, AP Souza, A.A.F. Garcia, M.S. Buckeridge, M. Meonossi, M.A. van Sluys, and G.M. Souza (2010). The Biotechnology Roadmap for Sugarcane Improvement. *Tropical Plant Biol.*, 3: 75–87.

Inman-Bamber N.G., D.M. Smith (2005). Water Relations in Sugarcane and Response to Water Deficits. *Field Crops Research*, 92: 185-202.

Jangpromma, N., S. Kitthaisong, K. Lomthaisong, S. Daduang, P. Jaisil, S. Thammasirirak (2010). A Proteomics Analysis of Drought Stress-responsive Proteins as Biomarker for Drought-tolerant Sugarcane Cultivars. *American J. Biochemistry and Biotechnology*, 6(2): 89-102.

Jayabal, V., S. Chockalingam (1990). Studies on Drought Management in Sugarcane. *Co-op. Sugar*, 21(8): 571-73.

Kathiresan, G., N. Balasubramanian (1991). Management of Drought in Sugarcane during Early Growth Phase. *Indian Sugar*, 41(5): 319-324.

Kavi Kishor, P.B., S. Sangam, R.N. Amrutha, P. Sri Laxmi, K.R. Naidu, K.R.S.S. Rao, K.J. Sreenath Rao Reddy, P. Theriappan, N. Sreenivasulu (2005) Regulation of Proline Biosynthesis, Degradation, Uptake and Transport in Higher Plants: Its Implications in Plant Growth and Abiotic Stress Tolerance. *Current Science*, 88: 424-438.

Kido, É.A., J.R.C. Ferreira Neto, R.L.O. Silva, V. Pandolfi A.C.R. Guimaraes, D.T. Veiga, S.M. Chabregas, S. Crovella and A.N. Benko-Iseppon (2012). New Insights in the Sugarcane Transcriptome Responding to Drought Stress as Revealed by superSAGE. *Sci. World J.*, 2: 1-28.

Kramer, P.J. and J.S. Boyer (1995). Water Relations of Plants and Soil. Academic Press, San Diego, CA.

Krishnamurthi, M. (1989). Sugarcane Genetic Resources and their Utilization through Conventional and Unconventional Approaches, in *Sugarcane Varietal Improvement* (eds K.M. Naidu, T.V. Sreenivasan and M.N. Premchandran), S.B.I. Coimbatore, India, pp. 163-176.

Lal, K. N., D. N. Mehrotra and J. N. Tandon (1968). Growth Behaviour, Root Extension and Juice Characters of Sugarcane in Relation to Nutrient Deficiency and Drought Resistance. *Indian J. Agric. Sci.*, 38(5): 790-804.

Larcher, W. (2006). Ecofisiologia Vegetal. Translation: Prado CHBA. 1st ed. São Carlos: Rima.

Leather, J.W. (1895). Chemical Composition of Sugarcane and Sugarcane Juice and of the Raw Sugars Obtained there from The Agricultural Ledger No, 1:1-39.

Lenka, S.K., A. Katiyar, V. Chinnusamy and K.C. Bansal (2011). Comparative Analysis of Drought-responsive Transcriptome in Indica Rice Genotypes with Contrasting drought Tolerance. *Plant Biotechnol. J.*, 9: 315-327.

Li, Y.R. and Solomon S. (2003). Ethephon: A Versatile Growth Regulator for Sugar Cane Industry. *Sugar Tech*, 5(4): 213-223.

Lopes M.S., J.L. Araus, P.D.R. van Heerden and C.H. Foyer (2011). Enhancing Drought Tolerance in C4 crops. *J. Experimental Bot.*, 62(9): 3135-3153.

Manoharan, M.L., K. Duraisamy and H. Vijayaraghavan (1990) Effect of Management Practices to Improve Cane Yield and Quality under Moisture Stress Conditions. *Bharatiya Sugar*, 15(10): 19-31.

Medeiros, D.B., E.C. Silva, H.R.B. Santos, C.M. Pacheco, R.S. Musser and R.J.M.C. Nogueira (2012). Physiological and Biochemical Response to Drought Stress in the Barbados Cherry. *Brazilian J. Plant Physiol.*, 24:181-192.

Medeiros, D.B., E.C. da Silva, R.J. Mansur Custodio Nogueira, M.M. Teixeira, M.S. Buckeridge (2013). Physiological Limitations in two Sugarcane Varieties under Water Suppression and after Recovering. *Theor. Exp. Plant Physiol.*, 25: 213–222.

Misra, Varucha, S. Solomon and Mohmmad Israil Ansari (2016). Impact of Drought on Post-Harvest Quality of Sugarcane Crop. *Advances in Life Sciences*, 20(5): 9496-9505.

Molinari, H.B.C., C.J. Marur, E. Daros, M.K.F. Campos, J.F.R.P. Carvalho, J.C. Bespalhok-Filho, L.F.P. Pereira, L.G.E. Vieira (2007). Evaluation of the Stress Inducible Production of Proline in Transgenic Sugarcane (*Saccharum* spp.): Osmotic Adjustment, Chlorophyll Fluorescence and Oxidative Stress. *Physiologia Plantarum*, 130(2): 218-229.

Nagarajan, R. (2003). Drought: Assessment, Monitoring, Management and Resource Conservation, Capital Publishing Company, New Delhi, p. 312.

Naidu K.M., T.R. Srinivasan and S.M. Raj (1983). Varietal Behaviour and Management Practices for Improvement of Sugarcane Yield and Quality under Moisture Stress. Paper Presented at the *Workshop of Drought Management of Sugarcane Crop and Drip Irrigation*, Trichy, June 18.

Negi, O. P., S. P. Naithani and S. Poddar (1971). Root Studies of Outstanding Sugarcane Varieties of Bihar, India. *Proc. International Soc. Sugar Cane Technol.*,14 : 733-738

Nepomuceno, A.L., N. Neumaier, J.R.B. Farias and T. Oya (2001). Drought Tolerance in Plants: Molecular and Physiological Mechanisms-Brazil. *Biotecnol. Ciênc. e Desenvol.*, 23: 12-18.

Nogueira, R.J.M.C., J.A.P.V. Moraes, H.A. Burity (2000). Modifications in Vapor Diffusion Resistence of Leaves and Water Relations in Barbados Cherry Plants under Water stress. *Pesquisa Agropecuária Brasileira*, 35:1331-1342.

Nogueira, R.J.M.C., J.A.P.V. Moraes, H.Á. Burity, N.E. Bezerra (2001). Modifications in Vapor Diffusion Resistance of Leaves and Water Relations in Barbados Cherry Plants under Water Stress. Revista Brasileira de Fisiologia. *Vegetal*, 13:75-87.

Oki, T., Shinjiro K. (2006). Global hydrological Cycles and World Water Resources. *Science*, 313: 1068–1072.

Pandey, Veena and Alok Shukla (2015). Acclimation and Tolerance Strategies of Rice under Drought Stress. *Rice Science*, 22(4): 147-161.

Parameswaran, P., M.S. Ramakrishnan, (1987). Measures to Alleviate drought Conditions in Sugarcane Due to Canal Closure in Wet lands. *Indian J. Sugarcane Technol.*, 4(2): 113-118.

Parida, S. K., K.K. Sanjay, K. Sunita, V. Dalal, G. He-maprabha, A. Selvi, A. Pandit, A. Singh, K. Gaikwad, T. R. Sharma, P. S. Srivastava, N.K. Singh and T. Moha-patra (2009). Informative Genomic Microsatellite Markers for Efficient Genotyping Applications in Sugarcane. *Theoretical and Applied Genetics*, 118(2): 327-338.

Perez Z. F., E.R. Romero, J. Scandaliaris and S. Sotillo (1996). Effect of the Drought of 1995 on Growth and Expected Yield of Sugarcane. *Advance Agroindustrial (Argentina)*, 16(64): 8-11.

Pimentel, C. (1999). Gas Exchange and Chlorophyll *a* Fluorescence of Sugarcane Varieties Submitted to Water Stress. *Pesquisa Agropecuária Brasileira*, 34:2021-2027.

Prasada Rao, K.K. (1989). Land Marks in Sugarcane Research at Anakapalle, in, *Platinum Jubilee Souvenir (1913-1988)*, (ed. K.K. Prasada Rao), Regional Agricultural Research Station, Anakapalle, India, pp. 21-31.

Palhares, I. (2014). Drought Causes Break up to 15% in Crops in the Region of Ribeirão Preto (Original in Portuguese: secaprovocaquebradeaté15%em safrasnaregiãodeRibeirãoPreto). Available online at: http://www1.folha.uol.com.br/cotidiano/ribeiraopreto/2014/10/1537883-seca-provoca-quebra-de- ate-15-em-safras-na-regiao-de-ribeirao-preto.shtml (Accessed on November 19, 2014).

Queiroz, R.J.B., D.M.M. Santos, S.D. Carlin, A. Marin, D.A. Banzatto, J.O. Cazetta (2008). Effects of Osmoprotectors on Sugarcane Plants Growing under different Water Deficit Levels. *Científica* 36:107-115.

Rajkumar, A.S., N.S. Kambar (1999). Drought Management in Sugarcane. *Bharatiya Sugar*, 24(9): 6-9.

Ramakrishna, Rao, S., J.S.N. Raju, K. Veerbhadra Rao, M. Padmanabhan, A. Sadanandachari, S. Ramapandu (1988). Effect of Trash Mulching and Nitrogen and Potash Nutrition on Rainfed Sugarcane. *Proc. Deccan Sugar Tech. Assoc.*, 38: 55.

Roach, B.T., J. Daniels (1987). A Review of Origin and Improvement of Sugarcane. *Proc. Copersucar International Sugarcane Breeding Workshop, Brazil*, pp.1-32.

Chen, Ru-Kai, Mu-Qing Zhang, Yi-Bo Lu (1995). Studies on the Effect of Water Deficits on Physiology in Sugarcane (*Saccharum officinarum*, L.), Sugarcane. http://en.cnki.com.cn/Article_en/CJFDTOTAL-GZZZ501.000.htm. 09.07.2016.

Sairam, R.K. (1994). Effect of Moisture Stress on Physiological Activities of two Contrasting Wheat Genotypes. *Indian Journal Experimental Biology*, 32: 594-597.

Saliendra, N.Z., F.C. Meinzer (1992). Genotypic, Developmental and Drought-induced differences in Root Hydraulic Conductance of Contrasting Sugarcane Cultivars. *J. Exp. Bot.* 43: 1209-1217.

Serraj, R., L. Krishnamurthy, J. Kashiwagi, J. Kumar, S. Chandra, J.H. Crouch (2004). Variation in Root Traits of Chickpea (*Cicer arietinum* L.) Grown under Terminal Drought. *J. Field Crop Res.* 88: 115-127.

Shao, H.B., L.Y. Chu, C.A. Jaleel and C.X. Zhao. 2008. Water-deficit stress-induced Anatomical Changes in Higher Plants. *Comp. Ren. Biol.*, 331: 215-225.

Shinozaki, K., K. Yamaguchi-Shinozaki (2007). Gene Networks Involved in Drought Stress Response and Tolerance. *J. Experimental Botany*, 58(2): 221-227.

Shrivastava, A.K., S.Srivastava (2012). Sugarcane: Physiological and Molecular Approaches for Improving Abiotic Stress Tolerance and Sustaining Crop Productivity. In *Improving Crop Resistance to Abiotic Stress* (Tuteja N., S S. Gill, A.F. Tiburcio and R. Tuteja, eds.) Vol. 2, Wiley-Blackwell, Germany, pp. 885-922.

Shrivastava, A. K. and M. K. Srivastava (2006). *Abiotic Stresses Affecting Sugarcane: Sustaining Productivity*, International Book distributing Co., Lucknow. India, pp. 322.

Shrivastava, A. K. and Sangeeta Srivastava (2012). Improving Crop Resistant to Abiotic Stress, Tuteja, N., S. S. Gill, A.F. Tiburcio and R. Tuteja (Eds.) Vol. II, Wiley-V.C.H. Verlag GmbH & Co. KGaA, pp 885-921.

Shrivastava, A. K., A. K. Ghosh and V. P. Agnihotri (1992). *Sugar Cane Ratoons*, Oxford & IBH Publishing Co. Pvt. Ltd., New Delhi, pp. 184.

Shrivastava A.K., Srivastava A.K. and S. Solomon (2011). Sustaining Sugarcane Productivity under Depleting Water Resources. *Current science*, 101(6): 748-754.

Shrivastava A.K., T.K. Srivastava, A.K. Srivastava, Varucha Misra, Sangeeta Shrivastava, V.K. Singh and S.P. Shukla (2016). Climate Change Induced Abiotic Stresses Affecting Sugarcane and their Mitigation. ICAR-Indian Institute of Sugarcane Research, Lucknow, Pp 108 (ISBN:978-93-5265-983-8).

Sindaçucar (2012). Drought Punishes Sugarcane Region with Only 5.7 mm of Raining November. (Original in Portuguese: secacastigaregiãocanavieiracom Apenas 5,7mmdechuvaemnovembro). Available online at: http://www. sindacucar-al.com. br/2012/12/seca-castiga-regiao-canavieira-com-apenas- 57-mm-de-chuva-em-novembro/ (Accessed on November 19, 2014).

Silva, M.A., J.L. Jifon, J.A.G. Silva, V. Sharma (2007). Use of Physiological Parameters as Fast Tools to Screen for Drought Tolerance in Sugarcane. *Brazilian J. Plant Physiology*, 19:193-201.

Silva, M.A., J.A.G. Silva, J. Enciso, V. Sharma, J. Jifon (2008). Yield Components as Indicators of Drought Tolerance of Sugarcane. *Sci Agric.*, 65: 620-627.

Silva, E.C., R.J.M.C. Nogueira, F.H.A. Vale, N.F. Melo, F.P. Araujo (2009). Water Relations and Organic Solutes Production in Four Umbu Tree (*Spondias tuberosa*) Genotypes under Intermittent Drought. *Brazilian J. Plant Physiol.*, 21: 43-53.

Silva, E.C., M.F.A. Silva, R.J.M.C. Nogueira, M.B. Albuquerque (2010). Growth Evaluation and Water Relations of *Erythrina velutina* Seedlings in Response to Drought stress. *Brazilian Journal of Plant Physiology*, 22: 225-233.

Silvam, E.C., M.B. Albuquerque, A.D. Azevedo Neto, C.D. Silva Junior (2013) Drought and Its Consequences to Plants from Individual to Ecosystem. In: Sener Akinci, editor. *Responses of Organisms to Water Stress. Croatia: InTech.* pp.17-47.

Singh, S., M. Reddy (1980). Growth, Yield and Juice Quality Performance of Sugarcane Varieties under Different Soil Moisture Regimes in Relation to Drought Resistance. *Proc. International Soc. Sugar Cane Technol.*, 17(1): 544-555.

Sircelj, H., M. Tausz, D. Grill, F. Batic (2005). Biochemical Responses in Leaves of two Apple Tree Cultivars Subjected to Progressing Drought. *J. Plant Physiol.*, 162: 1308-1318.

Smith, D.M., N.G. Inman-Bamber, P.J. Thorburn (2005). Growth and Function of the Sugarcane Root System. *Field Crop Res.*, 92: 169-183.

Solomon S. (2009). Post Harvest Deterioration. *Sugar Tech*, 11 (2): 109-123.

Songsri, P., S. Jogloy, C.C. Holbrook, T. Kesmala, N. Vorasoot, C. Akkasaeng, A. Patanothai (2009). Association of Root, Specific Leaf Area and SPAD Chlorophyll Meter Reading to Water use Efficiency of Peanut under different available Soil Water. *Agric. Water Manage.*, 96: 790-798.

Sreenivasan, T.V., K.V. Bhagyalakshmi (2001). *Recently Released Sugarcane Varieties,* Sugarcane Breeding Institute, Coimbatore, India, pp. 29.

Srinivasan, T.V. (2004) Improving Indigenous Sugarcane of India. *Sugar Tech,* 6(3): 107-111.

Thompson G.D., C.H.O. Paerson and T.G. Cleasby (1963). The Estimation of the Water Requirements of Sugarcane in Natal. *Proc. of South African Sugar Technologists Assoc.* 134-142.

Uprety, K.K., G.S.R. Murti, R.M. Bhatt (1999). Response of French Bean Cultivars to Water Deficits: Changes in Endogenous Hormones, Praline and Chlorophyll. *Biology Plant,* 40: 381-388.

Vinocur, B. and A. Altman (2005). Recent Advances in Engineering Plant Tolerance to Abiotic Stress: Achievements and Limitations. *Current Opinion in Biotechnology,* 16(2): 123-132.

Wang, W., B.Vinocur and A. Altman (2003). Plant Response to Drought, Salinity and Extreme Temperatures: Towards Genetic Engineering for Stress Tolerance. *Planta, 218: 1-14.*

Witcombe, J.R., P.A. Hollington, C.J. Howarth, S. Reader, K.A. Steele (2008). Breeding for Abiotic Stresses for Sustainable Agriculture. *Phil. Trans. R. Soc. B.,* 363: 703-716.

Xiong, L., R.G. Wang, G. Mao, J.M. Koczan (2006). Identification of Drought Tolerance Determinants by Genetic Analysis of Root Response to Drought Stress and Abscisic Acid. *Plant Physiol.,* 142: 1065-1074.

Zhao, D. and Y.R. Li (2015). Climate Change and Sugarcane Production: Potential Impact and Mitigation Strategies. *International J. Agronomy,* 1-10.

Index